THE IDEA OF HOME IN LAW

'Lorna Fox O'Mahony and James Sweeney's book bridges different branches of the law when examining the concept of home. The breadth of such an undertaking, which includes discussion on displacement in the context of conflict and the international legal implications of such, possession of the home from an English law perspective, human rights as well as home ownership in the US, is admirable. With leading scholars from a broad range of fields this book is likely to make a significant contribution to the legal field.'

Rachel Murray, University of Bristol, UK

Law, Property and Society

Series Editor:
Robin Paul Malloy

The Law, Property and Society series examines property in terms of its ability to foster democratic forms of governance, and to advance social justice. The series explores the legal infrastructure of property in broad terms, encompassing concerns for real, personal, intangible, intellectual and cultural property, as well as looking at property related financial markets. The series is edited by Robin Paul Malloy, and book proposals are welcome from all interested authors.

Robin Paul Malloy is E.I. White Chair and Distinguished Professor of Law at Syracuse University College of Law, USA. He is Director of the Center on Property, Citizenship, and Social Entrepreneurism. He is also Professor of Economics (by courtesy appointment) in the Maxwell School of Citizenship and Public Affairs, Syracuse University. Professor Malloy writes extensively on law and market theory and on real estate transactions and development. He has authored six books (one now in its third edition and another in its second edition), and edited five additional books. He has also written more than 25 scholarly articles, and contributed to 12 other books. His recent books include: LAW AND MARKET ECONOMY (2000, in English and translated into Spanish and Chinese); LAW IN A MARKET CONTEXT (2004); and REAL ESTATE TRANSACTIONS 3RD EDITION (with James C. Smith, 2007).

The Idea of Home in Law
Displacement and Dispossession

LORNA FOX O'MAHONY
University of Durham, UK
JAMES A. SWEENEY
University of Durham, UK

ASHGATE

Published by
Ashgate Publishing Limited
Wey Court East
Union Road
Farnham
Surrey, GU9 7PT
England

Ashgate Publishing Company
Suite 420
101 Cherry Street
Burlington
VT 05401-4405
USA

www.ashgate.com

British Library Cataloguing in Publication Data
The idea of home in law : displacement and dispossession.
-- (Law, property and society)
1. Right of property. 2. Eviction. 3. Refugee property.
4. Eminent domain (International law)
I. Series II. Fox O'Mahony, Lorna. III. Sweeney, James A.
346'.04-dc22

Library of Congress Cataloging-in-Publication Data
The idea of home in law : displacement and dispossession / Lorna Fox O'Mahony and James A. Sweeney.
p. cm.
Includes index.
ISBN 978-0-7546-7947-9 (hardback) -- ISBN 978-0-7546-9886-9 (ebook)
1. Right to housing. 2. Housing--Law and legislation. 3. Refugees--Legal status, laws, etc. 4. Home--Social aspects. I. Fox O'Mahony, Lorna. II. Sweeney, James A.

K738.I34 2010
344'.063635--dc22

ISBN 978 0 7546 7947 9 (hbk)
ISBN 978 0 7546 9886 9 (ebk)

MIX
Paper from responsible sources
FSC www.fsc.org FSC® C013056

Printed and bound in Great Britain by
TJ International Ltd, Padstow, Cornwall.

Contents

Notes on Contributors

Professor Susan Breau is Professor of International Law at Flinders University, Australia. She was formerly the Dorset Fellow in Public International Law at the British Institute of International and Comparative Law and Reader in International Law at the University of Surrey. Her monograph entitled *Humanitarian Intervention: The United Nations and Collective Responsibility* was published by Cameron May in 2005. Professor Breau is also co-author of K. Yildiz and S. Breau, *The Kurdish Conflict: Political Context, the Law of Armed Conflict, and Post-Conflict Mechanisms (*Routledge 2010); co-editor of E. Wilmshurst and S. Breau (eds), *Perspectives on the ICRC Study on Customary International Humanitarian Law* (Cambridge University Press, 2007) and J. Rehman and S. Breau (eds), *Religion, Human Rights and International Law (*Martinus Nijhoff, 2007). She has published several chapters and articles on various aspects of international law and the international protection of human rights.

Professor Susan Bright is a Professor in Land Law at New College, Oxford University. The majority of her publications are in the field of real property law. Her most recent book, *Landlord and Tenant Law in Context* (Hart, 2007), weaves together discussion of law and policy in both the residential and commercial property sectors. In her current research she is exploring legal models for the delivery of affordable housing, and the challenge of 'greening' commercial tenanted property.

Dr Antoine Buyse is Associate Professor at the Netherlands Institute of Human Rights (SIM), Utrecht University, where he teaches the courses International Human Rights at University College, and Economic, Social and Cultural Rights in the human rights LL.M. programme. His research interests are the European Convention on Human Rights (ECHR), human rights in post-conflict situations, housing rights, and the freedom of expression. He is author of *Post-Conflict Housing Restitution: The European Human Rights Perspective, with a Case Study on Bosnia and Herzegovina* (Intersentia: Antwerpen 2008), as well as several journal articles. His work has been awarded the *Erasmus Research Prize 2008*, the *Max van der Stoel Award 2008*, the *G.J Wiarda Prize 2008*.

Professor Rashmi Dyal-Chand is Professor of Law at Northeastern University. Professor Dyal-Chand's research and teaching focus on property law, poverty and economic development. Her recent projects examine credit, including microlending and credit card lending, as a means of economic development. Her current research explores property formalization and wealth accumulation by the poor in the United States. Professor Dyal-Chand's article, "Human Worth as Collateral," won the 2006 Association of American Law Schools' scholarly papers competition for new law teachers. Her work has appeared in journals including the *Stanford Journal of International Law, Tennessee Law Review*, and *Rutgers Law Journal*. She teaches Modern Real Estate Development, Intellectual Property and Property.

Professor Lorna Fox O'Mahony is Professor of Law at Durham University. She is author of *Conceptualising Home: Theories, Laws and Policies* (2006, Hart Publishing), which was awarded First Prize in the Society of Legal Scholars' Birks Prizes for Outstanding Legal Scholarship (2007), and was shortlisted for the Socio-Legal Studies Association Book Prize (2008). Her work to develop a legal concept of home is often cited as laying the foundations for new approaches to the idea of home in law, including giving content to rights to housing and home. Lorna is Associate Editor-in-Chief of the *International Encyclopaedia of Housing and Home* (Elsevier Publishing, 2011) and co-editor of *Unconscionability in European Private Financial Transactions: Protecting the Vulnerable* (Cambridge University Press, 2010) (with M. Kenny and J. Devenney). Her new monograph, *Home Equity and Older Owners: Between Risk and Regulation* will be published by Hart Publishing in 2011.

Dr Padraic Kenna lectures in land law and housing law and policy at the School of Law, National University of Ireland, Galway. He has published widely in the area of housing rights, socio-economic rights and related topics. Books include *Housing Law and Policy in Ireland* (Dublin: Clarus Press, 2006), *Housing Rights and Human Rights* (Brussels: FEANTSA, 2005) and *Housing Law, Rights and Policy* (Dublin, Clarus Press, 2010). A key area of his research work involves the development of socio-economic rights and their implementation in the areas of housing, land and property across the national and regional systems and approaches. His book, *Housing Law and Policy in Ireland* addresses both traditional legal areas as well as the developing issues arising from the International Law, ECHR, European Law and the movement towards equality, inclusion and rights-based approaches, both in the public and market spheres. He is a member of the Editorial Advisory Board of the *International Journal of the Law in the Built Environment*. Padraic has worked within a range of statutory and NGO agencies in the UK and Ireland in an advocacy role and in the development and management of housing.

Dr James A. Sweeney is Senior Lecturer in Law at Durham University. He is the founder and convenor of the 'Law and Conflict at Durham' research group. His research is about the after-effects of conflict; principally human rights law in transitional democracies and the rights of refugees. His work on the rights of asylum seekers to be free from destitution has been cited by the highest court in the UK. During 2009 he advised the European Union's Committee of the Regions as it drafted its responses to proposed amendments of the Common European Asylum System. His monograph *The European Court of Human Rights in the Post-Cold War Era: Universality in Transition* will be published by Routledge in 2011. Dr Sweeney has acted as an expert advisor to the Council of Europe on democratic transition and freedom of assembly in Armenia, Azerbaijan and Kosovo.

Professor A. J. van der Walt holds the South African Research Chair in Property Law at Stellenbosch University. He has been the recipient of the Alexander von Humboldt fellowship on several occasions and has been a visiting fellow commoner at Trinity College, Cambridge. Professor Van der Walt is author, co-author or editor of and contributor to more than 20 books on legal history, research methodology and property law, and has published more than 100 articles in legal journals. His most recent work is mainly concerned with constitutional property, land reform and property theory. His most recent books include *Constitutional Property Clauses: A Comparative Analysis* (Kluwer 1999); *Constitutional Property Law* (Juta 2005) and *Property in the Margins* (Hart 2009).

Acknowledgements

We would like to express our gratitude to Durham University's Institute of Advanced Study, Human Rights Centre, Centre for Criminal Law and Criminal Justice, and Institute for Commercial and Corporate Law who generously funded the Home Symposium held on the 29 June 2009 that gave rise to the work presented in this collection. We would like to thank all those who presented and participated in lively discussions on the day: Professor Susan C. Breau (Flinders University); Alan Brice, Medical Foundation for the Care of Victims of Torture; Professor Susan Bright (New College, University of Oxford); Dr Antoine Buyse (Netherlands Institute of Human Rights (SIM)); Professor Suzanne Fitzpatrick (Director of the Centre for Housing Policy, University of York); Dr Padraic Kenna (NUI Galway); Judy Nixon (Sheffield Hallam University); Simon Underwood, Head of the Social Inclusion Unit at Newcastle City Council; and Professor André van der Walt (Stellenbosch University). This symposium formed part of a wider series of events exploring the importance of 'Home' in 'Being Human' and we also want to thank all those who participated in the 'Home' theme, especially our colleagues Dr Divya Tolia-Kelly (Department of Geography, Durham University), Dr Simon James and Dr Benedict Smith (Department of Philosophy, Durham University), and Dr John Chapman (Department of Archaeology, Durham University). Their contributions and our shared discussions greatly enriched our understandings of the human experience of losing home.

The team at Ashgate have been wonderfully efficient in managing the publication process, and we'd especially like to thank Eric Levy, Pam Bertram and Helen Parry. Finally for their constant help and support, Lorna would like to thank David and Conor, and James would like to thank Sarah, Grace and Isla.

Professor Lorna Fox O'Mahony
Dr James A Sweeney
Durham Law School
November 2010

Chapter 1
The Idea of Home in Law: Displacement and Dispossession

Lorna Fox O'Mahony and James A. Sweeney[1]

(1) The Idea of Home in Law: Thinking about Loss of Home

The idea of home is both present and absent in law. In one sense, ideas concerning home – both in the sense of the dwelling place as a special type of property, and territorial claims to homeland – underpin many contemporary legal problems, typically where people have been displaced or dispossessed from their homes. For example, the significance of the home as dwelling place has been highlighted in the rise in repossession and foreclosure statistics following the recent crunch in the credit and housing markets.[2] Indeed, the global financial crisis triggered by the subprime mortgage lending crisis that began in 2007 has clearly demonstrated the potentially widespread risks of displacement and dispossession from our dwellings, bringing into sharp relief the adverse consequences associated with losing their home[3] to many individuals and households who might not previously have expected that they would have been exposed in this way.[4] As the crisis in the housing and mortgage markets has brought home to us our vulnerability to displacement and dispossession, we are well placed – perhaps more so than at any other time in recent years – to empathise with those people, whether in our own communities or elsewhere in the world, who have lost, or are at risk of losing, their homes and so becoming displaced or dispossessed. This presents an opportune moment to reflect on our shared human need for a secure dwelling place, and our vulnerability to loss of home. With this in mind, this collection sets out to examine some of the circumstances in which displacement and dispossession takes place, and argues that it is timely to consider how law and policy respond to such circumstances.

---

1 lorna.fox@durham.ac.uk / j.a.sweeney@durham.ac.uk

2 See for example, S. Bright, 'Dispossession for Arrears: The Weight of Home in English Law' and R. Dyal-Chand, 'Home as Ownership, Dispossession as Foreclosure: The Impact of the Current Crisis on the American Model of "Home"' in this volume.

3 See L. Fox, *Conceptualising Home: Theories, Laws and Policies* (Hart Publishing, Oxford 2006) 109–22.

4 See S. Bright, 'Dispossession for Arrears: The Weight of Home in English Law' and R. Dyal-Chand, 'Home as Ownership, Dispossession as Foreclosure: The Impact of the Current Crisis on the American Model of "Home"' in this volume.

There are a myriad of circumstances in which displacement and dispossession from home occurs, ranging from mortgage repossession to displacement following natural disaster.[5] This collection focuses primarily on those instances of displacement and dispossession which might be regarded as resulting from human agency, specifically, from either economic or political events or circumstances. There is a particular case for scrutinising law and policy responses to displacement and dispossession in these cases, as the causes of these home losses can be viewed as rooted in the human actions of law and policy agendas. In addition, as in any case of displacement and dispossession, the consequences of loss of home, particularly where it occurs on a widespread basis, generate costs which are borne not only by individuals but by society at large.[6] Where home loss results from economic or political circumstances the balancing exercise carried out by the policy maker in each context – between protecting home values and a range of countervailing demands – merits particular attention.

The importance of 'being at home in the world' for human flourishing, and the consequences of alienation when the connection with one's home is lost, are common philosophical themes,[7] and underpin much political philosophy, from Hegel to Heidegger. These perspectives have, in turn, influenced property theory as it has been brought to bear on issues in law and society. For Hegel,[8] the justification for private property was rooted in the role of property appropriation in the formation of identity. Property was identified as a vehicle through which the individual could manifest himself as a human being in the world; by appropriating property, the person confers personal meaning onto the property and expresses his identity outwardly through exercising his will in relation to the property.[9] Furthermore, the purpose of this appropriation was not merely to satisfy the

5 See, for example, Robin Paul Malloy (ed.), *Law and Recovery From Disaster: Hurricane Katrina* (Ashgate, Aldershot 2009) in this series.

6 See for example, S. Nettleton, 'Losing a Home through Mortgage Repossession: A "New" Public Health Issue' (1998) 8 *Critical Public Health* 47; S. Nettleton and R. Burrows, 'When a Capital Investment becomes an Emotional Loss: The Health Consequences of the Experience of Mortgage Possession in England' (2000) 15 *Housing Stud.* 463; L. Fox, *Conceptualising Home: Theories, Laws and Policies* (Hart Publishing, Oxford 2006), especially 115–22.

7 See, for example, D. Cooper, *The Measure of Things* (2nd edn, Oxford University Press, Oxford 2008) for a philosophical account of what it might mean to 'be at home in the world'. Levinas described the home as a precondition for existence, since: '[m]an abides in the world as having come from a private domain, from being at home with himself, to which at each moment he can retire'; E. Levinas, *Totality and Infinity* (Martinus Nijhoff, The Hague 1969), 152.

8 G.W.F. Hegel, A.W. Wood (ed.), H.B. Nisbet (trans.), *Elements of the Philosophy of Right* (Cambridge University Press, Cambridge 1991).

9 Ibid., s. 44 p. 76.

possessor's needs, but also to enable the human person to experience freedom;[10] and only from that position of freedom could the person then engage in civil society. While Hegel's analysis focused on private property more generally, and particularly on ownership of private property, the significance of housing and home for Hegelian self-development, and the implications this bears for law and policy, has been most notably developed through Radin's concept of property for personhood.[11]

The core of Radin's theory was the idea that an individual's attachment to particular property, for example their home, may be so strong that the particular property becomes constitutive of their personhood. Radin conducted a positivist analysis of the personhood perspective, and concluded that the relationship between property and 'personhood' had: 'commonly been both ignored and taken for granted in legal thought'.[12] However, the central premise of Radin's analysis was her normative argument 'that to achieve proper self-development – to be a *person* – an individual needs some control over resources in the external environment.'[13] Furthermore, in identifying those resources most essential to the person, Radin noted firstly that 'some property is worthier of protection than other property',[14] and – crucially – that the measure of whether property is 'worthier of protection' by virtue of its role in personhood, can be determined by considering the loss that would be suffered by the property holder if they were to be dispossessed of that property. Indeed, Radin proposed that the function of the personhood perspective was to 'serve as an explicit source of values for making moral distinctions in property disputes';[15] for example, by taking account of the impact of dispossession or displacement in contests where a certain type of property is at stake.

The occupied home is widely recognised as a quintessential example of 'worthy' property. In Radin's analysis, different forms of property were described as being located on a continuum, ranging from property that is constitutive of

10 'To have even external power over something constitutes *possession* just as the particular circumstance that I make something my own out of natural need, drive, and arbitrary will is the particular interest of possession. But the circumstance that I, as free will, am an object to myself in what I possess and only become an actual will by this means constitutes the genuine and rightful element in possession, the determination of *property*... In relation to needs – if these are taken as primary – the possession of property appears as a means; but the true position is that, from the point of view of freedom, property, as the first *existence* of freedom, is an essential end for itself'; ibid., s. 45 pp. 76–7.

11 See M.J. Radin, 'Property and Personhood' (1982) 34 *Stanford Law Rev.* 957; M.J. Radin, *Reinterpreting Property* (University of Chicago Press, Chicago 1993).

12 M.J. Radin, 'Property and Personhood' (1982) 34 *Stanford Law Rev.* 957.

13 Ibid.

14 M.J. Radin, *Reinterpreting Property* (University of Chicago Press, Chicago 1993) 48.

15 Ibid., 35.

personhood (described as 'personal property'[16]) to property that carries no meaning beyond its capital value (described as 'fungible property'). Radin argued that 'in our social context a house that is owned by someone who resides there is generally understood to be towards the personal end of the continuum.'[17] This argument was strengthened by the view that where certain types of property are constitutive of personhood, this is valued as a positive relationship between the person and the property. Radin claimed that '[t]here is both a positive sense that people are bound up with their homes and a normative sense that this is not fetishistic';[18] and so is a relationship which laws and policies should support.

The chapters in this collection develop this argument through analyses of various contexts in which the individual's personhood is threatened by loss of control over the 'resources' – both practical and symbolic – represented by control over or connection with *home*. The papers start from the premise that it is a necessary aspect of human existence that, at the most basic level, everyone must exist in some relationship with place and either with a meaningful connection to *home*; or, in the absence of such a meaningful connection, in a state of alienation.[19] Heidegger argued that the human condition – human 'being' – is rooted in these connections with home: people cannot 'be' without having some connection to a particular place.[20] This human need for connection to home can be described as 'multi-scalar',[21] in that it involves connections at various levels, from the attachment to home at the household level through the dwelling house itself, to the connection a person feels to a home-city or nation-state as home. As such, the issues of displacement and dispossession from home clearly go beyond considerations of private property, to encompass a set of issues relating to citizenship and exile from homeland. The importance of dwelling as the basis for human existence is brought into sharp relief by experiences of displacement and dispossession, and these multi-scalar attachments to home – from dwelling house to nation-state – are also reflected in this collection. These essays reflect on law and policy responses to disruptions ranging from repossession of the

16 Radin later conceded that this categorisation was not ideal, as it could potentially create confusion with the separate dichotomy between real property (land) and personal property (chattels and intangible property).

17 M.J. Radin, *Reinterpreting Property* (University of Chicago Press, Chicago 1993) 54.

18 Ibid. The notion of 'fetishism' is applied to distinguish between 'healthy' object relations, which are not fetishistic, and 'unhealthy' object relations.

19 M. Heidegger, 'Bauen, Wohnen, Denken' (1951) ['Building Dwelling Thinking'] and the 1951 lecture '…dichterisch wohnet der Mensch' ['…Poetically man dwells…'] in A. Hofstadter (trans.), *Poetry, Language, Thought* (Harper Colophon Books, New York 1971).

20 'The way in which you are and I am, the manner in which we humans are on the earth, is Buan, dwelling. To be a human being means to be on the earth as a mortal. It means to dwell…man is insofar as he dwells.' Ibid., 'Building, Dwelling, Thinking', Part I.

21 See A. Blunt and R. Dowling, *Home* (Routledge, Abingdon 2006) 27.

dwelling house, whether in a landlord or creditor possession action or at the hands of the state through compulsory acquisition, to the experiences of people who are both dispossessed from their properties and displaced from their homelands, often because of conflict or other political events. Yet a common thread connects the varied contexts considered in the essays: the impact of loss of home for the human person, and the extent to which this is present, or absent, in legal analyses.

The contribution of political philosophy is important in bridging the gap from a factual account of the ways in which a person identifies with a place as their home – towards an argument for the protection of 'settled expectations' that can support ideas of 'rights' and so generate a legal endorsement of a person's ability to exercise control within the territory that provides their housing and home. In the context of *property* rights, this argument appears to support the proposition that only those settled expectations generated by law – and so already protected – should be recognised.[22] Waldron argued that 'the principle of respect for expectations and the concomitant idea of identifying with a property object cannot be the *foundation* of a principle of entitlement; such a principle must already be generally respected before the relevant expectations can come into play.'[23] The question which remains concerning the origin of such principles of entitlement has been variously answered in theories of concerning first acquisition of property. Hegel, for example, argued that the recognition of property rights rooted in the expression of the person's will through possession was an essential precondition for the person to engage in civil society: that one achieves personality through the social anchor of property, which enables the person to become at home in the world.[24]

Yet, while Hegel's justification for private property recognises that property can function to anchor the person in the world, and Radin's theory of property for personhood provides a basis for arguing that certain types of property, most particularly the home, are worthy of special protection because of their role in constituting personhood, these property theories do not go so far as to advocate that housing or home should be available to all: 'There is no suggestion that each and every person can or should have certain sorts of property in order to be at home in the world…'.[25] This argument is, however, explicitly made in the statement on 'Progressive Property' published in the *Cornell Law Review* in

22 Waldron described the Benthamite argument as suggesting that 'Only when he can predict that by and large others will abide by some principle of respect for his acquisitions is he likely to form a settled expectation of keeping them'; J. Waldron, *The Right to Private Property* (Oxford University Press, Oxford 1988) 197.

23 Ibid.

24 G.W.F. Hegel, A.W. Wood (ed.), H.B. Nisbet (trans.), *Elements of the Philosophy of Right* (Cambridge University Press, Cambridge 1991) s. 33.

25 A. Ryan, *Property and Political Theory* (Blackwell, Oxford, New York, 1984) 124.

2009,[26] which proposed that our shared commitment to the values of 'life and human flourishing, the protection of physical security, the ability to acquire knowledge and make choices, and the freedom to live one's own life on one's own terms',[27] implicates moral and political conceptions that require property law to promote 'human flourishing'. While our perspectives are sympathetic with those underpinning progressive property, the question of 'property entitlements' is not one this book seeks to address. Rather, the papers in this collection seek to consider the significance of human relationships with housing and home not from a 'strong property rights' stance, but from alternative perspectives.[28] The emergent legal concept of home[29] focuses on the proposition that the relationship between a person and their home – distinct from any 'strong property rights' the person may or may not have in that home as an item of property – can potentially generate the basis for a legal claim which should be weighed in the balance against other types of claim. These papers develop that line of scholarship by considering normative questions concerning law and policy responses to displacement and dispossession from a variety of perspectives.

A key feature of the collection is the connection made between housing and home and human rights approaches. This provides a useful perspective because the proposition that particular rights or expectations are essential to human dignity or flourishing is one that is more typically encountered in the context of human rights discourse.[30] Writing on the subject of the universality of human rights, Jack Donnelly argued that the modern human rights movement is an historically bounded response to protecting human dignity inspired by the need for protection from the, 'economic, social and cultural intrusions into, and disruptions of, the traditional community [which] have removed the support and protection which would "justify" or "compensate for" the absence of individual human rights.'[31]

26 G.S. Alexander, E.M. Peñalver, J.W. Singer and L.S. Underkuffler, 'A Statement on Progressive Property' (2009) 94 *Cornell Law Rev*. 743.

27 Ibid.

28 For an extensive illustration of the insights to be gained through considering alternative perspectives to the 'strong property rights' paradigm, and arguing for a wider notion of what can be considered worthy of recognition as property 'interests', see A.J. van der Walt, *Property in the Margins* (Hart Publishing, Oxford 2009).

29 See, for example, L. Fox, *Conceptualising Home: Theories, Laws and Policies* (Hart Publishing, Oxford 2006); D.B. Barros, 'Home as a Legal Concept' (2006) 46 *Santa Clara L. Rev.* 255; M.J. Ballard, 'Legal Protections for Home Dwellers: Caulking the Cracks to Preserve Occupancy' (2006) 56 *Syracuse L. Rev*. 277; Tang Hang Wu, 'The Legal Representation of the Singaporean Home and the Influence of the Common Law' (2007) 37 *HKLJ* 81; A. Buyse, 'Strings Attached: The Concept of "Home" in the Case Law of the European Court of Human Rights' [2006] *EHRLR* 294.

30 See O. Schachter, 'Human Dignity as a Normative Concept' (1983) 77(4) *AJIL* 848.

31 J. Donnelly, 'Human Rights and Human Dignity: An Analytic Critique of Non-western Conceptions of Human Rights' (1982) 76 *Amer. Polit. Sci. Rev*. 303, 314.

Likewise Beyleveld and Brownsword have identified human dignity as the source for human rights in many human rights treaties.[32] It is particularly apposite to consider the human dignity aspect of rights to home in the context of a project that takes 'being human' as its initial stimulus, at a time when the human rights movement itself is at risk of being subverted by the recognition of 'human' rights for corporate and profit-making entities.[33] It is fascinating to see, for example, that the tenuous grasp that displaced and dispossessed people may have upon their human rights to 'home' is more difficult to conceptualise from the legal standpoint of the European Convention on Human Rights[34] than a corporation's right to 'home, family and private life' in the course of competition proceedings brought against it.[35]

International human rights law recognises some fusion of property law approaches and human rights approaches to the extent that the right to (peaceful enjoyment of) property is (sometimes) recognised as a human right itself. This is the case in Article 17 of the Universal Declaration of Human Rights;[36] the European Convention on Human Rights, where it is included in Article 1 of Protocol 1;[37] Article 14 of the African Charter on Human and Peoples' Rights;[38]

32 D. Beyleveld and R. Brownsword, 'Human Dignity, Human Rights and Human Genetics' (1998) 6 *MLR* 661. Indeed Beyleveld and Brownsword go further, and argue that in another more specific sense human dignity can become a species of human right itself. (In the context of personal autonomy and the right to profit from the use of one's own body, they argue that the notion of human dignity, if properly conceptualised, can help resolve complicated questions surrounding new technologies such as the cloning of genetic material, or even humans.)

33 See M.K. Addo, 'The Corporation as a Victim of Human Rights Violations', in Addo (ed.) *Human Rights Standards and the Responsibility of Transnational Corporations* (Kluwer, The Hague 1999) 187 (supporting this development); M. Emberland, *The Human Rights of Companies: Exploring the Structure of ECHR Protection* (Oxford University Press, Oxford 2006); cf. A. Grear, 'Challenging Corporate "Humanity": Legal Disembodiment, Embodiment and Human Rights' (2007) 7(3) *Human Rights Law Review* 511.

34 See Sweeney and Fox O'Mahony in this volume.

35 See *Société Colas Est and Others v. France* (2004) 39 EHRR 17 at [41] in particular, where the European Court held that, 'Building on its dynamic interpretation of the Convention, the Court considers that the time has come to hold that in certain circumstances the rights guaranteed by Article 8 of the Convention may be construed as including the right to respect for a company's registered office, branches or other business premises.'

36 Universal Declaration of Human Rights (adopted 10 December 1948) UNGA Res 217 A(III) (UDHR).

37 Convention for the Protection of Human Rights and Fundamental Freedoms (European Convention on Human Rights, as amended) (ECHR); Protocol to the Convention for the Protection of Human Rights and Fundamental Freedoms (European Convention on Human Rights, as amended) (ECHR).

38 African Charter on Human and Peoples' Rights (adopted 27 June 1981, entered into force 21 October 1986) (1982) 21 ILM 58 (African Charter).

Article 21 of the American Convention on Human Rights;[39] and Article 23 of the American Declaration on the Rights and Duties of Man;[40] although it is notably absent from both the International Covenant on Civil and Political Rights[41] and the International Covenant on Economic, Social and Cultural Rights.[42] The aim of this volume is to recognise the specific role of housing and home to human dignity. The research presented here opens up avenues for exploration of these related issues: it is not intended to promote a specific agenda for strong property rights (e.g. ownership), but rather to use ways of thinking about normative claims about the promotion of 'human rights' to shed new light on issues of displacement and dispossession.

(2) Displacement and Dispossession

The subject matter covered in the book addresses issues of major contemporary intellectual and policy interest. Both within states and globally, questions of forced evictions, displacement and dispossession, refugees and homelessness are of obvious current importance. On the global stage, the UN's Global Land Tools Network and the UN-Habitat Global Campaign for Secure Tenure have focused attention on issues such as the importance of security of tenure and the role of law and policy in protecting people who are vulnerable to forced eviction. Yet, despite the authenticity of home attachments, and the indisputable significance of access to housing and home for human flourishing, government policies, as expressed through law, struggle to attach significant weight to these home meanings or to their central role in relation to the occupier's experience of 'being human'. While scholarship on the legal concept of home has been a growing area in recent years, this collection progresses that debate into a new legal arena by shining a spotlight on the human rights and international law aspects of questions concerning displacement and dispossession from one's home.

The dispossession aspects include focusing on the relationship between 'home' and the law in relation to a range of circumstances, from responses to repossession triggered by inability to pay housing costs – including repossession for rent arrears or mortgage default in the UK (Bright) and foreclosure in the US (Dyal-Chand) – to dispossession caused by expropriation of land by the state for public purposes (van der Walt). The displacement theme draws the focus across to transnational

39 American Convention on Human Rights (entered into force 18 July 1978) (1969) 9 ILM 99.

40 Reprinted in 'Basic Documents Pertaining to Human Rights in the Inter-American System', OEA/Ser.L.V/II.82 doc.6 rev.1 at 17 (1992); (1949) 43 AJIL Supp. 133.

41 UNGA Res. 2200A (XXI), 21 UN GAOR Supp. (No. 16) at 52, UN Doc. A/6316 (1966); 999 UNTS 171; (1967) 6 ILM 368.

42 UNGA Res. 2200A (XXI), 21 UN GAOR Supp. (No. 16) at 49, UN Doc. A/6316 (1966); 993 UNTS 3; (1967) 6 ILM 368.

'home' issues: papers cover topics concerning the experience of displacement from home, for example for exiles and refugees (Breau), in the developing world and elsewhere in times of conflict (Buyse) and in the context of economic, social and cultural rights (Kenna, Breau). Bridging both themes, Sweeney and Fox O'Mahony analyse responses to the 'double displacement and dispossession' of asylum seekers and the intersecting issues of immigration and social welfare that characterise housing and home for asylum seekers in UK domestic and international human rights laws and norms.

This book brings together key protagonists across a range of interconnected global debates relating to the human experience of displacement and dispossession, to share insights into the role of law and policy in responding to displacement and dispossession from one's home, both at the national and international level, and to discuss priorities and strategies for future research in this important field. By bringing these perspectives together in a single work, we address a range of interconnected issues for the person experiencing displacement and/or dispossession from home, which are set out and examined in more detail in the concluding chapter. The papers address issues across a range of jurisdictions, including domestic legal approaches across the United Kingdom, United States of America, South Africa and Germany, and at different levels of legal system, including regional and international organisations such as the European Union, Council of Europe and United Nations, as well as public international law, international human rights law and international humanitarian law (otherwise known as the law of armed conflict).

(3) 'Being Human'

The impetus for this collection was a workshop held at the Institute of Advanced Study at Durham University on 29 June 2009, and we would like to acknowledge the generous support of the Institute in supporting and enabling the research collected in this volume. The workshop was the fourth in a thematic series focusing on 'Home' as an aspect of 'Being Human', which in turn formed part of the Institute of Advanced Study's 'Being Human' theme in the academic year 2008–2009. Durham University's Institute of Advanced Study is an ideas-driven institute, which is distinctive in organising the core of its work around a rolling programme of thematic priorities. Core themes have interdisciplinary appeal; they are controversial, lie at the cutting edge of research and require urgent attention from more than one perspective. Typically, themes run across one academic year, and provide a forum to gather together scholars, intellectuals and public figures of world standing or world promise from a varied range of backgrounds to address topics of major academic or public interest.

The 'Being Human' theme explored the fundamental question at the heart of human history: 'What does it mean to be human?'; specifically, what does it mean to be human at this moment in history, and including the proposition that there may be a case for the recovery of 'human being', at a time when 'many people around the world continue to be reduced to bare life or less…'.[43] The focus on being human reflected a suggestion that the decentring of humanity in our age requires urgent attention, focusing on contemporary developments, and creating space to consider, *inter alia*, 'the status as humans of the many locked in precarious work, abject poverty and societal inattention; changing institutional and state practices towards the "deserving" and the "undeserving"; and changes to ethics of care and responsibility spawned by new forms of human attachment.'[44]

The thematic focus on 'being human' is crucial to the analysis undertaken in this book. Although law is a system created by human beings to regulate human conduct, property law *per se* does not generally allow much scope for taking account of the human consequences of particular acts, events or decisions. English land law has been described by leading commentators as:

> display[ing] many of the features of a closed system of logic or an autopoietic order, prompting immediate analogies with mathematics and, more particularly, with the discipline of Euclidean geometry…every strategic move is dictated by an arbitrarily predetermined set of foundational principles…property in land 'behaves' in a manner just as predictable and verifiable as any other branch of rational science.[45]

Furthermore, if strict rationality is sometimes tempered by the rhetoric of human dealings, Gray and Gray have argued that where these relationships involve proprietary and contractual matters between landlords and tenants, mortgagor and mortgagee, they 'are strictly commercial, bargaining is hard-nosed, social bondings are minimal and the value attached to land is primarily, perhaps even exclusively, an "exchange value". Altruism is in very short support; we are talking money.'[46] In this context, Fox O'Mahony has argued that the 'human' dimensions of legal problems involving displacement and dispossession are often excluded or 'unvalued' – because (property) law as a discipline does not consider itself to have the tools with which to apply value to interests such as the occupier's interest in hanging on to her home. Thus: 'the idea of home in law has not carried much weight, particularly when balanced against easily measurable, legally definable, proprietary and contractual interests in the property.'[47]

---

43 http://www.dur.ac.uk/ias/themes/0809/

44 Ibid.

45 K.J. Gray and S.F. Gray, 'The Rhetoric of Realty' in J. Getzler (ed.), *Rationalizing Property, Equity and Trusts: Essays in Honour of Edward Burn* (Butterworths, London 2003) 204–205.

46 Ibid., 241.

47 See L. Fox, *Conceptualising Home: Theories, Laws and Policies* (Hart Publishing, Oxford 2006) 119–20.

Yet, for the essays collected in this book, the human consequences are central to the contemporary problems which the authors identify, and their analyses of the ways in which law does, or does not, respond to these problems place the human person experiencing the displacement or dispossession at the core. This reflects a shared acceptance of the proposition that home is an essential grounding of human identity, whether we are talking about dispossession from the home, with *home* as the meaningful relationship between people and their individual dwelling places, or whether we are talking about displacement from homeland (which is usually accompanied by dispossession from the dwelling house). The essays analyse law and policy responses to these displacements and dispossessions to consider what the idea of home in law can tell us about our concepts of housing and home, and the relationships between 'housing', 'home' and human rights. There are obvious but implicit synergies across the conceptual fields of shelter, housing and home: as Kenna has recently noted: '[h]ousing addresses the basic need for human shelter, but also facilitates the essential human requirement for a home.'[48] This book seeks to raise questions about the relationships between the idea of home in law and the 'rights' and norms associated with home, housing and being human. By focusing on the impact of displacement and dispossession from home on the human person, and bringing together experts who work across the areas of eviction and homelessness, dispossession at the domestic 'housing' level, exiles, refugees and transnational displacement from home, it is our hope that we have been able to stimulate some new perspectives on these problems.

---

48 P. Kenna, 'Globalization and Housing Rights' (2008) 15 *Ind. J. Global Legal Stud.* 397.

Chapter 2

Dispossession for Arrears: The Weight of Home in English Law

Susan Bright[1]

(1) Introduction

This chapter examines the extent to which the processes of dispossessing a debtor of his or her home enable weight to be attached to the importance of *this* home to *this* person.[2] The focus is upon what will be called the 'personal home story'.

English law implicitly accepts that forced loss of any home is likely to be a more serious business than deprivation of other kinds of real estate. For example, a court order is required before a landlord can recover possession of a rented home, but not other types of rented property.[3] Sometimes the law goes further where the reason given for dispossession of a home is non-payment of monies due, giving the occupier an opportunity to show to a judge that, given a reasonable time to do so, she will be able to sort out the arrears. An obvious example is the power a judge has to postpone possession if a mortgagee is seeking possession of a dwelling house.[4] Yet, while these rules ensure that the occupier does not lose her home without good lawful reason, they do not allow the unique 'meaning of *this* home' to be a consideration in deciding whether or not possession should be allowed on the facts. Whilst there is, then, a general weighting that is given to homes in the law, the question addressed in this chapter is whether the law ever allows more than this by making the 'personal home story' legally relevant.

Whilst losing a home will seldom be easy, the impact of loss will be much greater for some than others. A young person who has only recently rented a room in a shared house is unlikely to suffer serious harm if dispossessed of that room, whereas the picture may be very different for an elderly person whose home of many years has been specially adapted for her disability and whose network of carers live nearby. For some, a forced move will be devastating: there are financial, emotional, social and practical consequences. It may mean dislocation from communities of family, friends, school, work and other social groupings; it can

---

1 I would like to thank Janet Bettle, barrister, for her advice on the practice of possession hearings.

2 The legal and regulatory position discussed in this chapter is based on English law.

3 Protection from Eviction Act 1977 s. 3.

4 Administration of Justice Act 1970 s. 36.

lead to homelessness or overcrowding; it may exacerbate existing health problems or generate new ones, and it can lead to a profound sense of 'loss' and insecurity. The reach will often be far wider. It is not only the debtor herself who stands to lose the home, but other occupiers who share the property may also be made homeless. Loss of home impacts very differently upon different people depending upon their financial resources, expectations, health, family and social situation, and general resilience. Is this something that has any relevance in law?

(2) Arrears and Dispossession

There are a number of distinctions that will need to be drawn in discussing the relevance of the personal home story. The central ones relate to the type of arrears, the tenure of the debtor and the identity of the creditor, with clear connections between these.

The most obvious forms of arrears are those that relate to payment for occupation: rent and mortgage[5] payments. During 2009, the level of arrears was high. The number of residential mortgages in arrears had been steadily rising since early 2007 and by mid 2009 around 400,000 accounts were in arrears.[6] Precise figures on rent arrears are hard to obtain, but around one in three private landlords had a tenant in arrears in mid 2009.[7] Both forms of arrears can lead to dispossession, but the processes followed will depend upon the tenure and the identity of the creditor. In outline, rent arrears can lead to a mandatory ground for possession with a private landlord (including a registered provider of social housing),[8] but (usually[9]) only a discretionary ground for possession if there is a local authority landlord.[10] Mortgage default gives a right to possession and sale.[11]

---

5 Not all mortgage loans are taken out to purchase the property; business or other personal loans may be secured on the property but for ease the text treats mortgage payments as relating to occupation.

6 Financial Services Authority, Statistics on Mortgage Lending: June 2009 Edition.

7 According to the National Landlords Association (www.landlords.org.uk, accessed 10 July 2009).

8 Housing Act 1988 Sch. 2, Ground 8. Most social housing (low-cost accommodation provided for those unable to access housing at market rates) is provided either by the local housing authority or by 'registered providers'. Although these registered providers are subject to extensive regulation and may be in receipt of government funding, the legal rules governing their letting arrangements treat them as part of the private sector.

9 Most local authority tenants have 'secure tenancies', and the grounds for possession are discretionary. However, during the first year, or later following anti-social behaviour, there may be a form of tenancy that can be ended by notice.

10 Housing Act 1985 Sch. 2 Ground 1.

11 At common law there is a right to possession as soon as the mortgage is entered (*Four-Maids Ltd v Dudley Marshall (Properties) Ltd* [1957] Ch. 317), although this can be varied by contract, and in practice a mortgagee would usually only enter into possession in

Other forms of debt can also lead to loss of the home: judgment creditors, with unsecured debt, are able to apply for a charging order to be made if the debtor is a home owner with equity in the home,[12] and can then apply for an order for sale of the house. Almost 136,000 charging orders were made in 2008,[13] and Citizens Advice have expressed concern about the rising use of charging orders and the threat of orders for sale against their homes in order to intimidate debtors into paying what can be relatively small sums of money due.[14] Creditors can also make the debtor bankrupt, which can then also lead to loss of the home.[15]

In practice, the likelihood of losing a home because of money owed will depend not only on the legal rules governing the relationship between tenant and landlord or debtor and creditor, but on a variety of other factors, some formal, some less so. Different lenders and landlords may adopt different strategies towards arrears management, so that not all cases of arrears will result in court actions for immediate repossession,[16] and even when a possession case reaches court there is considerable variety in the likely outcome of the proceedings. In some arrears situations the judge has no discretion but to order possession if the grounds are made out. But a judge who is uncomfortable with evicting a family may try very hard to find some way of avoiding this outcome, perhaps by a scrupulous scrutiny of the paperwork.[17] In other cases a judge may have discretion whether to order possession or not, which can result in much local variation. Research by Hunter and others into the exercise of judicial discretion in rent arrears cases shows that

---

order to secure vacant possession prior to a sale. By statute the power to sell arises as soon as the debt is due (Law of Property Act 1925 s. 101) and can be exercised, inter alia, once interest payments are two months in arrears (Law of Property Act 1925 s. 103; although s. 103 is often excluded by contract so that the power of sale is exercisable as soon as there is default).

12 See Charging Orders Act 1979.

13 Ministry of Justice, 'Judicial and Court Statistics 2008' (2009; available at http://www.justice.gov.uk/publications/docs/judicial-court-stats-2008-full.pdf) 79. In 2004 this figure was just over 33,000.

14 CAB evidence briefing, 'Out of Order' (June 2009), available online at http://www.citizensadvice.org.uk/index/campaigns/policy_campaign_publications/evidence_reports/er_consumerandebt/out_of_order.htm (accessed 9 October 2009).

15 Insolvency Act 1986 s. 335A.

16 C. Hunter and J. Nixon, 'Better a Public Tenant than a Private Borrower Be: The Possession Process and The Threat of Eviction' in D. Cowan (ed.) *Housing: Participation and Exclusion* (Ashgate, Aldershot 1998), 92.

17 For example, a study by Hunter and others into how judges deal with rent arrears cases found that Ground 8 (the mandatory ground for rent arrears) was operating in a far from mandatory way: C. Hunter et al., 'The Exercise of Judicial Discretion in Rent Arrears Cases' (DCA Research Series 6/05, 2005; available at www.dca.gov.uk/research/2005/6_2005.htm), iv. Anecdotal evidence shows that judges also search for technical reasons not to grant possession in mortgage cases by means such as applying service rules and time limits very strictly, and refusing to proceed if relevant searches have not been done.

there are different patterns of decision between courts, and between individual judges in courts.[18] But it is not only formal legal rules and what happens in court that matter. Before reaching court there are a number of regulatory practices that may affect how much of the occupier's personal story is known to the creditor or landlord, and how likely the creditor or landlord is to bring possession proceedings. In recent years there have, for example, been pre-action protocols issued both for rent arrears and mortgage default.[19] Informal, extra-legal practices are also tremendously important. Since the credit crunch has struck the government has launched a number of initiatives designed to help borrowers stay in their homes, but it tends to be only the big high-street lenders that have signed up to these.[20] Borrowers from sub-prime lenders are much more likely to lose their homes not simply because their repayments are often at the margins of affordability but also because these lenders tend to be inflexible and hasty.[21] Likewise, some landlords will be more patient and willing and able to allow time for payment whereas others may rush to recover possession.[22]

(3) Different Opportunities to Tell Different Personal Stories

It is, of course, always possible for a creditor or landlord to listen to personal home stories when considering how to respond to arrears: there is no compulsion to recover possession. In terms of formal responses, however, there are three broad categories within which cases can be considered.

First, are those cases in which the personal home story is not legally relevant. By using 'Ground 8', for example, a private landlord has a mandatory ground for possession on the basis of two months' rent arrears.[23] If the ground is proven, the judge has to order possession: there is no requirement for the landlord to engage with the tenant, there is no opportunity for a judge to hear the tenant's story and the judge has no discretion. Thus, a 'non-social' private landlord can recover possession without the judge or landlord knowing anything of the tenant's personal circumstances. Where Ground 8 is being used by a social landlord, however, the landlord cannot simply rely on Ground 8 but must follow regulatory guidance which provides an opportunity for personal stories to be aired to the landlord. Unlike the wholly private landlord, a social landlord should comply both with

18 C. Hunter et al., 'The Exercise of Judicial Discretion in Rent Arrears Cases' (DCA Research Series 6/05, 2005; available at www.dca.gov.uk/research/2005/6_2005.htm) ii.

19 Pre-action Protocol for Possession Claims based on rent arrears; and Pre-Action Protocol for Possession Claims based on Mortgage or Home Purchase Plan Arrears in Respect of Residential Property: both available from www.justice.gov.uk.

20 See text below following n. 80.

21 See text below following n. 67.

22 See text below following n. 67.

23 Housing Act 1988 Sch. 2 Ground 8.

the good practice guides on rent arrears management[24] and the pre-action rent arrears protocol.[25] Collectively these good practice guidelines encourage greater communication between the landlord and tenant and promote 'eviction…as a last resort' only. Once the case reaches court, however, possession must follow if the ground is proven even if it is a social landlord bringing the action.

Secondly, there are cases in which what can be described as the occupier's 'personal *financial* story' is legally relevant but the wider home story is not. The personal financial story includes the occupier's financial circumstances, the explanations as to why she has fallen into debt and the prospects of her being able to make future payments and pay any arrears due. Mortgage cases come into this group as a court has power to stay, suspend or postpone possession if the mortgagor is likely to be able within a reasonable period to pay any sums due under the mortgage.[26] In these cases, the judge has some discretion in relation to the decision as to whether (and when) possession should be given, but is allowed only to take account of financial matters.

Finally, there are cases in which both the personal financial and home stories can be taken into account. It is this category that gives the widest discretion to the judge. This degree of discretion is explicit in cases involving the Trusts of Land and Appointment of Trustees Act 1996 (TLATA) where a creditor is seeking possession based on a security interest against part of a co-owned property. It is also present, though with no express reference to home meanings, in tenancy cases that require the landlord to prove that it is 'reasonable' for possession to be ordered, because 'reasonableness' is wide enough to encompass both financial and home stories if the judge wishes to take them into account.[27] This will include any case in which a local authority landlord is seeking to recover possession on the grounds of rent arrears,[28] as well as where private and (other) social landlords are seeking possession for rent problems but are not relying on Ground 8.[29]

Looking only at strict legal relevance tells only part of the story however. As seen in the Ground 8 cases, the law is the same for both private landlords and registered providers of social housing. The practice of dispossession operates very differently, however. The behaviour of landlords is not governed solely by legal rules, but is influenced by other processes, some formally required, others to do with the perceived 'mission' of the landlord. So, for example, social landlords in receipt of public funding need to comply with regulatory guidance issued by the

24 ODPM, 'Improving the Effectiveness of Rent Arrears Management; Good Practice Guidance' (June 2005), and DCLG, 'Guide on Effective Rent Arrears Management' (August 2006), both available from www.communities.gov.uk.

25 Pre-action Protocol for Possession Claims based on rent arrears; available from www.justice.gov.uk.

26 Administration of Justice Act 1970 s. 36.

27 These cases are discussed below in the text accompanying n. 93.

28 Housing Act 1985 Sch. 2 Ground 1.

29 Housing Act 1988 Sch. 2 Grounds 10 and 11.

Tenant Services Authority. In addition, as will be seen below, even though the rent arrears protocol is not binding law it does impact on judicial behaviour. The same kinds of issues can be seen operating in mortgagee repossession. The likelihood of losing a home for debt is affected at least as much by extra-legal considerations, both 'soft law' and the personality of the creditor, as it is by legal processes.

(4) Personal Stories through Human Rights: a Trump Card?

Although the Human Rights Act 1988 came into force in October 2000, it remains unclear exactly how the Convention rights given effect under this Act apply to cases involving the repossession of homes, notwithstanding several cases that have been heard in the House of Lords. The right most directly applicable to dispossession for arrears is contained in Article 8 paragraph 1, which provides that everyone has the right to respect for his home. This is qualified by paragraph 2 which provides that there can be no interference with this right by a public authority except in accordance with the law and (inter alia) as necessary in a democratic society in the interests of the economic well-being of the country or for the protection of the rights and freedoms of others. It has been clear since the case of *Kay v London Borough of Lambeth* that a possession action does involve an interference with the right to respect for home, even in cases when there is no continuing lawful right to occupy.[30] It is also clear that where there is a lawful right to recover possession there will usually be justification for this interference as the housing needs of others is accepted as a legitimate aim,[31] as is protecting the rights of the lawful owner.[32] What remains obscure is the extent to which the decision to end a lawful right to occupy (which would apply to tenancies being terminated for rent arrears), to commence possession proceedings and then to evict must be reasonable in the light of the occupier's personal circumstances which are known (or perhaps, ought to be known) to the owner.

Although the law is still evolving in this area it does appear to have reached the point whereby a direct human rights challenge to possession is unlikely to succeed in English law. This sits uncomfortably alongside the approach taken in the European Court of Human Rights in *McCann v United Kingdom* where there was a clear statement about the need for there to be some balancing carried out before someone loses their home:

> the loss of one's home is a most extreme form of interference with the right to respect for the home. Any person at risk of an interference of this magnitude should in principle be able to have the proportionality of the measure determined by an independent tribunal in the light of the relevant principles under Article

30 [2006] UKHL 10 [2006] AC 465.
31 *Blecic v Croatia* (2004) 41 EHRR 185.
32 *McCann v United Kingdom* (App No 19009/04) [2008] LGR 474.

> 8 of the Convention, notwithstanding that, under domestic law, his right of occupation has come to an end ...[33]

Cases before the European Court of Human Rights where Article 8 has been found to be violated have taken account of the impact of loss having regard to the personal home story, including the longevity of occupation.[34] In contrast, English courts have been reluctant to allow consideration of personal circumstances under the human rights umbrella and the most recent case in the House of Lords (the top appellate court), *Doherty v Birmingham City Council*,[35] reveals a clear judicial discomfort with the approach taken in *McCann v United Kingdom*. The tension between the domestic and European courts continues, and further cases are due to be heard in Strasbourg.

In the meantime, human rights law has not been completely without impact on domestic law. 'Convention ways of thinking' are influencing public law remedies. This means that a local authority landlord (and quite possibly registered social providers[36]) must take account of relevant facts when taking possession action, which may include having regard to the personal circumstances of the occupier and the length of occupation.[37] Furthermore, notwithstanding the judicial caution revealed in cases such as *Doherty*,[38] it may be that the court itself must also give some consideration to the personal circumstances of the occupier in deciding whether to order possession.[39] In practice, however, unless the court has a statutory discretion as to whether or not to order possession at all (as to which, see below), it may be that the most that the court will be able to do is defer possession for a short period. This is because section 89 of the Housing Act 1980 (which applies, inter alia, to Ground 8 possession cases) provides that possession should not be deferred for more than 14 days unless this would cause

---

33 *McCann v United Kingdom* (App No 19009/04) [2008] LGR 474 [50].

34 See *Connors v UK* (App No 66746/01) (2004) 40 EHRR 189 (ECtHR). At [85] the Court noted the seriousness of the interference: 'The applicant and his family were evicted from the site where they had lived, with a short absence, for some fourteen to fifteen years, with consequent difficulties in finding a lawful alternative location for their caravans, in coping with health problems and young children and in ensuring continuation in the children's education. The family was, in effect, rendered homeless, with the adverse consequences on security and well-being which that entails.'

35 [2008] UKHL 57 [2008] 3 WLR 636.

36 The Court of Appeal in *London & Quadrant Housing Trust v Weaver* [2009] EWCA Civ 587 held that termination of a tenancy by a housing trust was a public act sufficient to bring it within the Human Rights Act 1998.

37 *Doran v Liverpool CC* [2009] EWCA Civ 146; *Central Bedfordshire Council v Taylor* [2009] EWCA Civ 613.

38 *Doherty v Birmingham City Council* [2008] UKHL 57 [2008] 3 WLR 636.

39 *Central Bedfordshire Council v Taylor* [2009] EWCA Civ 613.

exceptional hardship, and even then it cannot be deferred for more than six weeks from the making of the order.[40]

The state of the Article 8 jurisprudence is unclear. In practice, notwithstanding the torrent of case law, Article 8 has had very little impact on the outcome in possession cases to date. It is possible that the personal home story may be part of what a public authority landlord and the court have to take into account; if so, it may well buy a few extra weeks for the occupier but this is a jurisdiction that the courts already have through section 89 where possession would cause exceptional hardship. The discussion that follows is subject to the possibility that personal stories may become relevant through the development of the human rights jurisprudence. However, in the absence of a clear indication that English law is prepared to give real substance to Art 8 in the context of possession actions, the following sections consider other 'domestic' avenues through which these stories may be taken into account by a court.

(5) Personal Stories: No Legal Relevance

There are two main types of case in which personal stories have no legal relevance. The first is where the property is both tenanted and subject to a mortgage on which the landlord has defaulted, and the landlord's mortgagee takes an action for possession. The second is where a private landlord seeks possession on Ground 8 because the tenant has defaulted on payment of rent.

Tenanted Properties

Rates of landlord mortgage default rose during the credit crunch that started in 2007,[41] and in 2009 the repossession rate for 'buy-to-let' (BTL) properties became marginally higher than that for owner-occupier mortgages.[42]

40 This limitation does not apply to mortgagee possession actions or discretionary grounds for tenancy possession. See also *Central Bedfordshire Council v Taylor* [2009] EWCA Civ 613: but this was a case where the occupier had no lawful right to remain.

41 Statistics are available only for buy-to-let (BTL) mortgages (not for hidden 'unauthorised' lettings). In the second quarter of 2009, 2.49 per cent of all BTL mortgages were in arrears of three months or more, down 17 per cent from the peak of 3.06 per cent in the previous quarter. Source: Council of Mortgage Lenders (CML). The Department of Communities and Local Government (DCLG), estimated around 2,000–3,000 unauthorised tenants would be evicted for landlord default in 2009: DCLG, 'Lender Repossession of Residential Property: Protection of Tenants – Consultation' (August 2009) para 1.17.

42 Around 1,400 BTL mortgaged properties were taken into possession in the second quarter of 2009 (0.12 per cent of all BTL mortgages); (compared to 11,400 owner-occupier possessions; 0.1 per cent of all owner occupation mortgages). The more common mortgagee remedy for BTL mortgages is to appoint a receiver (who collects the rent and passes it on to the mortgagee, whilst allowing the tenant to remain in place). In the second quarter of 2009,

If a mortgagee repossesses a property that has been let, the occupier (the tenant) has no opportunity to tell his personal story. Some lettings, especially those granted by landlords who have financed the purchase of the house with a BTL mortgage, will bind the lender, but generally these can be ended on two months' notice.[43] With unauthorised lettings, for example those granted by owner-occupiers in breach of the terms of the mortgage, the tenant can be immediately evicted. Studies reveal that tenants are extremely vulnerable in these situations. Often they will have virtually no notice of the possession hearing;[44] but even if aware of the hearing the tenant has no standing, and the judge has no power to defer possession because of the tenant's circumstances. Further, until recently, in these circumstances the occupier often had little or no warning of imminent eviction.[45] Recent changes to the Civil Procedure Rules (lengthening the notice period and requiring notification of a hearing to be addressed to 'the tenant or the occupier')[46] increase the likelihood of the tenant learning of the possession hearing, and it is likely that the law will change further so that all tenants can ask for two months' notice before eviction.[47] But even if the most 'tenant friendly' version of these proposals becomes law the tenant will still have to move out; he may just have a bit longer to prepare for it.

Ground 8

Ground 8 can be used by a landlord to recover possession when the tenant is two months in arrears with rent and, unless the arrears are paid by the time of the

there were 2,500 receivers newly appointed (0.91 per cent of all BTL mortgages), and this was a stunning increase from a year earlier when only 0.09 per cent had a receiver in place. Source: CML (www.cml.org.uk/cml/media/press/2358; accessed 19 October 2009).

43 Housing Act 1988 s. 21.

44 Crisis, Citizens Advice Bureau, Shelter, Chartered Institute of Housing, 'A Private Matter? Private Tenants: the Forgotten Victims of the Repossessions Crisis' (2009, available at www.citizensadvice.org.uk/a_private_matter).

45 Crisis, Citizens Advice Bureau, Shelter, Chartered Institute of Housing 'A Private Matter? Private Tenants: the Forgotten Victims of the Repossessions Crisis' (2009, available at www.citizensadvice.org.uk/a_private_matter). In a survey of advisers, 10 per cent of respondents said that the tenant had no notice at all, and nearly a quarter said that the most common outcome was that the tenant became homeless.

46 The changes were introduced in April and October 2009.

47 Crisis and others called for legislative amendment so that possession can be deferred, taking into account the interests of vulnerable occupiers and the household's economic circumstances: Crisis, Citizens Advice Bureau, Shelter, Chartered Institute of Housing 'A Private Matter? Private Tenants: the Forgotten Victims of the Repossessions Crisis' (2009, available at www.citizensadvice.org.uk/a_private_matter) 6. The government consultation on this issue closed on 14 October 2009: DCLG, 'Lender Repossession of Residential Property: Protection of Tenants – Consultation' (2009, available at www.communities.gov.uk/documents/housing/pdf/1304815).

hearing, the judge must order possession.[48] The only – very limited – discretion conferred on the court is that in section 89 of the Housing Act 1980, which allows the court to extend the usual 14-day period for possession to up to six weeks in cases of 'exceptional hardship'. The judge is unable to listen to any stories, personal or otherwise, that might give a reason for not ordering possession. This is so even though a common cause of arrears is administrative delay with the payment of housing benefit.[49] There is considerable judicial disquiet about Ground 8 and it was described by Dyson LJ in *North British Housing Association Ltd v Matthews* as 'potentially draconian in its application'.[50] The use of Ground 8 by social landlords is controversial. It is thought, by some, to go against their 'social housing' mission, while others make regular use of it.[51]

Although Ground 8 allows no opportunity for the occupier to tell his personal story to the judge, there may well be opportunities tell this story at an earlier stage if there is a social landlord. Social landlords should follow both the good practice guides to rent arrears management, and the pre-action rent arrears protocol (PRAP).[52] Both aim to promote communication between the landlord and tenant so that eviction is used only as a last resort. The PRAP requires parties to try to agree an affordable way of the tenant paying arrears, and for the landlord to assist the tenant in any housing benefit claims. The court is directed to take into account whether the protocol has been followed when considering what orders to make and sanctions for non-compliance are specifically provided: if the landlord unreasonably fails to comply with the protocol, the court can impose an order for

48 It is two months if the rent is paid monthly, with different arrears periods for different payment methods.

49 See, for example, H. Pawson et al., 'The Use of Possession Actions and Evictions by Social Landlords' (ODPM, 2005; available at www.communities.gov.uk/publications/housing/203568).

50 [2004] EWCA Civ 1736 [33]. All but one of the judges interviewed by Hunter and others expressed some distaste for its use: C. Hunter et al., 'The Exercise of Judicial Discretion in Rent Arrears Cases' (DCA Research Series 6/05, 2005; available at www.dca.gov.uk/research/2005/6_2005.htm) 90.

51 Research published in 2005 shows one third of housing associations (and half of London housing associations) making use of Ground 8: H. Pawson et al., 'The Use of Possession Actions and Evictions by Social Landlords' (ODPM, 2005; available at www.communities.gov.uk/publications/housing/203568). A small-scale study by CAB shows that of 10 housing associations they contacted that do use Ground 8 and have full sets of figures, half evicted no tenants on the basis of Ground 8 whereas one said that Ground 8 evictions represented 93 per cent of all tenants evicted: CAB evidence, 'Unfinished Business' (2008; available at http://www.citizensadvice.org.uk/index/campaigns/policy_campaign_publications/evidence_reports/er_housing/unfinished_business.htm) Table 1.

52 ODPM, 'Improving the Effectiveness of Rent Arrears Management; Good Practice Guidance' (June 2005), and DCLG, 'Guide on Effective Rent Arrears Management' (August 2006), both available from www.communities.gov.uk. Pre-action Protocol for Possession Claims based on rent arrears; available from www.justice.gov.uk.

costs, and, in non-mandatory grounds cases, the court may adjourn, strike out or dismiss claims. Research by the Citizens Advice Bureau (CAB) indicates that the PRAP has had a broadly positive effect in preventing unnecessary court action, although the extent of compliance varies.[53]

Of course, the fact that Ground 8 is used does not necessarily mean that the landlord is acting unreasonably. It may already have exhausted all other realistic options. Certainly, this was the view taken by the housing manager for London and Quadrant Housing Trust, which makes 'regular use of ground 8'.[54] His evidence in *R (Weaver) v London and Quadrant Housing Trust* stated:

> our principal objectives are to avoid arrears occurring in the first place, but where they do to deal with them without the need for service of a NoSP[55] and certainly without the necessity then to issue proceedings let alone pursue them as far as a hearing…In those cases where the arrears are high and neither a lump sum nor a suitable agreement is forthcoming, then obtaining an outright order under Ground 8 may be the only realistic or sensible option from the tenant's point of view as much as LQHT's.[56]

Richards LJ in the Divisional Court agreed that the fact that LQHT had relied on Ground 8 did not mean that it had failed to use all reasonable alternatives.[57]

Although most social landlords who use Ground 8 may do so sensitively, this leaves tenants in a vulnerable position. The CAB is highly critical of the continued use of Ground 8 by a minority of housing associations as it prevents independent scrutiny by the courts as to the reasonableness of the landlord's claim for possession.

(6) Personal Financial Story Bears Legal Relevance

Although the personal home story is not legally relevant in owner-occupation mortgage cases, the personal financial story is. The usual process for mortgagee sale is for the mortgagee first to obtain a court order for possession of the property

---

53 It found there 'was considerable variation in the level of compliance, both between housing associations and in terms of the different elements of the protocol itself': CAB evidence, 'Unfinished Business' (2008; available at http://www.citizensadvice.org.uk/index/campaigns/policy_campaign_publications/evidence_reports/er_housing/unfinished_business.htm).

54 This is taken from the Audit Commission report on LQHT referred to in *R (Weaver) v London and Quadrant Housing Trust* [2008] EWHC 1377 (Admin) [74].

55 A 'NoSP' is a notice seeking possession.

56 *R (Weaver) v London and Quadrant Housing Trust* [2008] EWHC 1377 (Admin) [77].

57 Ibid. [89].

so that it can be sold with vacant possession.[58] The court has a discretion to defer possession, but only taking into account the borrower's ability to pay 'monies due'.[59] 'Home meanings' do not count. The process before the court gives little opportunity to ask detailed questions even within the confines of investigating the financial position of the borrower: earlier studies have found that, in practice, only around one half of borrowers attend possession hearings (although attendance rates may have increased since) or make written submissions to the court, and the average length of a repossession hearing is five minutes.[60]

This means that what happens before the case reaches the judge is important. Unless lenders are perceived to be supportive and sympathetic early on in the process, borrowers may simply abandon hope and walk away. More than one in four possessions is voluntary.[61] Other borrowers, fearing repossession, have resorted to sale and rent back deals, in the hope that this will enable them to stay in their home.[62]

There is some regulation of mortgagee behaviour. Most mainstream lenders are regulated by the Financial Services Authority (FSA) which provides guidance on arrears and repossessions in the Mortgage Conduct of Business Rules (MCOB).[63]

---

58 A lender may take possession without a court order (see *Ropaigealach v Barclays Bank* [2000] QB 263 (CA)) but this is unusual because of the risk of committing a criminal offence. Judicial control can also be bypassed by selling mortgaged property subject to the mortgage. Once the purchaser discharges the mortgage the occupiers will have no right to remain: *Horsham Properties v Clark and Beech* [2008] EWHC 2327 (Ch) [2009] 1 WLR 1255. The CML has issued a voluntary statement that its members will not sell owner occupied properties without first seeking a court order for possession (save for vacant and abandoned properties): http://www.cml.org.uk/cml/policy/issues/4707 (accessed 19 October 2009).

59 Administration of Justice Act 1970 s. 36.

60 C. Hunter et al., 'The Exercise of Judicial Discretion in Rent Arrears Cases' (DCA Research Series 6/05, 2005; available at www.dca.gov.uk/research/2005/6_2005.htm) 10 and 106.

61 These figures were supplied by the Council of Mortgage Lenders and are based on possession by CML members (membership is open to lender organisations that are authorised and regulated by the Financial Services Authority (FSA)). Of course, walking away does not discharge the contractual debt.

62 Many of such schemes are disadvantageous and fail to offer the security sought and promised: see OFT, 'Sale and Rent Back: An OFT Market Study' (October 2008, OFT 1018) available at http://www.oft.gov.uk/shared_oft/reports/consumer_protection/oft1018.pdf. The sale and rent back market is a recent phenomenon (around 50,000 transactions entered by the time of the OFT study), and evidence suggests that around 60 per cent of individuals resorting to it were facing repossession: para 3.56. The FSA introduced an interim regime to regulate sale and rent back in summer 2009, with a view to there being a full regulatory regime in place by the second quarter of 2010.

63 The mortgage contracts regulated by the FSA are defined by paragraph 61 (3)(a) of the Financial Services and Markets Act 2000 (Regulated Activities) Order 2001, SI 2001/544. Broadly, this covers mortgages to consumers that involve a first legal charge on

The MCOB guidance on arrears and possession places information disclosure requirements on lenders, but there is nothing that requires them to find out about the circumstances of the occupier before acting, or that in any other way tempers the legal right of the lender to seek possession. Possession claims may well be brought as soon as two months' arrears have accrued,[64] and even if there is a simple and temporary explanation for the default the lender may never learn of it.

Ironically, the effect of the credit crunch and fall in property values is that lenders are generally showing greater forbearance towards borrowers. The emphasis is less on the strict 'pay or possess' policy of the past and more on the aim of minimising or stabilising arrears and supporting the borrower through difficult circumstances.[65] This customer-focused approach, which involves a degree of listening to personal stories, has been driven by a number of different factors; in part economic drivers that seek to reduce balance sheet losses, but also the changed regulatory climate and increased government scrutiny.[66]

As at the end of 2009, it is unclear how much lender type still influences arrears and repossession practices. A study by the FSA only a year earlier revealed considerable differences between 'mainstream' and 'specialist' lenders (specialist lenders include those lending to people with impaired credit ratings, using self-certification, and BTL landlords).[67] Specialist lenders were less likely to take account of the borrower's circumstances, more ready (in fact, the FSA say 'too

---

a dwelling. It does not cover 'buy-to-let' mortgages or second charges. The section of the MCOB dealing with arrears and possessions is MCOB 13, available at http://fsahandbook.info/FSA/html/handbook/MCOB. Second mortgages come within the Consumer Credit Act 1974, but there does not appear to be comparable guidance for the second mortgagees.

64 A small-scale survey by the Citizens Advice Bureau (CAB) found that in 15 per cent of cases the lender took court action before three months: Citizens Advice, 'Mortgage Remedies (Possession and Sale) Review Lines of Inquiry: Response by Citizens Advice to the Ministry of Justice' (Citizens Advice, London 2009) replies to q14. A two-month wait is required under the MCOB. Statute provides that the right to sell is exercisable after two months' arrears: Law of Property Act 1925 s. 103. More recent research notes that possession actions are often much later: J. Ford and A. Wallace, 'Uncharted Territory? Managing Mortgage Arrears and Possessions' (Shelter, 2009; available at http://england.shelter.org.uk/__data/assets/pdf_file/0017/203705/Uncharted_Territory.pdf) 22.

65 J. Ford and A. Wallace 'Uncharted Territory? Managing Mortgage Arrears and Possessions' (Shelter, 2009; available at http://england.shelter.org.uk/__data/assets/pdf_file/0017/203705/Uncharted_Territory.pdf) 24.

66 Ibid.

67 FSA/PN/087/2008, 5 August 2008. This pre-dated the introduction of the Mortgage Arrears Pre-action Protocol at the end of 2008 (discussed below in text). Other, earlier, studies likewise found considerable variation in lender practices, and the imposition of unreasonable charges on borrowers as soon as they fall into arrears: see P. Tutton and S. Edwards, 'Set Up to Fail: CAB Clients' Experience of Mortgage and Secured Loan Arrears Problems' (CAB, London 2007); L. Whitehouse, 'The Impact of Consumerism on the Homeowner' in D. Cowan (ed.), *Housing: Participation and Exclusion* (Ashgate, Dartmouth 1998) 138. See also L. Whitehouse, 'The Homeowner: Citizen or Consumer?'

ready') to take court action, and had lower standards of controls in place. All lenders could have done more to consider customers' individual circumstances and offer options as to how to resolve arrears issues: they tended to be inflexible and not willing to accommodate suggested alternative repayment schedules (the common response was 'pay in full or face legal proceedings'), and would initiate court proceedings when the borrower had accrued around three months' of arrears.[68] Interestingly, whereas most borrowers were not happy with the treatment received from lenders when they were in arrears the research found that consumers felt that *courts* were more willing to be sympathetic and hear their stories, offering a managed solution. Research commissioned by Shelter which reported in July 2009 noted a cultural shift in lenders' management of mortgage arrears towards 'managed forbearance' but the authors also observed that this change was not universal.[69] It remains unclear as yet just how widespread this shift is from the hard policy of 'pay or possess' amongst lenders, and whether it will be sufficiently entrenched to continue into periods of economic growth.

As rising possession figures came to the fore in the latter half of 2008,[70] the government introduced a raft of measures designed to help owner-occupiers to be able to stay in their homes. This included the introduction of a Mortgage Pre-action Protocol (MPAP).[71] The aim is to keep the borrower fully informed of the amount of their indebtedness and to encourage lenders to see if there is some way of sorting out the problem short of seeking possession. The impact of the protocol is, however, variable and the extent of compliance is affected by the identity of the mortgagee. The protocol is a further example of guidance that occupies the fuzzy area between law and good practice, setting out to describe 'the behaviour the court will normally expect of the parties prior to the start of a possession claim'.[72] According to surveys conducted by advice agencies, not all lenders are following the protocol.[73] Although mainstream lenders have largely improved their arrears and repossession practices following its introduction, sub-prime and second charge

---

in S. Bright and J. Dewar (eds), *Land Law: Themes and Perspectives* (Oxford University Press, Oxford 1998).

68 'Mortgage Effectiveness Review: Arrears Findings' (FSA, 2008; available at www.fsa.gov.uk/pubs/other/mer_report.pdf).

69 J. Ford and A. Wallace, 'Uncharted Territory? Managing Mortgage Arrears and Possessions' (Shelter, 2009; available at http://england.shelter.org.uk/_data/assets/pdf_file/0017/203705/Uncharted_Territory.pdf) 6.

70 CML figures show 40,000 properties taken into possession (this includes voluntary possessions) in 2008, up from 25,900 in 2007.

71 Pre-action Protocol for Possession Claims based on Mortgage or Home Purchase Plan Arrears in respect of Residential Property. This is available on the Civil Justice Council website (http://www.civiljusticecouncil.gov.uk/files/Mortgage_Pre-Action_protocol_21_Oct.pdf) accessed 16 September 2010. It came into force in November 2008.

72 Preamble 1.1.

73 'Mortgage and Secured Loan Arrears: Adviser and Borrower Surveys' (research from AdviceUK, Citizens Advice, Money Advice Trust and Shelter, 2009; available at

lenders have not.[74] There are no sanctions for failing to use the protocol,[75] and it is unclear whether courts can impose a costs sanction.[76] The tone of the protocol is much weaker than that of the PRAP discussed earlier, and the changes between the initial draft and the final version of the protocol suggest that the strong lobbying arm of the mortgage industry was effective to water down the proposals.[77]

The MPAP has, however, had some positive effects. Surveys suggest that judges now ask more questions about whether lenders tried to reach agreement before taking court action, and there is a willingness by many judges to adjourn cases where the lender has not followed the protocol.[78] Following the introduction of the protocol there was a significant reduction in the number of possession orders being made: 19,064 possession *orders* were granted in the county courts in the second quarter of 2009, 39 per cent lower than in the same period a year earlier.[79] The MPAP also coincided with a fall of around 50 per cent in the number of new mortgage repossession *claims* being issued.[80]

Other government initiatives have also contributed to the reduction in the number of possession orders. For example, an agreement was reached with major

---

http://england.shelter.org.uk/_data/assets/pdf_file/0004/192685/Mortgage_and_secured_loan_arrears_Final_Report.pdf).

74 The Adviser and Borrower Surveys looked at: arrears collection practices, arranging arrears payment plans, considering other options, granting time to sell their property (where there is equity in the property), capitalising arrears and/or extending mortgage term, and agreeing to change the payment date.

75 In contrast to the explicit sanctions in the rent arrears protocol discussed below, and in the draft MPAP.

76 The Adviser and Borrower Surveys note that case law authority suggests that courts have power to disallow costs where they have been unreasonably incurred (n. 13), but the position is not clear.

77 Whitehouse describes it as 'an opportunity lost in the attempt to reform the law of mortgage': L. Whitehouse, 'The Mortgage Arrears Pre-action Protocol: an Opportunity Lost' (2009) 72 *MLR* 793, 814. She argues that the draft sought to challenge three fundamental tenets of the law of mortgage: the economic rationale for regulation, the inherent right to possession and the freedom of contract principle. The final version is an 'ideological volte-face' (801).

78 Anecdotal evidence suggests that many district judges apply MPAP strictly, and effectively give it the force of law.

79 Ministry of Justice, 'Statistics on Mortgage and Landlord Possession Actions in the County Courts – Second Quarter 2009' (statistics bulletin, 2009; available at http://www.justice.gov.uk/publications/docs/mortgage-landlord-possession-stats-notice.pdf). These figures do not indicate how many properties have actually been repossessed. Repossessions can occur without a court order, and not all court orders result in repossession.

80 Figures taken from the daily and weekly numbers of new mortgage repossession claims being issued in the courts as evidenced from administrative records: Ministry of Justice, 'Statistics on Mortgage and Landlord Possession Actions in the County Courts – Second Quarter 2009' (statistics bulletin, 14 August 2009; available at http://www.justice.gov.uk/publications/docs/mortgage-landlord-possession-stats-notice.pdf).

lenders that they would wait at least three months before initiating repossession proceedings.[81] Another scheme, the Homeowner Mortgage Support Scheme, allows mortgagors to defer a proportion of the interest payments for up to two years.[82] The period which a borrower has to wait before welfare payments to assist with mortgage interest payments are payable has also been reduced.[83] There is also a mortgage rescue scheme, which enables qualifying borrowers,[84] with the assistance of social landlords, to stay in their home notwithstanding mortgage difficulties, either by reducing the size of the commercial mortgage (by changing to 'shared equity'[85]) or by becoming renters (through 'mortgage to rent').[86] However, mortgage rescue and the homeowner mortgage support scheme are available only with the major lenders. This is a serious limitation. The more vulnerable borrowers – those with poor credit histories, illnesses and unreliable income levels – are much more likely to fall into arrears and to have borrowed from the sub-prime lenders who, as we have seen, pursue more aggressive arrears and repossession policies and are not participants in several of these more progressive government initiatives.

The thrust of these measures is to enable borrowers in financial difficulties to be able to stay in their home by working out some kind of arrangement with the lender. However, unless they are able to prove that there is a reasonable prospect of paying (all) the arrears within a reasonable time they have no *right* to stay, only a hope of the lender's indulgence. In practice the likelihood of arrears leading to loss of the home is heavily dependent upon the attitude of the lender. The personal

---

81 Announced by the Department for Communities and Local Government on 24 November 2008; available at http://www.communities.gov.uk/news/corporate/1071959.

82 The scheme came into effect after 14 April 2009; for details see www.direct.gov.uk. The government guarantees the *deferred* interest payments in return for banks' participation in the scheme. It is too recent to have been included in the research for the Adviser and Borrower Surveys.

83 From 39 weeks to 13 weeks for new working age claims. The capital limit for eligible loans has also been increased. These changes came into effect 5 January 2009. The payment is known as SMI, Support for Mortgage Interest.

84 To qualify borrowers must be eligible for homelessness assistance and in priority need, and there is a cap on the value of the property against which the scheme can be applied. Initially it could not be used for those in negative equity, but this has been changed from 1 May 2009.

85 The details are complex, but in substance it is as if the borrower now owns only part of the house and a non-commercial lender (usually a provider of social housing) provides a low – or no – cost mortgage on the balance.

86 In mortgage to rent, the borrower sells the house to a provider of social housing but can remain in occupation, paying rent. For figures on the uptake of the mortgage rescue scheme, see: http://www.communities.gov.uk/documents/housing/xls/table1303.xls. It was introduced in January 2009; in the period to the end of May 2009 only six households had been approved for mortgage rescue (but approval takes around three and a half months, and 743 households applied for mortgage rescue during the period January to end May 2009).

home story will be wholly irrelevant unless the borrower is able to appeal to the goodwill of the lender.

(7) Personal Stories with a Legal Voice

There are some situations in which a judge is able to take account of the debtor's personal story when deciding whether to order possession. However, as will be seen, in the majority of cases the judge is most likely to focus on financial considerations rather than the personal home story.

Local Authority Tenancies

Most local authority tenants have security of tenure (effectively a right to stay for life unless the landlord can prove a ground for possession).[87] Even if there are rent arrears, possession is never automatic and can be granted only if the court considers it reasonable to make the order.[88] The court also has a discretion as to whether possession should be 'immediate' or 'postponed'.[89] Suspended or postponed possession orders are much more common than outright orders: in the social housing sector there were 43,972 suspended possession orders and 26,184 outright orders made in 2008.[90] In practice, as many of the arrears cases involving social landlords are caused by systemic delays in the payment of housing benefit, the standard order in rent arrears cases has become an adjournment or suspension.[91]

The fact that possession is not automatic means that there is room to hear argument about the occupier's personal home story. The question of reasonableness

87 But it may start as non-secure. CLG Table 601 (http://www.communities.gov.uk/documents/housing/xls/141431.xls) shows that in 2007/08, 69 per cent of new lettings to new tenants were non-secure. Most of these will be 'introductory' tenancies which will usually become secure after one year. In the three years before the introduction of introductory tenancies in 1996, 8 per cent of new lettings to new tenants were non-secure; this suggests that around 90 per cent of local authority lettings are likely to end up as secure tenancies. Introductory tenancies (and demoted tenancies – secure tenancies downgraded following anti-social behaviour) can be ended simply by notice. In these cases, there is no opportunity to tell a personal story, and (apart from the Housing Act 1980 s. 89) no judicial discretion to delay or refuse possession at the request of a landlord, in the event of arrears.

88 Housing Act 1985 Sch. 2, Ground 1.

89 Housing Act 1985 s. 85.

90 Ministry of Justice, 'Judicial and Court Statistics 2008' (2009; available at http://www.justice.gov.uk/publications/docs/judicial-court-stats-2008-full.pdf). Note that these figures – which cover England and Wales – include both local authority and housing association possession cases (even though they are governed by different regimes) and are not confined to rent arrears cases.

91 C. Hunter et al., 'The Exercise of Judicial Discretion in Rent Arrears Cases' (DCA Research Series 6/05, 2005; available at www.dca.gov.uk/research/2005/6_2005.htm) 18.

gives the court a very wide discretion.[92] Lord Greene MR said in *Cumming v Danson*:

> In considering reasonableness...it is...perfectly clear that the duty of the judge is to take into account *all relevant circumstances* as they exist at the date of the hearing. That he must do in what I venture to call a broad, common-sense way as a man of the world, and come to his conclusion giving such weight as he thinks right to the various factors in the situation. Some factors may have little or no weight, others may be decisive, but it is quite wrong for him to exclude from his consideration matters which he ought to take into account.[93]

In deciding whether it is reasonable to order possession the judge must consider the effect that possession would have on *each* party. In *Cresswell v Hodgson* Somervell LJ said: 'I do not see how it is possible to consider whether it is reasonable to make an order unless you consider its effect on landlord and tenant, firstly, if you make it, and secondly, if you do not.'[94]

Given that so few possession cases are reported, however, it is difficult to know what effect 'home meanings' have upon the exercise of judicial discretion. Further, although trial judges are required to consider reasonableness and not merely 'rubber stamp' pre-agreed deals, there is a perception that many judges show 'enormous respect' for pre-arranged deals, while others are more willing to reopen them.[95] Research by Hunter and others into the decisions of district court judges in rent arrears possession cases show that the personal characteristics of judges makes a difference to the outcome. The individual judge injects his or her own view of a case depending on factors such as constructed models of worthiness,[96] perceptions as to whether the cause of arrears is a systemic or individual failure, whether the problem is perceived as a social welfare problem or a simple contractual debt, and the judge's perception of the judging role.[97]

92 In *Whitehouse v Lee* [2009] EWCA Civ 375 Rimer LJ said that 'reasonableness' was a question of fact entrusted to the trial judge, akin to the exercise of a discretion [23].

93 [1942] 2 All ER 653 (CA) 655 (emphasis added). In *Williamson v Pallant* [1924] 2 KB 173 (DC) 176, Swift J said: 'I can hardly conceive any circumstance which affects the relationship of the tenant to the premises which is not a proper circumstance for him to consider.'

94 [1951] 2 KB 92 (CA) 96.

95 See discussion in S. Bright, *Landlord and Tenant Law in Context* (Hart, Oxford 2007) 601.

96 D. Cowan and E. Hitchings, '"Pretty Boring Stuff": District Judges and Housing Possession Proceedings' (2007) 16 *Social and Legal Studies* 363, 374–5.

97 D. Cowan et al., 'District Judges and Possession Proceedings' (2006) 33 *Journal of Law and Society* 547. The Law Commission has noted concerns about the variability of decisions on reasonableness: Law Commission, 'Renting Homes' (Law. Com. No. 284, 2003) 9.83.

In arrears cases, attendance at the court, payment history and the level of arrears have been shown to be important factors in the exercise of discretion, as has knowledge of the tenant's personal circumstances (such as dependent children, old age and mental health issues).[98] District judges are more likely to exercise their discretion in the tenant's favour if he is present in court. Why this is so is unclear, although the fact that the tenant has 'bothered' to turn up may make a difference, as well giving the tenant an opportunity to tell his side of the story. It is also a harder act to make homeless a person whom you can see.[99] Knowledge of the tenant's personal circumstances is important, but seemingly not because of 'home meanings' (that is, the importance of this home as a link to memories, local networks etc.) but because of the *impact* that being made homeless may have. Judges are particularly concerned about the effect that repossession will have on the welfare of children.

There are some reported cases in which the personal home story is considered, but most are cases where possession is sought on the grounds of suitable alternative accommodation being available (not on the ground of rent arrears). In these cases, there is often strong and direct reference to personal home meanings. In *Bracknell Forest BC v Green*, where possession was sought on the grounds that the tenant occupied, with his sister, a property bigger than required for his needs, the judge referred to the tenant's long occupation (over 50 years) of the property with his family, which had given rise to a 'genuine emotional attachment' to the property 'as part of the family', the fact that 'decades of family memories which they hold dear' were located in this home, and that the property provided a 'profound sense of security – connected as it is with their family memories – which sustains them.'[100] Likewise, in finding it not reasonable to order possession in *Whitehouse v Lee*, the Court of Appeal made the importance of home clear: the couple had lived in the home for 45 years, the home was 'one which they loved, where they had brought up their family and in which they had established themselves as valuable, popular and respected members of a local community.'[101]

It may be that district judges do look at similar considerations in arrears cases, but whereas home meanings may provide a reason for refusing to order possession in cases which are determined according to whether suitable alternative accommodation is available, they are unlikely to in rent arrears cases. The nature of the decision is quite different between these situations. Where the suitability

98 C. Hunter et al., 'The Exercise of Judicial Discretion in Rent Arrears Cases' (DCA Research Series 6/05, 2005; available at www.dca.gov.uk/research/2005/6_2005.htm).

99 In the research by Hunter and others, one district judge observed that when he first became a judge it was difficult to look people in the eye if you were going to repossess their home: C. Hunter et al., 'The Exercise of Judicial Discretion in Rent Arrears Cases' (DCA Research Series 6/05, 2005; available at www.dca.gov.uk/research/2005/6_2005.htm) 58.

100 [2009] EWCA Civ 238 [15–17]. See also *Battlespring v Gates* (1984) 11 HLR 6 (CA).

101 [2009] EWCA Civ 375 [33].

of alternative accommodation is in issue, it is natural to take account of the home meaning to decide if it is reasonable to force a move elsewhere. But where the landlord is owed money, it is a given that the landlord should not be burdened with a non-payer, and home meanings appear irrelevant. The fact is that when money is owed, possession will usually follow, even if it is suspended.

Owner-occupation and Creditors

While the discussion above has considered the process for applications for possession and sale by a mortgagee of a sole owner, such applications may also be brought by other types of creditor, and there are various routes by which this may take place. One is where an ordinary, unsecured judgment creditor seeks security for the debt and applies for a charging order on the property. Armed with a charging order the creditor can then apply for an order for sale.[102] Another route is to make the debtor bankrupt; the trustee in bankruptcy then steps into the bankrupt's shoes and has a duty to realise his assets, which may include the home, in order to satisfy the creditors.[103] If the home is co-owned, then it may be necessary to apply for an order for sale under section 14 of the Trusts of Land and Appointment of Trustees Act 1996 (TLATA). Similarly, if the judgment debtor has mortgaged the home but the mortgage operates only as a charge on the debtor's beneficial interest the lender will have to use TLATA to seek sale, rather than the more usual mortgagee remedies.

In each of these contexts, it might be thought that there would be more scope for 'home meanings' to come into play. In the case of the charging order, the debt was not initially a secured debt and it is not obvious that it should take priority over the home interest. Likewise in cases of co-ownership it is not obvious why the creditors' interests should take priority.[104] Whenever sale is sought in a co-ownership situation using TLATA the court is directed by section 15 to take account of a range of (non-exclusive) factors, including the welfare of any minor living in the home, and the circumstances and wishes of the co-owners. The court can make such order 'as it thinks fit'. Similar considerations apply when the court exercises its discretion as to whether to order sale following a charging order.[105] If one of the co-owners is bankrupt and it is the trustee in bankruptcy seeking sale, it is not section 15 that then applies but section 335A of the Insolvency Act 1986. Again the court has discretion to 'make such order as it thinks just and reasonable' and is specifically directed to take account of the needs and financial resources of the bankrupt's partner, the needs of any children, and all the circumstances (other

102 By the Charging Orders Act 1979 s. 3(4) 'a charge imposed by a charging order shall have the like effect and shall be enforceable in the same courts and in the same manner as an equitable charge created by the debtor by writing under his hand.'

103 Insolvency Act 1986 s. 305.

104 After all, the co-owner's interest was first in time.

105 *Close Invoice Finance Ltd v Pile* [2008] EWHC 1580 (Ch).

than the needs of the bankrupt). Likewise if the property is solely owned by the bankrupt, but there are others who occupy it as home and who enjoy statutory 'home rights' under the Family Law Act 1996, the court has discretion in similar terms to section 335A.[106]

In each of these differing situations it is clear that the court is able to take account of 'home meanings', and in some reported decisions, we can clearly see the first instance judges attaching weight to 'home'. In *Edwards v Lloyds TSB Plc*, for example, the judge postponed sale until the youngest child reached majority (which would be around five years) because immediate sale 'would be unacceptably severe in its consequences upon Mrs Edwards and her children.'[107]

Shortly after TLATA came into force there were signs that it could signal a new approach to applications for sale in co-ownership cases. In *The Mortgage Corporation v Shaire*, Neuberger J referred to the fact that the interest of secured creditors is only one of the factors that section 15 directs the court to have regard to and 'there is no suggestion that this is to be given any more importance than the interests of the children residing in the house…'.[108] Indeed, Neuberger J clearly engaged with the balancing of home and security interests.[109] His solution was to try to meet both parties' interests by encouraging the occupier to agree to convert The Mortgage Corporation's (TMC's) equity into a loan, which would enable TMC to receive a return, and would allow Mrs Shaire to stay in her home.

Yet, notwithstanding the flexibility which is possible under TLATA, sale remains the usual outcome. This is surprising, especially where the home is occupied by a co-owner who is not the judgment debtor and whose property interest was first in time. Noting an increasing number of 'non-priority' mortgagees applying for sale, Dixon has commented that 'it might be thought entirely proper that the lender should have to show exceptional hardship in order to obtain sale and thereby reverse the possessory priority enjoyed by the equitable owner.'[110] He suggests that sale should be more difficult to achieve – both for mortgagees without priority ('who should not be able to translate forcibly the equitable owner's proprietary priority into cash priority') and for trustees in bankruptcy ('sale against the wishes of an innocent equitable owner should be more difficult to achieve').[111]

The judicial preference for sale is also seen in the other creditor contexts. Noting the seriousness of converting a charging order into an order for sale, 'particularly where the property to be sold is the debtor's home', Floyd J nonetheless said it will be justified if it is the only way of the debt being paid.[112] This argument is even

106 Insolvency Act 1986 ss 336 and 337.

107 [2004] EWHC 1745 (Ch) [33]. The bank's security was safe on the facts.

108 [2001] Ch 743, 758.

109 [2001] Ch 743, 763–4.

110 M. Dixon, 'Equitable Co-ownership: Proprietary Rights in Name Only?' in E. Cooke (ed.), *Modern Studies in Property Law, Vol 4* (Hart, Oxford 2007) 41, 47.

111 Ibid.

112 *Royal Oak Property Co Ltd v Iktilat* [2008] EWHC 1703 (Ch) [9].

stronger when bankruptcy is involved. If the application for sale of the property is made more than one year after the bankrupt's estate vests in the trustee, the court is required to assume that the interests of the bankrupt's creditors will 'outweigh all other circumstances' unless the circumstances are 'exceptional'. Exceptional circumstances are rare in practice.[113] In *Re Citro*, Hoffmann J postponed sale until the youngest child reached 16, taking into account the fact that there was not much money coming into the house, that the children's education would be upset if the family had to move; and that it would be difficult for the family to afford 'proper accommodation' if they had to move. The Court of Appeal disagreed with this approach. Sale would be only briefly postponed as the facts were not exceptional.[114] In the words of Nourse LJ:

> it is not uncommon for a wife with young children to be faced with eviction in circumstances where the realisation of her beneficial interest will not produce enough to buy a comparable home in the same neighbourhood, or indeed elsewhere. And, if she has to move elsewhere, there may be problems over schooling and so forth. Such circumstances, while engendering a natural sympathy in all who hear of them, cannot be described as exceptional. They are the melancholy consequences of debt and improvidence with which every civilised society has been familiar.[115]

In most cases where exceptional circumstances have been found to justify a delay in possession, the 'home story' has included serious ill-health on the part of an occupier. In this context, courts tend not to refer to the kind of home meanings that we saw at work in relation to some of the discretionary grounds for possession of council tenancies (longevity, community ties, memories etc.). What must instead be shown is that a forced move would have a very severe impact, usually linked to serious illness.[116] In *Nicholls v Lan*, for example, the co-owner suffered from schizophrenia and medical evidence showed that a forced move could be devastating for her, giving rise to the 'probability of recurrent future hospitalisation' and loss of independence.[117] Sale was postponed for a minimum

113 The meaning given to 'exceptional' in some cases would not suggest such a level of rarity: Paul Morgan QC referred to them as 'out of the ordinary course, or unusual, or special, or uncommon' in *Hosking v Michaelides* [2004] All ER (D) 147 (Ch). Even if there are exceptional circumstances, the judge must still decide what is just and reasonable taking into account all the circumstances, including the interests of the creditors: *Nicholls v Lan* [2006] EWHC 1255 (Ch) [10].

114 [1991] Ch 142; there were in fact two properties and two families involved; the facts are simplified in the text.

115 [1991] Ch 142, 157.

116 In *Barca v Mears* [2004] EWHC 2170 (Ch) Strauss QC questioned whether such a narrow approach to exceptional circumstances was compliant with human rights law [39]–[42].

117 [2006] EWHC 1255 (Ch) [35] (the findings of the district judge).

of 18 months. In *Brittain v Haghighat* the home had been adapted to deal with the severe disability of the eldest child and this was found to be exceptional, justifying possession being deferred for three years (the time likely to be necessary for the local authority to provide suitable alternative accommodation).[118]

It thus appears that in all of the creditor contexts it will take unusual circumstances for the 'solid tug of money'[119] not to prevail. The general attitude of the courts is that it will be 'very unfair' to keep creditors – secured or otherwise – waiting for their money 'with no prospect of recovery…and with the debt increasing all the time.'[120] There is little evidence of the personal home story being taken into account unless there is serious illness. Occasionally the presence of children may make a difference, but seldom do other home meanings come into play even though this is quite within the jurisdiction of the judge. Of course, we only see the reported cases. Most cases will be heard in the county court and not reported. Furthermore, it is not unusual for an appellate court to order immediate sale, overturning the decision of the first instance judge.[121] It would be interesting to know more about the outcomes in the unreported cases, and, if there is more of a tendency to postpone or refuse sale at first instance, perhaps because the judge has heard the personal story and listened to the voice of the occupiers.

(8) The Randomness of It All

As the foregoing shows, the formal processes for possession take little account of the personal home story. From the perspective of the individual, it may appear random that the likelihood and speed of losing the home will depend so heavily upon factors such as the form of tenure and the identity of the creditor. A simple (and common) maladministration of housing benefit may lead to loss of the home if a registered provider landlord decides to use Ground 8, but this mandatory ground is not available to a local authority landlord and a judge asked to exercise discretion

---

118 [2009] EWHC 90 (Ch). It was the shorter of three years or three months after the disabled eldest child ceased to live in the property. For further illustrations of exceptional circumstances, see: *Claughton v Charalambous* [1998] BPIR 558 (Ch) (ill-health, special housing needs and sale proceeds would be absorbed by costs); *Re Bremner* [1999] BPIR 185 (Ch) (old age and terminal illness led to postponement until after death of husband); *Close Invoice Finance Ltd v Pile* [2008] EWHC 1580 (Ch) (sale postponed from the 120 days sought to 18 months, taking account of the effect on cancer treatment, the disturbance to education and the sizeable equity in the house).

119 A phrase used in the context of trusts of the family home: *Hofman v Hofman* [1965] N.Z.L.R. 685, 800 (Woodhouse J).

120 *Bank of Ireland v Bell* [2001] 2 FLR 809 (CA) [31]; but this was said in the context of a debt that already exceeded what would be realised on sale.

121 See, for example, *Edwards v Lloyds TSB Bank Plc* [2004] EWHC 1745 (Ch); *Bank of Ireland v Bell* [2001] 2 FLR 809 (CA); *First National Bank v Achampong* [2003] EWCA Civ 487.

is unlikely to find possession 'reasonable'. Even in discretionary possession cases, the study by Hunter and others suggests that the attitude of the district judge and the physical presence of the occupier at the hearing will affect the outcome. In the case of non-social private landlords, bad payers may be evicted through use of Ground 8, but most likely the landlord will simply fail to renew the tenancy. If there is a personal home story to be heard, it probably will not be. And if a BTL tenant is a good tenant but it is the landlord who is in default, there is nothing to be done. The occupier has no voice, and will be lucky to receive much notice of having to move.

Similarly, the vulnerability of owner-occupiers to losing the home will depend a great deal upon the identity of the creditor. Once a mortgage case reaches court, there is nothing a judge can do if the occupier is unable to pay the arrears within a reasonable time. But the likelihood of the case reaching court and of the occupier having a chance to tell his story will turn on the attitude of the mortgagee, on its willingness to engage in meaningful conversations with the borrower and to respond flexibly to the borrower's difficulties. Sub-prime lenders are the least likely to show tolerance. In practice, the legal rules provide only a minimal amount of protection; and home stories will be taken into it only by those lenders who follow regulatory guidance and choose to adopt good practice. Again, it is the home that is at stake and the probability of debt leading to its loss should not be so heavily dependent upon the attitude of the lender.

(9) The Home as a Weak or No-Right

The (un)importance of home in rent arrears cases provides an illustration of what van der Walt describes as the 'rights paradigm': the argument, developed in his book *Property in the Margins*, that the outcome of property disputes is determined by a hierarchy of rights in which ownership rights are privileged over weaker or no property rights. Only rarely is there a fundamental challenge to this paradigm, that is, an:

> instance where a party with a weaker right or without any property right is allowed to challenge and prevent eviction by the…person with a stronger right... purely because of contextual factors or personal considerations that are unrelated to the relative rights of the parties.[122]

The strongest challenge to this rights paradigm that we have seen in this chapter is in the context of the discretionary ground for possession in local authority tenancies. Why? Is there something about the nature of ownership by public bodies, or the perceived welfare responsibilities of public bodies, that means that the rights paradigm does not apply with equal force to their ownership rights?

---

122 A.J. van der Walt, *Property in the Margins* (Hart, Oxford 2009) 32.

In the context of competing claims to property (the co-ownership cases), however, it is not always the one with the stronger property right that will win when it comes to disputes between an owner with a priority property right and a creditor with a secured property right. In this battle, it will almost invariably be the creditor that triumphs, even if the competing claim is from a co-owner (with a strong, prior, property right) who is living in the property and for whom the home carries many meanings beyond a 'mere' investment. It is simply the case that creditors, because of who they are as a type of litigant, almost always win no matter who, or what, the competing claims.

(10) A New Approach?

Home meanings seldom play a part when it comes to deciding whether possession (or sale) should be granted. Even when judges have discretion to take account of any relevant circumstances, there is little evidence that they consider the impact that losing the home will have. This is particularly evident in the way that human rights jurisprudence is developing: where the property owner has an undisputed right in law to recover possession it is most unlikely that the 'right to respect for the home' will trump the owner's property right. It is surprising that the legal system attaches so little weight to the personal home story: there is a considerable body of empirical evidence focusing on the psychological and health impacts of losing one's home for the dispossessed individual, and there are also clear financial, administrative and resource costs for wider society.[123]

It is not satisfactory that the probability of losing your home following debt should depend so much on the vagaries of factors such as who the judge is or how tolerant your mortgagee is. At the same time, home means different things to different people, and this is something that the law needs to acknowledge. Two suggestions follow as to how this might occur.

First, there should always be an opportunity for an occupier to air personal stories – whether financial, home or other – before an independent tribunal, before losing the home. This would be quite a radical change. Of course, in the vast majority of cases it is right and necessary for property owners to be able to recover their property, and there is 'economic importance…[in] ensuring that there is an efficient machinery for the enforcement of debt obligations'.[124] Further, if the occupier's financial position is such that postponing possession is simply delaying the inevitable, then it will often be better for him to move sooner rather than later in order to avoid mounting debt. Balancing personal stories against the interests of property owners and creditors is difficult. As Hoffmann J noted in *Re Citro*, in the context of an application for sale brought by a trustee in bankruptcy:

---

123 L. Fox, *Conceptualising Home* (Hart, Oxford 2007) 109–22, and references therein.

124 *Close Invoice Finance Ltd v Pile* [2008] EWHC 1580 (Ch) [12].

> The two interests are not in any sense commensurable. On the one hand, one has the financial interests…On the other, one has personal and human interests of these two families. It is very hard to see how they can be weighed against each other, except in a way which involves some value judgment on the part of the tribunal.[125]

Nonetheless, the occupier should be able to ask for such a balancing exercise to take place in exceptional cases. The Law Commission recommended a similar approach in the context of discretionary grounds for possession of rented homes, suggesting that there should be a structured discretion to guide judges when deciding whether to order possession. It suggested that, on the one hand, the court would have to consider the likely effect of an order on the home, family and private lives of occupiers, taking account of how long it is likely to take them to find somewhere else and how they will be affected by not having a home. On the other hand, the judge should consider the effect of not making the order on the landlord's interests, which would include its financial interests.[126]

As we have seen, the courts already take account of some of these factors in TLATA cases, but what is suggested here is both that the ability to require the court to undertake a balancing exercise in exceptional cases should apply to all possession cases involving the home (not simply TLATA), and that there should be a broader approach to exceptionality, to encompass not merely illness and disability but other exceptional home meanings. It may be that proving that certain factors exist should trigger the need for a special case to be made for possession, or at least for immediate possession. These could include longevity of occupation, the fact that the house has been adapted for special needs, serious illness of a household member or severe disruption to education.[127] Procedures should ensure that the occupier has the opportunity to alert the court to the fact that there are special circumstances or that the consequences of losing the home would be

---

125 [1991] Ch 142 (CA) 150. Hoffmann J was the first instance judge, being referred to in the Court of Appeal.

126 Law Commission, 'Renting Homes' (Law Com No 284, 2003) 9.82–9.89. It is unlikely that these proposals will be adopted as there is no political appetite for radical reform of the law on renting homes.

127 South African law provides an interesting model, although the political and economic context is very different. Under the Prevention of Illegal Eviction from and Unlawful Occupation of Land Act 19 of 1998 the court can grant an order for eviction only if it is just and reasonable taking into account all the relevant circumstances, including the rights and needs of the elderly, children, disabled persons and households headed by women. If an unlawful occupier has been in occupation for more than six months the court must also consider whether land has been made available for relocation. This has (controversially) been held to apply to those who were initially lawfully in occupation as well as those who began with unlawful occupation: *Ndlovu v Ngcobo; Bekker v Jika* 2003 (1) SA 113 (SCA). Further, in determining the date for eviction the court must have regard to all relevant factors, including the length of occupation.

unusually severe. In these exceptional situations the case will need to be listed for more than a simple five-minute hearing. There would be an inconvenient impact on the court timetable; in *Whitehouse v Lee* a considerable amount of evidence was adduced to support the measure of the occupier's loss, and this necessitated a three-day trial.[128] The importance of the issues at stake, both in terms of the impact on the lives of the debtor and other family members and for wider society, does, however, justify such a commitment of resources.

If the court finds that the case is made out and immediate possession would cause significant harm, the court should be able either to refuse to grant possession if the interests of the creditor can be sufficiently protected without the grant of possession, or to defer possession for more than the six weeks currently allowed by section 89 of the Housing Act 1980. There are examples of both responses in the context of TLATA case law.[129]

Secondly, there is a much broader issue underlying this discussion. In order for personal stories to be counted a better framework needs to be developed for proving and measuring the impact of loss of home. If courts are to move towards making these wider enquiries, then they will need to be supplied not only with information about the financial risk to the creditor if possession is deferred or denied, but also with evidence that enables them to have detailed information about the occupier's circumstances (emotional, physical and financial), alternative housing arrangements, and how woven the occupier is into local communities.[130] This means that a methodology needs to be developed for attaching weight to home. In *Re Citro* Hoffmann J pointed to the difficulty of weighing incommensurable interests.[131] Economic interests are readily quantifiable and the tools for measurement are well established.[132] The same cannot be said of social interests. Social measures involve contested value judgments and are not as readily given to quantitative assessment. Economic and social measures cannot be weighed against one another in a simple exercise, but each must be taken into account as part of an overall assessment as to what is the appropriate course of action. For this reason it is necessary to develop better tools to evaluate social measures. By way of illustration as to what can be done, the Relationships Foundation has begun to develop ways of measuring 'relational links', as a means of testing the impact

---

128 [2009] EWCA Civ 375 [37].

129 *Mortgage Corporation v Shaire* [2001] Ch 743; *Brittain v Haghighat* [2009] EWHC 90 (Ch).

130 See *First National Bank v Achampong* [2003] EWCA Civ 487, and *Telecom Plus Plc v Hatch* [2005] EWHC 1523 (Ch) where (in the context of applications for sale) the judges comment on the need for courts to be provided with evidence about the impact on welfare etc.

131 [1991] Ch 142 (CA) 150.

132 The remainder of this paragraph draws heavily on the work of the Relationships Foundation, particularly the booklet, 'The Triple Test, Integrating Economic, Environmental and Social Policy' (January 2009). For further information, see http://www.relationshipsfoundation.org/.

that policy measures are likely to have on relationships. Towards this goal, it has developed a framework – the Relational Proximity Model – that explores issues of connectedness, continuity, breadth, power and purpose in relationships. Loss of home may cause severe disruption to the occupier's relationships with others. It is not only the relational impact of loss of home that will need to be measured. There is also a need to find ways of measuring the impact on the physical and mental health and well being of the occupiers. It is a difficult challenge, but it is a just challenge. These personal stories should matter in law.

Postscript

Since writing this chapter some of the details have changed. Mortgage and rent arrears are down a little, and mortgagee repossessions have fallen. There has been (a narrow) consultation on the mortgagee's power of sale, and some adjustment of the measures in place to assist mortgagors in difficulties. The only substantive reform is the Mortgage Repossessions (Protection of Tenants etc.) Act 2010 which helps those tenants whose landlords have let the property without the consent of the mortgagee: the court is now able to delay possession for two months and lenders must give notice of the proposed execution of the order. The broad landscape remains the same however: there is still little scope for the personal home story to get a legal airing.

Chapter 3

Home as Ownership, Dispossession as Foreclosure: The Impact of the Current Crisis on the American Model of 'Home'[1]

Rashmi Dyal-Chand

(1) Introduction

With its strong roots in civic republican traditions, American society has long embraced a relatively unitary conception of the home. Populist belief and investment, and the laws supporting them, treat home as ownership and dispossession as foreclosure. The strength of these equations in American society marginalises protection for investments by tenants in rental property as well as for homeless persons. But the unitary nature of this conception sometimes obscures the fact that it has been refined in recent decades, by market forces and by law.

This essay focuses on the 'fine print' surrounding the American understanding of home and dispossession by examining the impact of recent federal regulatory responses to the financial crisis. I begin, in the first section, by delineating the model that existed prior to the financial crisis, having developed from colonial times into a quite particular vision of risk taking and negative rights of individualised market access. In the second section, I outline the major federal regulations and proposals aimed at stemming the foreclosure crisis and rejuvenating the markets for credit. In the third and final section, I analyse the changes in the fine print. I conclude that the American vision of home and dispossession has changed in nuanced but important respects.

(2) The American Model of Home

Before it became a catchphrase of the second Bush administration, the term 'ownership society' referred to the idea that the United States is a nation of homeowners. From its origins in civic republican ideals to its recent use as a term with enormous political cachet, the ownership society symbolises the predominant social, political and legal conceptualisation of home in the United States.

1 I am grateful to Benjamin Ericson for his comments on a prior draft and to Danielle Beaver for terrific research assistance.

Perhaps because no less a luminary than Thomas Jefferson championed civic republican ideals, the notion that property ownership is essential to productivity, political participation, and citizenship has deep and abiding roots in American society.[2] In his Draft Constitution for the Commonwealth of Virginia, Jefferson included a provision that: 'Every person of full age...shall be entitled to an appropriation of 50 acres...in full and absolute dominion.'[3] Far from being a quaint philosophy that modern ideals could easily supersede, civic republicanism has many modern manifestations, not the least of which is the political and social backlash against recent uses of the government's eminent domain power for the purpose of economic development – at least when such development is led by private corporations.[4] The corollary image of the 'home as castle',[5] as a locus of individual dominion and power as against the world, is another contemporary expression of the civic republican impulse.[6]

One legal consequence of the 'ownership society' model of the 'home' is an enormous reluctance, in American law and society, to limit alienability of the home. Thus, while the former Soviet bloc countries contemplate 'Fourth Way'

2 Cited in William E. Forbath, 'Caste, Class, and Equal Citizenship' (1999) 98 *Mich. L. Rev.* 1, 14 ('To Madison or Jefferson, the socioeconomic key to individual freedom and citizenly independence was ownership of productive property, and at various times both men said citizens had a right to sufficient property upon which to work to support themselves and their families and championed broad distributive policies on that basis').

3 Ibid., 14 (citing Jefferson's Draft Constitution for Virginia). See also Mark E. Brandon, 'Home on the Range: Family and Constitutionalism in American Continental Settlement' (2003) 52 *Emory L. J.* 645, 665–7 (describing Thomas Jefferson as 'a progenitor of a strand of American ethos known as agrarian republicanism'); S. Candice Hoke, 'Preemption Pathologies and Civic Republican Values' (1991) 71 *B.U. L. Rev.* 687, 704 ('Civic republicanism is committed to principles of civic virtue, open-minded deliberation, substantive political equality, and participatory citizenship').

4 The recent US Supreme Court case of *Kelo v City of New London*, 545 US 469 (2005) and its aftermath exemplify this phenomenon. For commentary on *Kelo*'s aftermath, see George Lefcoe, 'After Kelo, Curbing Opportunistic TIF-Driven Economic Development: Forgoing Ineffectual Blight Tests; Empowering Property Owners and School Districts' (2008) 83 *Tul. L. Rev.* 45; David A. Dana, 'The Law and Expressive Meaning of Condemning the Poor after Kelo' (2006) 101 *Nw. U. L. Rev.* 365; D. Benjamin Barros, 'Home as a Legal Concept' (2006) 46 *Santa Clara L. Rev.* 255.

5 Joseph William Singer, 'The Ownership Society and Takings Of Property: Castles, Investments, And Just Obligations' (2006) 30 *Harv. Envtl. L. Rev.* 309.

6 For one critique of civic republicanism and its traditional roots, see Linda K. Kerber, 'The Republican Civic Tradition: Making Republicanism Useful' (1988) 97 *Yale L. J.* 1663, 1665 (discussing traditional civic republicanism's 'tendency to homogeneity and the tyranny of the majority as well as liberalism's tendency to enshrine private property rights'). Kerber remarks that 'classical republican tradition assumed that deliberation was possible only in small and exclusive communities; the absence of the dependent classes – defined by race, gender, and property – was essential to the republican view of the world, not an easily correctable accident.' Ibid.

approaches to property use and ownership,[7] in America limitations on the ability to build equity in individual homes are acceptable only in the narrow realm of affordable housing development. For the 'unsubsidised' majority of American homeowners,[8] William Simon's intriguing recommendations to limit alienability *in pursuit* of republican ideals are ignored in favour of the private government achieved by modern 'common interest communities.'[9]

Another legal consequence of the 'ownership society' model of 'home' is the massive level of investment in homeownership that pervades federal laws and regulations. These include federal tax deductions and credits, most prominently in the form of the federal income tax deduction for interest paid on mortgage loans.[10] But perhaps the most extensive regulatory support of homeownership in America is the privileging of mortgage-based credit.[11] Indeed, both the regulations that historically protected mortgage borrowers and the deregulation over the past several decades that purported to increase access to credit have been justified as necessary means of stimulating and expanding the market for homes.[12] For example, even after the widespread federal pre-emption of state law regulation of mortgage-based credit, the equity of redemption exists in every state in the United States.[13] In addition, courts have long protected mortgage borrowers with a range of interventions focusing on contract formation and interpretation. A textbook example is that of a contract for an outright conveyance of land that the court determines to be a mortgage transaction on the basis of parol evidence.[14]

Not surprisingly, the consistent federal (and state-level) support for homeownership has produced meaningful results. Prior to the current financial

---

7 See Gregory S. Alexander and Graznya Skapska (eds), *A Fourth Way? Privatization, Property, and the Emergence of New Market Economies* (Routledge, New York 1994); William H. Simon, 'Social-Republican Property' (1991) 38 *UCLA L. Rev*. 1335, 1343–4, 1357.

8 I use the term 'unsubsidised' in quotations here, because in fact the federal regulatory support for middle- and upper-class homeowners is enormous.

9 For a recent and iconic discussion of common interest communities in America, see, e.g., Evan McKenzie, *Privatopia: Homeowner Associations and the Rise of Residential Private Government* (Vail-Ballou, Binghamton 1994).

10 A. Mechele Dickerson, 'The Myth of Home Ownership and Why Home Ownership is Not Always a Good Thing' (2009) 84 *Indiana L. J.* 189, 194–5.

11 Ibid.

12 Rashmi Dyal-Chand, 'From Status to Contract: Evolving Paradigms for Regulating Consumer Credit'(2006) 73 *Tenn. L. Rev* 303.

13 Marshall E. Tracht, 'Renegotiation and Secured Credit: Explaining the Equity of Redemption' (1999) 52 *Vand. L. Rev*. 599, 610. In addition, courts and legislatures carefully guard against 'clogging' of the equity of redemption.

14 Justice Field's majority opinion in *Pierce v Robinson* is a typical reaction to parol evidence in the mortgage context. 13 Cal. 116, 125 (1859); see also Gerald Korngold and Paul Goldstein, *Real Estate Transactions* 356 (4th edn Foundation, New York 2002).

crisis, 69 per cent of Americans owned their own homes.[15] The vast majority of these homes were financed with mortgages.[16] In addition, as of 2003, home equity borrowing[17] was a vast industry, totalling US$415 billion.[18] In recent decades, the ownership society had also expanded to include poor people, 44 per cent of whom owned their own homes at the turn of the millennium.[19]

Also not surprisingly, the American equation of 'home' as 'owned home' can be measured along racial lines. Important treatises on economic development among racial minority groups, such as *American Apartheid* and *Black Wealth/ White Wealth*, have traced the negative impact of segregated homeownership on wealth accumulation among African Americans.[20] The seemingly universal response to such studies is a redoubling in efforts among both lawmakers and advocates to increase homeownership among African Americans and other racial minorities. It seems appropriate, if a bit obvious, to point out that this is not the only option. As Mechele Dickerson has astutely argued in a recent article, many of

15 US Census Bureau, 'Housing Vacancies and Homeownership' http://www.census.gov/hhes/ (available at www/housing/hvs/annual04/ann04t12.html, accessed 9 January 2010).

16 According to 2003 Census figures, approximately 65 per cent of homeowners had mortgages of some sort on their homes. US Census Bureau, 'American Housing Survey for the United States: 2003' (available at http://www.census.gov/hhes/www/housing/ahs/ahs03/tab315.htm, accessed 9 January 2010).

17 A home equity loan is 'secured by a homeowner's residence other than loans used solely to purchase or construct the residence, to refinance a purchase money loan, or to make home improvements.' Julia Patterson Forrester, 'Mortgaging the American Dream: A Critical Evaluation of the Federal Government's Promotion of Home Equity Financing' (1994) 69 *Tul. L. Rev.* 373, 377. Consumers use such loans to finance everything from school tuition to groceries or luxury items.

18 David Myron, 'Home Equity Debt Soars' [2004] American Demographics (available at http://www.findarticles.com/p/articles/mi_m4021/is_9_26/ai_n6344044, relying on statistics maintained by the Federal Deposit Insurance Corporation).

19 The National Consumer Law Center recently found that over 44 per cent of low-income Americans own their own homes. National Consumer Law Center, 'Stop Predatory Lending 17' (Report) (2002). See also National Low Income Housing Coalition 1 'Low Income Housing Profile, 21' (2001) (available at http://www.nlihc.org/doc/profile.pdf, accessed 9 January 2010) (tabulation of 1999 American Housing Survey found 44 per cent homeownership by the 'very poor', defined as under 30 per cent of area median income). But see Raphael W. Bostic and Brian J. Surette, 'Have the Doors Opened Wider? Trends In Homeownership Rates by Race and Income' (2000) 19–21, 27 tbl.1.D (Federal Reserve Bd) (analysis of the 1989 and 1998 April supplement to the Current Population Survey finds that increases in homeownership during the 1990s are strongly correlated with income in the middle-income quintiles; in the lowest income quintile, growth in homeownership is not explained by increases in income).

20 Douglas S. Massey and Nancy A. Denton, *American Apartheid* (Harvard, Cambridge MA 1993); Melvin L. Oliver and Thomas M. Shapiro, *Black Wealth/White Wealth: A New Perspective on Racial Inequality* (Routledge, New York 1997).

the goals inherent in the pursuit of housing integration could also be accomplished by means of regulatory support for renters.[21]

This particularised image of the home in America produces an equally particularised image of dispossession. In legal terms, such an image could largely be defined by two types of regulations. The first is the regulatory response to foreclosure, which over time, was heavily regulated by states in order to protect the borrower.[22] Even today, despite the deregulation of foreclosure, in all but two states[23] foreclosure requires the lender to go through a public sale to obtain fee title to the collateral.[24] In the 40 percent of states that allow only judicial foreclosure, such regulations typically include requirements of adequate notice,[25] a hearing,[26] regulation of the method of sale and a process for determining rights to any surplus.[27] Even those states allowing non-judicial foreclosure, most prevalently the power of sale, regulate notice and other aspects of the foreclosure process.[28] It is important to note, nonetheless, that once a foreclosure proceeding begins, a borrower has very few defences available to her. Moreover, after foreclosure, it is difficult to overturn a foreclosure sale on grounds such as the inadequacy of the sales price.[29]

The second type of regulation that defines the American legal image of dispossession from home is regulatory support for access to credit *in times of economic recession or crisis.* The regulatory rejuvenation of the mortgage market both during the New Deal and during the late 1970s and early 1980s, both times

21 A. Mechele Dickerson, 'The Myth of Home Ownership and Why Home Ownership is Not Always a Good Thing' (2009) 84 *Indiana L. J.* 189, 194–5.

22 Eventually, some of these regulations were removed. For example, although foreclosure prototypically required court action, non-judicial foreclosure is now allowed in 60 per cent of jurisdictions. Grant S. Nelson and Dale A. Whitman, *Real Estate Finance Law* (4th edn West, St Paul 2002) 512.

23 Most states no longer allow strict foreclosure, a process by which the mortgagee receives title upon the mortgagor's default without having to bid at a sale, though Connecticut and Vermont continue to use this procedure, and other states allow it in certain circumstances. See Conn. Gen. Stat. Ann. § 8-256; 735 Ill. Comp. Stat. Ann. 5/15-1403 (allowing strict foreclosure only when three conditions are met); Vt. Stat. Ann. tit. 9A, § 9-620 (2001).

24 In other words, the remedy of foreclosure is not aimed at giving the lender title to the collateral, but rather at giving the lender proceeds from the sale of the collateral. Ann M. Burkhart, 'Lenders and Land' (1999) 64 *Mo. L. Rev.* 249, 269.

25 George E. Osborne, *Handbook on the Law of Mortgages* (2nd edn West, St Paul 1970) 683.

26 Grant S. Nelson and Dale A. Whitman, *Real Estate Finance Law* (4th edn West, St Paul 2002) 492.

27 Ibid.

28 Ibid., 513; George E. Osborne, *Handbook on the Law of Mortgages* (2nd edn West, St Paul 1970) 733–6.

29 Grant S. Nelson and Dale A. Whitman, *Real Estate Finance Law* (4th edn West, St Paul 2002) 589.

of economic stagnation, exemplify this point. During the New Deal, federal regulation standardised the mortgage market, spawning the development of the now sprawling secondary market in residential mortgages.[30] Four decades later, broad federal pre-emption of state regulations effectively eliminated usury caps, and enabled widespread entry by mortgage brokers and non-depository lenders into the residential mortgage market.[31]

The American equation of 'dispossession' with foreclosure and lack of access to credit also has distinctive race implications. The most recent, and perhaps most archetypal, example of a distinctive racialised impact is the extraordinary connection between predatory and sub-prime lending practices and race. As the story of the sub-prime meltdown unfolds in courts, popular media and empirical analyses, the details of reverse redlining and race-based predatory behaviour and their impact on minority neighbourhoods become hauntingly apparent.

(3) Home as Opportunity during a Deregulatory Period

The purpose of the previous section was to present the predominant American images of home and dispossession. The 'home,' in America, is the 'owned home.' It may be reductionist, but it is not inaccurate, to say that other images of the home are either corollaries of this predominant motif or they are marginalised. Meanwhile, our understanding of 'dispossession' supports the image of 'home' by focusing on protections against loss of homeownership and market stimulations to regain or attain homeownership.

The purpose of this brief section is to add one fragment of historical perspective to the largely ahistorical account in the previous section by detailing our ending point just prior to the current financial crisis. In this section, I undertake an interim appraisal of the socio-legal images of 'home' and 'dispossession' that the most recent decades of regulation produced. My hope in doing so is to set forth a more detailed and precise understanding of these concepts prior to the crisis as a means of facilitating my analysis of what, if any, meaningful changes the recent federal responses to the crisis have wrought. I focus particularly on three key extensions of these images: the predilection towards the risk-taking model of homeownership, away from the model of home as security of tenure; the valourisation of negative rights to 'home' over positive rights; and the incentivising of individualised opportunity-seeking over group-based rights.

30 See Richard K. Green and Susan M. Wachter, 'The American Mortgage in Historical and International Context' (2005) 19 *J. Econ. Persp*. 93, 94–6.

31 See Elizabeth R. Schiltz, 'The Amazing, Elastic, Ever-Expanding Exportation Doctrine and Its Effect on Predatory Lending Regulation' (2004) 88 *Minn. L. Rev.* 518, 540-69; Cathy Lesser Mansfield, 'The Road to Subprime "HEL" Was Paved with Good Congressional Intentions: Usury Deregulation and the Subprime Home Equity Market' (2000) 51 *S.C. L. Rev*. 473, 521, 526.

Surely the most noteworthy development in the legal understanding of 'home' in the United States over the last half century resulted from the deregulation that occurred in the mortgage-based credit market. Whatever other purposes deregulation served, it was explicitly justified as a powerful engine for increasing access to credit – and thus homeownership. But somewhere along the way, as deregulation contributed to the exponential expansion of the secondary market, which contributed to the explosion in home equity lending and the subprime markets, implicit assumptions about the fundamental *purpose* of homeownership changed quite radically. Although the rhetoric of the ownership society emphasised the importance of building equity, the market incentivised something markedly different: the use of home equity as a means of leverage, a means of risk taking in pursuit of greater wealth.[32] How else could the use of home equity for consumption purposes and practices such as house-flipping be justified?

In complementary fashion, as deregulation incentivised exuberant risk taking, homeownership became a decreasingly apparent means of achieving security of tenure. Even as sub-prime lenders targeted marginalised borrowers with an opportunity to achieve the American dream of home as permanence, the exotic loans they pedalled severely destabilised the chances of actually achieving a meaningfully permanent level of tenure. In this respect, it is important to note that prior to the current crisis, American regulation protected not the security implicit in 'home,' but quite the opposite. The behaviour privileged by American housing policy was risk taking, rather than shelter building. Indeed, it was not really 'home' that American law protected at all; rather, it was the use of the home as a means of accessing the market for credit. Seen in this light, the apparent regulatory uninterest in protecting the rental market is more explicable.

A second and related extension of the 'ownership society' model of home that occurred prior to the current crisis was the valourisation of negative rights of access to housing, defined primarily as access to the real estate and credit markets, over positive rights to 'shelter', defined with reference to human rights conventions. The former rights are much more akin to the rights conceptualised by human rights laws as civil and political rights, including the right to liberty and equal protection.[33] And indeed, they have been protected as such by laws such

32 The market focus on risk taking is the subject of more extensive discussion in Nestor Davidson and Rashmi Dyal-Chand, 'Property in Crisis' (2009) 78 *Fordham L. Rev.* 101–54.

33 Universal Declaration of Human Rights, G.A. Res. 217A, art. 3, 7, U.N. GAOR, 3d Sess., U.N. Doc. A/810 (Dec. 12, 1948). See also Berta E. Hernández-Truyol and Jane E. Larson, 'Sexual Labor and Human Rights' (2006) 37 *Colum. Hum. Rts. L. Rev.* 391, 409–10 ('It does not cost a government much to implement individual rights to be free from state intervention. Civil and political rights are such rights. By contrast, rights that require the state to take positive action and that create obligations to provide welfare to the individual cost much more. Social and economic rights are of the latter variety'); Jennifer Prah Ruger, 'Toward A Theory of a Right to Health: Capability and Incompletely Theorized Agreements' (2006) 18 *Yale J.L. & Human.* 273, 282 ('The "liberal consensus"

as the Equal Credit Opportunity Act[34] and the Fair Housing Act.[35] The latter are conceptualised as economic, social and cultural, including the right to shelter, income, health and food.[36] Viewed in this light, access to the real estate and credit markets is a negative right, because it does not guarantee an improvement in welfare, but merely provides opportunity for welfare enhancement. Importantly, the unitary emphasis in housing policy on access to credit deemphasised other policy goals. Both federal dollars and rhetoric moved away from the notion of a right to shelter, rather than developing it in any meaningful sense.

A third extension of the ownership society, focusing a bit more explicitly on the consequences of dispossession, was the incentivising of individualised opportunity-seeking over group-based rights. It could be argued that even the negative group-based rights embodied in the civil rights and equal access statutes of the 1960s took a back seat in the last decade to market-based approaches to increasing individual access to the credit and real estate markets. The example of reverse redlining again provocatively demonstrates this point. In an earlier era, the targeting of people of colour by predatory lenders would have been a likely basis for a successful lawsuit under these laws (as indeed it is again now – in light of the current crisis). But in the decade prior to the crisis, the regulatory reaction to this practice was to favour it as a means of increasing access for individuals who had previously been excluded from the market.

These three extensions of the 'ownership society' model of 'home' all contributed to a distinctive vision of the market, and particularly, the state's role in regulating and developing the market. It bears repeating that the state could have chosen instead to develop the market for rental real estate. Instead, federal policy focused on enhancing individualised opportunity, risk taking and reward.

(4) Home Post-crisis

I will leave it to others to speculate about how self-sustaining such a model of homeownership could possibly be. For my purposes, it suffices to note that the enormity of the current crisis demanded a forceful federal response. In this section, I will describe the bulk of the response by summarising first the federal government's efforts to stem the foreclosure crisis from approximately the time President Obama took office. I will then briefly review recent efforts to restore the

---

in human rights scholarship and practice generally takes a libertarian approach, endorsing the fulfillment of "negative rights" (civil and political rights) but failing to endorse the fulfillment of "positive rights"').

34 15 U.S.C. § 1691 (2000).

35 42 U.S.C. § 3601 (2000).

36 Universal Declaration, art. 25. See generally Jeanne M. Woods and Hope Lewis, *Human Rights and the Global Marketplace: Economic, Social and Cultural Dimensions* (Transnational, Ardsley 2004).

market for consumer credit. I should note here that my purpose is by no means to provide a comprehensive overview of these efforts, but rather to capture the main thrusts of these efforts in a thematic overlay.

In short, since the change of administrations, the federal government's response to the foreclosure crisis has been to incentivise re-financings and modifications of residential mortgage loans as a means of staving off foreclosure and making individual loans more affordable over their entire terms. The centrepiece of these efforts has been the Obama administration's Homeowner Affordability and Stability Plan (HASP), which consists of three main initiatives. First, HASP expects to provide opportunities for up to four or five million homeowners to refinance loans owned or guaranteed by the two government-sponsored entities, Fannie Mae and Freddie Mac. Second, using a mix of incentives and mandates, HASP seeks to provide loan modification opportunities to three or four million homeowners in order to make their monthly payments more affordable. Finally, as a means of increasing confidence in Fannie Mae and Freddie Mac, HASP has increased stock purchases in, and purchases of toxic debt from, these two entities.[37] The new president has supplemented these programmes with a so-called Second Lien Program, the purpose of which is to automatically modify second mortgages when first mortgages are refinanced,[38] and a programme to develop foreclosure alternatives such as short sales and deed-in-lieu-of-foreclosure settlements.[39]

Arguably the most noteworthy programme to have been established since President Obama took office is the Protecting Tenants at Foreclosure Act, enacted in May of 2009.[40] This new statute requires purchasers of foreclosed properties[41] to honour the lease terms of renters, allowing them to stay in the properties until the end of the lease period. For month-to-month or at-will renters, or in cases where the new owner intends to occupy the property, the Act requires a 90-day pre-eviction notice. By virtue of its focus on renters, this new programme is a marked departure from the 'ownership society' focus of other federal housing initiatives undertaken both before and since the crisis.

Beyond efforts to stem the foreclosure crisis, the federal government has taken a multi-pronged approach to restoring the market for consumer credit. As previously noted, President Obama has begun to follow through on his campaign commitment

37 USA Dep. of Treasury, 'Homeowner Affordability and Stability Plan Fact Sheet' (available at http://www.treasury.gov/initiatives/eesa/homeowner-affordability-plan/FactSheet.pdf, accessed 9 January 2010).

38 USA Dep. of Treasury Press Release (28 April 2009; available at http://www.treas.gov/press/ releases/tg108.htm).

39 USA Dep. of Treasury, 'Homeowner Affordability and Stability Plan Fact Sheet' (available at http://www.treasury.gov/initiatives/eesa/homeowner-affordability-plan/FactSheet.pdf, accessed 9 January 2010).

40 Protecting Tenants at Foreclosure Act of 2009, Pub. L. No. 111-22, §§702-703 (2009).

41 The statute refers to 'successors in interest'; ibid.

to use Troubled Asset Relief Program (TARP) funds to purchase toxic debt owned by the federal government sponsored entities. President Obama has also proposed a new Consumer Financial Protection Agency, the purpose of which would be to regulate the sale of consumer credit. In addition to consolidating authority for regulating lenders and other servicers in the consumer credit market (an important function given the current lack of coordination and oversight of the industry),[42] the main purpose of this new agency would be to test the safety of consumer loans much as toasters and other consumer products are currently tested.[43]

Finally, in May of 2009, President Obama signed into law the Credit Card Accountability, Responsibility, and Disclosure Act[44] (Credit CARD Act) which provides much more extensive regulation of the credit card industry than previous laws. Consistent with recent federal regulation of consumer credit, this new statute requires more clear and specific disclosures about loan terms. But the most noteworthy aspects of the Act are its outright bans on certain practices, including increasing annual percentage rates and other key terms on outstanding balances, engaging in double cycle billing and charging interest on certain transaction fees. The statute also imposes certain limitations on penalty fees and payment terms.

(5) Home as Responsibility

A cursory review of the most recent American responses to the foreclosure crisis might bring to mind the adage: 'the more things change, the more they stay the same.' But I believe that a careful examination reveals that the more appropriate description of recent federal responses is that incremental and nuanced, but meaningful, changes are occurring. Specifically, although the blunt American ideals of 'home' as 'owned home' and 'dispossession' as 'foreclosure and lack of access to credit' remain almost completely intact, recent federal responses to the foreclosure crisis have weakened the more refined extensions of these ideals that flourished just prior to the crisis.

Let me begin with what has stayed the same during this time of extraordinary economic upheaval. As both the federal efforts to stem foreclosures (in the form of HASP) and the multifaceted approaches to rejuvenating the markets for credit demonstrate, the federal government has responded to this crisis by investing vast amounts of resources in buttressing the ownership society model of 'home'. In association with these efforts, the government has also shored up

42 Adam J. Levitin, 'The Consumer Financial Protection Agency' (available at http://ssrn.com/ abstract=1447082, accessed 16 September 2010).

43 Zachary A. Goldfarb and others, 'U.S. May Add New Financial Watchdog' *Washington Post* (20 May 2009; available at http://www.washingtonpost.com/wp-dyn/content/article/2009/05/19/ AR2009051903061.html, accessed 9 January 2010).

44 Credit Card Accountability, Responsibility, and Disclosure Act of 2009, H.R. 627, 111th Cong. (2009).

the dispossession as foreclosure equation. Thus, HASP has allocated billions of dollars in foreclosure relief which takes the form of propping up mortgage loans. As a theoretical matter, HASP's focus is noteworthy in two respects. The first is the federal government's determination to respond to populist notions that those most 'dispossessed' in this crisis were not the banks on the one hand, nor the many Americans who became homeless because they lost rented properties on the other. Rather, if dollars are an indicator of priorities, home*owners* were the primary victims suffering dispossession. The second noteworthy theoretical point about HASP is that foreclosure relief has largely been provided within the parameters of the borrower–lender relationship. The federal government has reaffirmed the importance of credit in the real estate market by relying mostly on incentives to convince lenders to modify loans. This approach effectively acknowledges the American conviction that lenders must not be made to suffer losses at the hands of their borrowers if those losses could lead to future contractions in the market for mortgage credit. For the same reasons, although we may yet see changes to foreclosure laws that would privilege borrowers more than the pre-crisis ascendancy of the power-of-sale regime has done, such changes have not been the leading force in post-crisis reform.

Of course, the federal efforts to keep credit flowing at all levels of market participation are a more straightforward version of the same story. Thus, in connection with the mortgage market, the Obama administration's proposed Consumer Financial Protection Agency is described as a means of eliminating bad practices among lenders and debt servicers as a means of encouraging widespread market participation. Similarly, the Credit CARD Act is billed as a way of eliminating predatory behaviour in order to increase the flow of 'good' credit. Meanwhile, we see TARP funds being used to re-establish the good name and reliability of the government-sponsored entities, which are so critical to the functioning of the secondary market. At all levels, these 'corrections' are meant to contribute to responsible access – and ultimately to responsible ownership.

Federal focus on this set of reforms has thus far still marginalised proposals that would more explicitly limit access to credit. For example, suitability, which some argued should lead reform efforts because of its imposition of responsibility on lenders to determine whether a loan is suitable for a borrower, still has not garnered much attention from lawmakers. The apparent concern is that such an imposition would overly restrict access to credit. Nor, for the same reasons, have proposals to impose a fiduciary duty on mortgage lenders and brokers been seriously considered.

In sum, the civic republican underpinnings of the 'ownership society' conception of home retain enormous force in shaping legal reform in the American response to the crisis. Far from considering a different model to govern appropriate uses of credit, leave alone a different model of 'home', federal efforts have defaulted to many of the same types of market-based incentives, including tax and other financial incentives for both individual borrowers and lenders, to protect what remains a paramount public goal in American society. Moreover, the extension of the 'ownership society' model to include the notion that access to credit rewards risk taking continues to restrain lawmakers from considering the benefits of limiting alienability. Because credit is privileged, it is much more difficult to regulate against the negative externalities created by real estate speculators and house flippers. Moreover, the privileging of credit, which still today does not limit the opportunity to borrow on home equity, also privileges risk taking over tenure building.

Finally, on the question of race, recent court cases against sub-prime lenders and other market participants confirm that the underlying goal of remedying race discrimination in the market for housing still is to increase homeownership by African Americans and other racial minorities.[45] Thus, in targeting reverse redlining as a racist practice, plaintiffs are battling for the marketing of good loan products to minority groups, certainly not to limit access to credit so that resources can be redirected toward developing other meaningful housing alternatives.

But even as we see a reaffirmation of the 'ownership society' model of home, we also see a meaningfully different refinement of this model than the version that existed just prior to the crisis. Simply put, whereas the pre-crisis version of the ownership society emphasised individualised risk taking and access, the post-crisis version emphasises responsibility. Indeed, it is on the subject of risk taking that the most marked change has occurred. Key aspects of both the foreclosure response and the credit market reforms currently underway suggest a renewed interest in the tenure building model of homeownership. For example, the US$75 billion loan modification initiative that is the centrepiece of HASP applies only to loans no larger than the conforming limits of the government-sponsored entities, and on homes that are owner-occupied. Although it would be a stretch to conclude that these limitations evidence an interest in limiting alienability of homes, the explicit rationale of excluding 'speculators' and 'house-flippers'[46] reveals a move toward preserving equity building over risk taking.

Similarly, the explicit justification for the provisions targeting homeowners whose house values have declined or who are 'underwater', creating an 'insurance' fund against housing price declines, and allowing judicial modifications of home mortgages in bankruptcy proceedings are to provide 'families with security' and 'neighborhoods with stability' and to 'stabilize home prices for homeowners in neighborhoods hardest hit by foreclosures'.[47] While it is possible that the main concern underlying these efforts is to reduce the negative externalities from widespread foreclosure, it is also possible to discern a desire to reinvigorate a model

---

45 Michael Powell, 'Bank Accused of Pushing Mortgage Deals on Blacks' *New York Times* (6 June 2009) A16 (available at http://www.nytimes.com/2009/06/07/us/07baltimore.html, accessed 9 January 2010).

46 USA Dep. of Treasury, 'Homeowner Affordability and Stability Plan Fact Sheet' (available at http://www.treasury.gov/initiatives/eesa/homeowner-affordability-plan/FactSheet.pdf, accessed 9 January 2010).

47 Ibid.

of homeownership that preserves the benefits of equity in the home. Likewise, it is possible to see a desire to limit unmitigated risk taking in the recent proposals to regulate consumer mortgages and in the Credit CARD Act. In these arenas as well, the focus appears to be on imposing a baseline level of responsible behaviour on both borrowers and lenders rather than on allowing borrowers to take whatever risks they can in order to achieve access to the market for credit.

Certainly, the most provocative move away from the risk-taking version of the ownership society toward the notion of responsible ownership is the new statute protecting tenants at foreclosure. This statute evidences a clear acknowledgement that the home is something more than an asset to be leveraged. It is also a shelter – whether it is owned or rented. The requirement that tenants be given the benefit of the entire lease period affirms tenants' expectations about the use of rental properties to 'settle' and build tenure. The requirement of 90-day pre-eviction notices even for at-will tenants communicates some appreciation that the consequences of dispossession from the home take time to sort out.

If federal regulations have begun to affirm the tenure model of home, legal academics are going much further in exploring this possibility. For example, Rachel Godsil and David Simunovich recently acknowledged that prior to the crisis:

> it is possible that the potential for rapid appreciation in home values created an expectation of homeownership not as a means of 'constitut[ing] ourselves as continuing personal entities in the world' but as nothing more than an investment vehicle.[48]

Godsil and Simunovich argued against such a model of ownership, however, focusing instead on protecting the broader and more diffuse benefits of homeownership status.

Mechele Dickerson is even more direct in her focus on tenure:

> Though inconsistent with the home ownership myth, the time has come for consumers to start ignoring the immediate, likely short-term, end result of achieving the status of homeowner. To force consumers to consider the long-term risks on investing in a house, home ownership subsidies should encourage renters and potential homeowners to focus on the likely long-term benefits of the investment itself.[49]

48 Rachel D. Godsil and David V. Simunovich 'Protecting Status: The Mortgage Crisis, Eminent Domain, and the Ethic of Homeownership' (2008) 77 *Fordham L. Rev.* 949, 995.

49 A. Mechele Dickerson, 'The Myth of Home Ownership and Why Home Ownership is Not Always a Good Thing' (2009) 84 *Indiana L. J.* 237.

As I have already asserted, to the extent the 'ownership society' model of home has changed since the current crisis began, the change has been most apparent in the movement away from risk taking toward greater responsibility. It is still, I think, accurate to describe our current system as embodying a 'negative rights' approach to homeownership focusing on the individual rather than the group. Nevertheless, the recent legislation on tenants' rights signals some movement even in these two respects – towards shelter, rather than investment, as a defining image. The same can be said of the outright bans on certain predatory behaviour included in the Credit CARD Act as well as the anticipated work of the proposed Consumer Financial Protection Agency. The credit reforms in particular signal an awareness that borrowers as a group require certain status-based protections beyond the more individualised, contract-based protections embodied in the disclosure oriented laws of the last few decades.

The importance of this shift in American law cannot be overemphasised. From the perspective of many consumer advocates, it is the first meaningful recognition by lawmakers that the market for credit cannot fully protect the multiple and nuanced meanings of 'home'.

Chapter 4
Housing Rights in the Intersection between Expropriation and Eviction Law

A.J. van der Walt[1]

(1) Introduction

Eviction is a powerful legal instrument; a remedy with which a landowner can enforce her superior right to exclusive possession against almost any occupier. The most striking characteristic of the right to evict is the way in which it illustrates the presumptive power of ownership[2] by forcing anybody who wants to resist eviction to prove a right that can withstand the owner's claim to exclusive possession.[3] A right that could successfully resist eviction could derive from the landlord's grant or from legislation,[4] but in the common-law tradition eviction

1 Thanks to Sue-Mari Maass for invaluable research and editing assistance and comments and to Gustav Muller, Eduardo Peñalver, Lorna Fox O'Mahony and participants in the Durham Institute for Advanced Study seminar for useful feedback. The views expressed in this chapter are those of the author and should not be attributed to any of these institutions or to the Institute of Advanced Study, Durham University.

2 The phrase 'presumptive power of property', in the sense of favouring ownership by placing the onus of proof on anyone who challenges or opposes the owner's right to evict, is used by J.W. Singer, *Entitlement — The Paradoxes of Property* (Yale University Press, New Haven 2000) 3; L.S. Underkuffler, *The Idea of Property: Its Meaning and Power* (Oxford University Press, Oxford 2003) 65–70.

3 In South African law the landowner evicts an occupier with the *rei vindicatio*. The plaintiff merely has to prove that she is the owner of property occupied by the defendant; it is then up to the defendant to prove that he has a valid right of occupation that is enforceable against the owner. The owner does not have to establish that the defendant's occupation is unlawful; once ownership has been proved, the defendant has to raise and prove a valid right of occupation. The requirements were set out in *Chetty v Naidoo* 1974 (3) SA 13 (A), recently confirmed by the Supreme Court of Appeal in *Dreyer NO and Another v AXZS Industries (Pty) Ltd* [2006] 3 All SA 219 (SCA) para. 4 and by the Constitutional Court in *Van der Merwe v Taylor NO* 2008 (1) SA 1 (CC) paras 131–2. The principles were recently confirmed specifically in the context of eviction in *De Villiers v Potgieter and ors NNO* 2007 (2) SA 311 (SCA) paras 12–13 and *Jackpersad NO and ors v Mitha and ors* 2008 (4) SA 522 (D) 528H–529A.

4 Most countries have legislation that regulates the termination of a lease and that may therefore shield a tenant from eviction, which is usually premised upon lawful termination of the lease. In some cases, tenants may in terms of legislation be distinguished from and

will not be prevented or even postponed by considerations emanating from the socio-economic context or the parties' personal circumstances – the right to evict is said to rely abstractly on the stronger right to possession.[5] Purely on the level of common-law property rights, a landowner (or a landlord) can therefore only be prevented from or delayed in evicting an occupier from her property if the occupier can prove a stronger occupation right or if eviction is regulated by legislation.

In the liberal state, governments routinely use legislation to regulate the hierarchical domination of ownership (and the right to exclusive possession) over weaker occupation rights or home interests,[6] according to changing

---

have a stronger (property) right to occupy than licensees. In South African law the most important law is the Rental Housing Act 50 of 1999. In German law, tenant protection is based on §§ 535–580 of the Civil Code (*Bürgerliches Gesetzbuch*; BGB) and the Landlord-Tenant Framework Act (*Mietrechtsrahmengesetz*) 2001. Similar protection appears in the Dutch Civil Code (*Burgerlijk Wetboek*; BW) 7:201–7:282. In English law tenant protection is based on a patchwork of legislation, the most relevant of which are the Rent Act 1977, the Housing Act 1985 and the Housing Act 1988. Apart from tenants, legislation can also protect other categories of lawful occupiers or even unlawful occupiers or squatters against arbitrary or otherwise unjust eviction. South African examples include the Extension of Security of Tenure Act 62 of 1997 (lawful occupiers of rural land) and the Prevention of Illegal Eviction from and Unlawful Occupation of Land Act 19 of 1998 (unlawful occupiers of all land). An important English example is the Mobile Homes Act 1983.

5 Abstract enforcement of the right to exclusive possession means that the right is enforced without reference to the personal circumstances of the parties, such as the hardship that eviction might cause for the occupier. In Roman-law-based civil law jurisdictions, the landowner's right to evict is founded on the so-called absolute right of ownership, which is the origin of the entitlement of exclusive possession. In English common law jurisdictions, eviction is based on the relatively stronger right to possession, which may or may not accrue to the 'landowner', in so far as such a notion exists. See S. Bright, *Landlord and Tenant Law in Context* (Hart Publishing, Oxford 2007) 48–9, citing W. Swadling, 'Property: General Principles' in P. Birks (ed.), *English Private Law vol I* (Oxford University Press, Oxford 2000) 218: strictly speaking, English land law has no concept of ownership since property in land is protected as possession. Despite the differences, eviction amounts to the enforcement of the stronger right to possession in both systems and therefore I do not distinguish between English Common Law and South African (Roman-Dutch) common law, at least not for purposes of this paper. See R. Zimmermann and D.P. Visser, 'Introduction: South African Law as a Mixed Legal System' in R. Zimmermann and D.P. Visser (eds), *Southern Cross: Civil Law and Common Law in South Africa* (Oxford University Press, Oxford 1996).

6 The jurisprudential meaning and significance of the notion of the home interest was worked out most comprehensively by L. Fox, *Conceptualising Home: Theories, Laws and Policies* (Hart Publishing, Oxford 2007). See further L. Fox, 'The Meaning of Home: A Chimerical Concept or a Legal Challenge?' (2002) 9 *Journal of Law & Society* 580. Given the nature of the collection I will not repeat or summarise Fox's idea of the home interest here, but see n. 98.

social, economic and political circumstances. In the modern regulatory state, legislation has generally replaced or expanded the restrictions that the common law might have imposed on enforcement of the right to exclusive possession. In most instances, statutory regulation of this nature assumes the form of mostly procedural protection against arbitrary and unfair eviction.[7] In some countries, statutory restrictions on the right to evict have been imposed or expanded specifically under the influence or inspiration of constitutional or other, similar (domestic, regional or international) human rights instruments.[8] In some of these cases, human rights inspired legislation grants courts the discretion to either allow or refuse an eviction order or to postpone its execution, depending upon considerations of justice, usually to be determined with reference to contextual considerations such as the socio-economic situation, the personal circumstances of the occupier and her family and the availability of alternative housing.[9] Regulatory restrictions of this kind can amend the law regarding

7 Most countries have legislation that regulates eviction by proscribing arbitrary and abusive eviction and imposing minimum due-process guarantees. In South African law arbitrary eviction is prohibited in s. 26(3) of the Constitution of the Republic of South Africa 1996; the most important legislation promulgated to give effect to this provision is the Prevention of Illegal Eviction from and Unlawful Occupation of Land Act 19 of 1998 (see n. 7). In English law the anti-eviction protection of the Protection from Eviction Act 1977 is both complemented and qualified by the Housing Act 1985, the Housing Act 1988 and the Anti-Social Behaviour Act 1996. The Dutch and German civil codes regulate the eviction of tenants (n. 3 above), while eviction of illegal occupiers is regulated in § 138 of the Dutch Criminal Code and § 123 of the German Criminal Code; see A.J. van der Walt, *Property in the Margins* (Hart Publishing, Oxford 2009) 137–43.

8 In South African law eviction is regulated by s. 26(3) of the Constitution, which provides that no one may be evicted from their home, or may have their home demolished, without an order of court made after considering all the relevant circumstances. Legislation may not permit arbitrary evictions. In response to this constitutional obligation the legislature has promulgated the Prevention of Illegal Eviction from and Unlawful Occupation of Land Act 19 of 1998, which regulates eviction of unlawful occupiers. Several other statutes regulate eviction of lawful occupiers; see A.J. van der Walt, *Constitutional Property Law* (Juta, Cape Town 2005) 308–53 for an overview. In terms of the European Convention for the Protection of Human Rights and Fundamental Freedoms (European Convention on Human Rights, as amended) (ECHR) (1950) Art. 8 provides that everyone has the right to respect for his private and family life, his home and his correspondence; the reference to 'his home' is treated as a human rights regulation of eviction. The impact of this instrument of regional human rights law on domestic English law, where tenants and other occupiers of residential property already enjoyed either substantive or procedural protection (or both) against eviction in terms of legislation, was mediated through the Human Rights Act 1998. See the references in S. Bright, *Landlord and Tenant Law in Context* (Hart Publishing, Oxford 2007) 281–4, 610–13 and compare nn. 8, 9, 15.

9 The South African Prevention of Illegal Eviction from and Unlawful Occupation of Land Act 19 of 1998 provides in s. 4(6) that, when the occupation was for less than six months, a court may grant the eviction order if it is of the opinion that it is just and equitable

eviction either marginally or quite drastically, particularly by transforming context sensitivity into (direct or indirect) occupation rights.[10] For the most part, however, statutory reforms of this nature are intended to restrict the power of eviction.

It should be noted that this kind of restriction on ownership and the right to evict does not necessarily diminish the presumptive power of ownership. Even when contextual factors enter the equation, courts' professional tendency to enforce the law of eviction 'normally', 'neutrally' or 'objectively' will more often than not still privilege the protection of stronger rights and result in more or less mechanical eviction of unlawful or weak occupiers who are unable to prove legal occupation rights that are strong enough to trump the owner's right.[11] Apart from instances where the legislature has changed the law explicitly,[12] so that courts cannot interpret anti-eviction provisions restrictively

---

to do so, after considering all the relevant circumstances, including the rights and needs of the elderly, children, disabled persons and households headed by women. S. 4(7) adds that, when the occupation was for longer than six months, the court must also consider whether suitable alternative accommodation has been or could be made available to the occupiers. In English law, reasonableness or the availability of suitable alternative accommodation (or both) features in eviction actions involving public tenancies; in some private tenancies reasonableness may also be a factor. When reasonableness has to be considered, the courts have to look at the context of the case as a whole, including factors that pertain to the personal circumstances of the tenant: S. Bright, *Landlord and Tenant Law in Context* (Hart Publishing, Oxford 2007) 599, 601–602; K. Gray and S.F. Gray, *Elements of Land Law* (5th edn Oxford University Press, Oxford 2009) 4.7.31–34.

10 See nn. 7, 8, 15; and compare *Connors v UK* (App no 66746/01) (2005) 40 EHRR 9 [68], [69], where it was confirmed that a summary eviction of gypsies from a local authority site was an interference with their Art. 8 ECHR right to respect for private life, family life and home. In *Chapman v UK* (App no 27238/94) [2001] 33 EHRR 399 [73] it was held that there is a positive obligation on the contracting ECHR states in terms of Art. 8 to ensure that it is possible for gypsies to maintain their identity and to lead their lives according to tradition, and the recent decision of the UK House of Lords in *Doherty v Birmingham City Council* [2008] UKHL 57 allows for context to be taken into account through judicial review of public authority decisions to evict. However, in Dutch case law and commentaries from the 1970s it was confirmed that context-sensitive protection of urban squatters against arbitrary eviction did not establish an indirect or so-called 'reflexive' right to occupy: see A.J. van der Walt, *Property in the Margins* (Hart Publishing, Oxford 2009) 140–41.

11 K. Klare, 'Legal Culture and Transformative Constitutionalism' (1998) 14 *South African Journal of Human Rights* 146, 167 explains that lawyers, trained to regard the 'intellectual sensibilities' and assumptions of their legal culture as normal, see the authority and force of its arguments as innate to the types of argument used and not as contingent cultural artefacts. Consequently, in the absence of critical reflection, lawyers become so embedded in their legal culture that they are 'unaware or only partially attentive to' the power of the cultural code to shape their ideas and steer their reaction to legal problems.

12 See n. 8. The South African courts have generally had little difficulty in applying the reasonably clear anti-eviction provisions in s. 4 of the Prevention of Illegal Eviction from

– in favour of tradition and the landowner's presumptive right to evict – and except for a small number of exceptional decisions in which the courts were willing to go beyond the clear wording of legislation,[13] the law of eviction generally tends to entrench the presumptive power of strong rights to enforce exclusive possession.[14] As a rule, really significant reforms only take place when the state introduces regulatory restrictions on eviction quite deliberately and explicitly, often under the influence of human rights principles or standards. It is important to note this conservative (in the non-political sense) tendency of law for the purposes of this essay, because it implies that any justice or human rights inspired advances that have been made in restricting arbitrary or unfair evictions should be guarded against erosion. My focus in this essay is on one potential source of such erosion.

It has become customary to discuss state regulation of eviction law within the human rights context from the point of departure that the state's role in the reform of eviction law is to promulgate legislation to protect vulnerable and weak property interests – particularly housing or home interests[15] – against common-law eviction by strong and possibly exploitative landowners. At least to a certain extent, this perception of the dynamic between the common law, legislation and human rights law in enabling or restricting eviction is certainly

---

and Unlawful Occupation of Land Act 19 of 1998, but they have been less open to reformist interpretations of the less explicit s. 26(3) of the Constitution. For similar reasons, anti-eviction measures in other land reform laws, which may seem to offer stronger protection because they confer occupation rights, are in fact used less often because these other laws do not specify the circumstances where eviction is restricted as clearly and the courts therefore tend to interpret them more restrictively. See A.J. van der Walt, *Constitutional Property Law* (Juta, Cape Town 2005) 338–53.

13 Three cases decided by the South African Constitutional Court are discussed below: *Port Elizabeth Municipality v Various Occupiers* 2005 (1) SA 217 (CC); *Occupiers of 51 Olivia Road, Berea Township, and 197 Main Street, Johannesburg v City of Johannesburg and ors* 2008 (3) SA 208 (CC); *Residents of Joe Slovo Community, Western Cape v Thubelisha Homes and ors (Centre on Housing Rights and Evictions and Community Law Centre, University of the Western Cape,* amici curiae*)* [2009] JOL 23711 (CC).

14 There is evidence that the obligation to consider reasonableness in some eviction cases does not always work in English law, in that the participation of tenants and the courts' actual consideration of the reasonableness factors are limited in fact: S. Bright, *Landlord and Tenant Law in Context* (Hart Publishing, Oxford 2007) 599, 601–602. In South African law, courts have been loath to amend the strong owner-oriented common law eviction procedure, even in view of the direct authority of s. 26(3) of the Constitution, unless they are explicitly or very clearly instructed to do so by clear and unambiguous legislation: *Brisley v Drotsky* 2002 (4) SA 1 (SCA) paras 40–41. Compare n. 11.

15 The notion of the 'home' interest in the context of tenure security and eviction has been highlighted particularly by L. Fox, *Conceptualising Home: Theories, Laws and Policies* (Hart Publishing, Oxford 2007). See further L. Fox, 'The Meaning of Home: A Chimerical Concept or a Legal Challenge?' (2002) 9 *Journal of Law & Society* 580.

accurate.[16] In this regard it could probably be said that the law regarding eviction has recently been developed or reformed more or less successfully under the influence of human rights and constitutional law, to a point where arbitrary and grossly unfair evictions are largely prohibited or restrained; where all occupiers of residential property enjoy a certain minimum of procedural protection against eviction; and where tenants and some other lawful occupiers cannot be evicted before the legal basis of their occupation has been terminated lawfully and fairly. In addition, eviction can in certain exceptional cases be prevented permanently or postponed temporarily, regardless of the legality of the occupation and the relative rights of the parties, purely because of justice considerations related to the social and economic context or the personal circumstances of the occupiers.

Moral, social and doctrinal justifications for these reforms of eviction law have been proposed and discussed over the last few decades. However, my goal in this article is not to discuss the development of eviction law under the influence of human rights instruments and standards, important and fascinating as that subject is.[17] For the present, I will simply take it as given that substantial progress has been made in this area and that eviction from residential property is now significantly restrained by constitutional and statutory conditions and requirements. Instead, I wish to focus on instances where residential occupiers are evicted specifically by the state[18] and where the state justifies the eviction

16 It is at least accurate to say that anti-eviction legislation has been promulgated or amended in view of human rights requirements in a number of jurisdictions and that eviction law is thereafter applied with due regard for human rights standards. In South African law, s. 25(6) of the Constitution places an additional obligation (on top of the anti-eviction provision in s. 26(3)) on the state to provide tenure security for persons and communities whose tenure of land is legally insecure because of apartheid. Residential tenants, especially in the former black townships, certainly fall within this category. In the UK a similar effect was created by promulgation of the Human Rights Act 1998 and the consequent incorporation of the ECHR into English law – subsequent case law (see the references below) clearly demonstrates the effect that the human rights perspective has had on the development of common law and statutory eviction law, despite the fact that English pre-1998 landlord–tenant legislation had already accomplished some of the goals associated with human-rights inspired protection against eviction. See further S. Bright, *Landlord and Tenant Law in Context* (Hart Publishing, Oxford 2007) 281–4, 610–13; K. Gray and S.F. Gray, *Elements of Land Law* (5th edn Oxford University Press, Oxford 2009) 4.7.31–34.

17 For South African law, some aspects of this development are discussed in A.J. van der Walt, *Constitutional Property Law* (Juta, Cape Town 2005) ch. 6; A.J. van der Walt, *Property in the Margins* (Hart Publishing, Oxford 2009) chs 2–5. For English law see K. Gray and S.F. Gray, *Elements of Land Law* (5th edn Oxford University Press, Oxford 2009) ch. 4.7; see generally S. Bright, *Landlord and Tenant Law in Context* (Hart Publishing, Oxford 2007).

18 In landlord–tenant law it is important to distinguish between private and public tenancies; see n. 8. In civil law jurisdictions, it is important to distinguish between eviction from private and from state land, since the landowner would usually initiate eviction proceedings. Of course, the state can also act as a private landowner to evict unlawful

of individuals and communities from residential property with an appeal to supposedly stronger or more urgent state interests, in a way that might in the long run indirectly undermine the progress that has been made in statutory law regarding eviction of tenants and unlawful occupiers or squatters. From this perspective, the state sometimes relies on and makes use of legislation and common law – and even constitutional and human rights law – not to regulate and impose controls upon eviction, but to reach exactly the opposite effect, namely to facilitate eviction in cases where it is in the interests of the state to vacate (specifically residential)[19] premises regardless of the socio-economic context, the personal circumstances of the occupiers or the effect that eviction may have on the occupiers. More specifically, I am interested in instances where the state uses its powers (either of expropriation or of land use regulation) to evict (lawful or unlawful) residential occupiers of land in order to clear the land for purposes of economic development or more beneficial use.[20] I am particularly interested in the fact that debate about these dispossessions and displacements for the sake of economic development tends to remain focused on the lawful or otherwise proper exercise of the state power that drives them and fails to engage with the housing or home interest issues that have gained currency in eviction law elsewhere. My hypothesis is that, unless these instances of state eviction for economic development are judged according to the same human rights inspired justice standards that have been developed to protect the home interest of occupiers of residential property against arbitrary or unjust evictions, any justice-promoting advances that have been made in eviction law might have been hollow or futile. Stated differently, I argue that the human rights inspired progress made in eviction law generally needs to be expanded to also cover the intersection between housing and expropriation law.

---

occupiers from state land. However, it is always possible for the state to initiate an eviction, even from private land, for instance in terms of regulatory legislation that protects public health and safety. For the moment I am only interested in evictions initiated by the state, regardless of whether the land is privately or state owned. Because of my focus I do not dwell on distinctions that might otherwise have been important, such as whether the land is privately or state owned, whether the occupation was lawful or unlawful, whether the tenancy (if there was one) was private or public and whether the occupier was a tenant or a licensee.

19 Of course the procedure I describe also applies to agricultural, industrial or commercial property, but for the present I am particularly interested in the effect that it has on occupiers of residential property, that is, on what Lorna Fox describes as the home interest.

20 In some of the cases I discuss, eviction follows from expropriation, condemnation or compulsory acquisition of the land, but in others the land already belongs to the state and is merely cleared for development; in yet others the land remains in private hands but the state uses its land-use regulatory powers to clear the land for development. What ties these cases together for my purposes is the exercise of state power, intended to promote economic development that involves eviction of the current residents.

The evictions I refer to mostly take place in the context of expropriation or regulatory state control over land use, such as slum clearance or economic redevelopment, where the proposed sanitation or redevelopment of land apparently justifies expropriation or dispossession and eventual eviction of the current occupiers of the land. Obviously, any form of expropriation that affects residential property, for any legitimate public purpose, will result in the eviction of the former occupiers and therefore it cannot be maintained (nor will I argue) that something like a home interest should always trump exercises of the power of eminent domain – if this were an inflexible rule, expropriation for clearly legitimate state actions such as the development of transport, electricity and water infrastructure or even social housing might well be impossible. In some of the instances I aim to discuss, the expropriation and concomitant eviction are inspired – and apparently justified – by apparently legitimate state purposes such as redevelopment of the area for social housing. Despite the apparent legitimacy of the land clearance for the sake of developing social housing, the evictions that follow from it often meet with resistance because of the personal and social disruption that these dislocations cause. In other cases, the expropriation and eviction are justified with reference to far less convincing state purposes such as vaguely defined slum clearance, upgrading of economically inactive areas and economic redevelopment, without any guarantee that new or more houses would be built or that the homeless or those affected by the displacement would benefit from it. Expropriations of the latter kind also elicit public outcry and litigation, but with some exceptions the focus in the ensuing debate is mostly on the legitimacy or justifiability of the compulsory acquisition and not on the eviction or the effect it has on the former residents. The context and the personal circumstances of the individuals and groups affected often do not even feature in the discussion.

In what follows I will first of all discuss two striking cases where state expropriation of land for economic development resulted in eviction of residential occupiers from their homes, under circumstances where it may well be asked whether the state purpose of (or public interest in) the expropriation indeed outweighed, or should have outweighed, the arguably equally important state purpose of (and public interest in) protecting the sanctity of home and the cohesion of established communities. The discussion of these two cases is contextualised by references to other similar or comparable decisions from various jurisdictions. Subsequently I will discuss three South African cases that were decided against the backdrop of recent advances in the human rights or justice inspired regulation and restriction of evictions that result in people losing their homes and where the purpose of the displacement was specifically to build social housing. Finally, I will pose the question whether the expropriation for development cases might be decided differently in a context where the home interest is protected more stringently or, stated differently, in a context where the progressive interaction between common law, legislation and human rights is conceived differently.

(2) Eviction Caused by Expropriation for Economic Development

Kelo v City of New London

By now, every property lawyer is familiar with the decision of the US Supreme Court in Kelo v City of New London.[21] The facts are well known.[22] The City of New London, Connecticut, approved an integrated development plan designed to revitalise its ailing economy. In 1996, the federal government had closed the Naval Undersea Warfare Center in the Fort Trumbull area of New London, an institution that had employed over 1,500 people. In 1998, the city's unemployment rate was nearly double the state average for Connecticut and its population of just under 24,000 residents was at its lowest since 1920.

The city council intended to turn around the downward trend by redeveloping the Fort Trumbull area. An integrated development plan was drawn up and the New London Development Corporation (NLDC), a private non-profit entity established earlier to assist the city in planning economic development, was reactivated. The plan envisaged developments in the Fort Trumbull area that would create more than 1,000 jobs, increase tax and other revenues and revitalise the economically distressed city. The developments would include a park, a waterfront conference hotel at the centre of a 'small urban village' with restaurants and shopping, marinas for recreational and commercial uses, approximately 80 new residences organised into an urban neighbourhood, a new US Coast Guard museum, at least 90,000 square feet of research and development office space, as well as office and retail space, parking, and water-dependent commercial uses. The city council hoped that a US$300 million research facility that the pharmaceutical company Pfizer Inc, would build on a site immediately adjacent to Fort Trumbull would draw new business to the area and serve as a catalyst for the area's rejuvenation.

To implement the development plan the city, through its development agent, purchased from willing sellers most of the private property in the Fort Trumbull area that had been earmarked for the project. The litigation that ended in the *Kelo* decision was sparked when the owners of the remaining properties in the area refused to sell and the city initiated condemnation (expropriation) procedures against them. Ms Susette Kelo and her fellow petitioners brought action in the state court claiming, inter alia, that the taking of their properties would violate the 'public use' restriction in the Fifth Amendment's Takings Clause. The trial court granted a permanent restraining order prohibiting the taking of some properties. The Connecticut Supreme Court, relying on earlier decisions of the US Supreme

21 545 US 469 (2005).

22 My summary of the facts relies on the judgment of Stevens J for the court, 545 US 469 (2005) 472–7, and on Institute for Justice, press release 'Susette Kelo Lost her Rights, She Lost her Property, but She has Saved her Home' (available at http://www.nolandgrab.org/archives/2006/07/institute_for_j.html, accessed 3 September 2009).

Court in cases such as *Berman v Parker*[23] *and Hawaii Housing Authority v Midkiff*,[24] upheld the proposed takings. On further appeal, a slender 5/4 majority of the US Supreme Court[25] upheld the Connecticut Supreme Court's finding that the city's proposed use of the petitioners' property for urban renewal qualified as a 'public use' within the meaning of the Takings Clause.[26]

The majority of the US Supreme Court acknowledged that the city was not planning to open all of the expropriated land to use by the general public, but reiterated that the court had long ago rejected the literal requirement that property may only be expropriated if it is actually opened up to or used by the public or the state. Instead, the court has embraced the broader interpretation of public use as 'public purpose'.[27] In terms of this broader interpretation, the city could not take land simply to confer a private benefit on a particular private party, but takings executed pursuant to a carefully considered plan such as the comprehensive development plan in the *Kelo* case might well satisfy the public use requirement. Considering the thorough deliberation that preceded adoption of the New London development plan and the limited scope of the court's review in such cases,[28] the Supreme Court thought it appropriate to assess the challenges of the individual owners in light of the entire plan and not on an individual basis. This approach inevitably placed the focus on the potential economic value of the development and away from its effect on individual landowners affected by it. The court decided that the development plan unquestionably served a public purpose and that the takings therefore satisfied the public use requirement in the Fifth Amendment.[29] The majority declined the invitation to develop a new 'bright line' test that would outlaw takings for economic development on the basis of the public use requirement.[30]

Despite the city's success in the US Supreme Court, not much has come of the development plan since July 2005. Following determined activism, the City of New London abandoned its plans to charge those who had resisted

23 348 US 26 (1954).

24 467 US 229 (1984).

25 Stevens J delivered the majority opinion, in which Kennedy, Souter, Ginsburg and Breyer JJ joined. Kennedy J filed a concurring opinion. O'Connor J filed a dissenting opinion, in which Rehnquist CJ and Scalia and Thomas JJ joined. Thomas J filed a dissenting opinion. Interestingly, O'Connor J wrote the majority opinion for the court in *Hawaii Housing Authority v Midkiff* 467 US 229 (1984), setting out the deference approach on which the *Kelo* decision is based, but she dissented from the majority in *Kelo*.

26 I do not propose to analyse the decision in detail here; see the literature referred to below. What follows is just a brief overview of salient points for purposes of the argument in this essay.

27 *Kelo v City of New London* 545 US 469 (2005) 480.

28 Ibid. 480–2, referring to the deferential approach adopted in *Berman v Parker* 348 US 26 (1954) and *Hawaii Housing Authority v Midkiff* 467 US 229 (1984).

29 *Kelo v City of New London* 545 US 469 (2005) 484.

30 Ibid. 486–7.

expropriation for back rent for the five years since the case began.[31] A group of New London residents who opposed the development plan formed a local political party, One New London. This group was unsuccessful in gaining control of the New London City Council, but they gained two seats on the city council and continued to oppose implementation of the plan. In June 2006 State Governor M. Jodi Rell intervened in the conflict between residents and the city council; officials thereafter proposed that the homeowners involved in the case should be granted property in the Fort Trumbull neighbourhood so that they might retain their homes.[32] The city also agreed to pay substantial additional compensation to the expropriated homeowners.[33] With the assistance of the Institute for Justice, the private organisation that litigated the case on Kelo's behalf, Susette Kelo's house was saved from demolition and moved wholesale to a new plot, not far from where it originally stood.[34] Other properties were demolished. By the end of 2008, after government expenditures of US$80 million, no redevelopment has taken place. The site of the Fort Trumbull redevelopment project (where Kelo's and her neighbours' homes originally stood) has been demolished almost completely and continues to be an unused lot. The preferred developer for part of the site, Corcoran Jennison, missed its final deadline to secure financing for building on the site and was terminated as the 'designated developer'.[35] Of the whole development, just one building was renovated for a Coast Guard museum.[36]

Politically, the *Kelo* decision has met with opposition as well, even from within federal and state government circles. On 23 June 2006 former president George W. Bush issued an Executive Order on the protection of the property rights of the American people, in which he prohibited abuses of the right of eminent domain for economic development purposes that are not clearly 'public use' as meant in

31 See Institute for Justice press release 'Susette Kelo Lost her Rights, She Lost her Property, but She has Saved her Home' (available at http://www.nolandgrab.org/archives/2006/07/institute_for_j.html, accessed 3 September 2009).

32 Ibid.

33 Ibid. However, three years later, the additional compensation has not yet been paid and it looks uncertain that it ever will: Bizzy Blog, 'The Kelo-New London Calamity Continues' (2008) (available at http://www.bizzyblog.com/2008/06/03/the-kelo-new-london-calamity-continues-barren-land/, accessed 3 September 2009).

34 The newly erected house at 36 Franklin Street in the heart of New London was dedicated on Saturday 21 June with a weekend celebration and a ribbon-cutting ceremony. See FCTO, 'Pink House that Inspired a Nation Reopened this Weekend' (available at http://www.ctact.org/default.asp?callcontent=yes&file name=Kelo.htm%20%20%20&location=eminent_domain&buttonname=Eminent%20Domain, accessed 26 May 2009).

35 See FCTO, 'Pink House that Inspired a Nation Reopened this Weekend' (available at http://www.ctact.org/default.asp?callcontent=yes&filename=Kelo.htm%20%20%20&location=eminent_domain&buttonname=Eminent%20Domain, accessed 26 May 2009).

36 See Institute for Justice press release 'Susette Kelo Lost her Rights, She Lost her Property, but She has Saved her Home' (available at http://www.nolandgrab.org/archives/2006/07/institute_for_j.html, accessed 3 September 2009).

the Fifth Amendment. The policy of the US, the Executive Order states, is that the taking of private property is limited to situations where the taking is for a public use 'and not merely for the purpose of advancing the economic interest of private parties to be given ownership or use of the property taken'.[37] Apart from this order, at least one private bill has been tabled in the US Senate, and several in the House of Representatives, to prevent abuses of the power of eminent domain to take (especially small) private property for development purposes that benefit a private developer rather than the public at large.[38] At the state level, there has also been reaction against the decision. Prior to the *Kelo* decision only eight states[39] specifically prohibited the use of eminent domain powers for economic development.[40] By July 2007, 42 states had enacted reform legislation in response to the *Kelo* decision, 21 of which now severely inhibit development takings such as the one allowed by the *Kelo* decision, while the rest placed at least some limits on the power of municipalities to invoke the power of eminent domain for economic development.[41]

---

37 The Executive Order states that 'It is the policy of the United States to protect the rights of Americans to their private property, including by *limiting the taking of private property by the Federal Government to situations in which the taking is for public use,* with just compensation, and *for the purpose of benefiting the general public and not merely for the purpose of advancing the economic interest of private parties to be given ownership or use of the property taken*' (emphasis added). See G.W. Bush, 'Executive Order: Protecting the Property Rights of the American People' (2006) (available at http://georgewbush-whitehouse.archives.gov/news/releases/2006/06/20060623-10.html6, accessed 3 September 2009). Most takings of the *Kelo* type take place on the state or local level and therefore the Executive Order will have no direct effect, although the increase of statutory prohibitions against takings for development suggests that the effects of anti-*Kelo* reaction might be felt on the state level as well. See the references to state reactions in nn. 37–9 below. See further I. Somin 'Post-*Kelo* America: Assessing the Progress of Eminent Domain Reform' (2007) (available at http://www.reason.com/news/show/119766.html, accessed 3 September 2009), who argues that the Executive Order is ineffectual in that it allows 'takings for private owners who promise to use the land for both private and "public" development', which is more or less the argument accepted in the *Kelo* decision.

38 See Wikipedia, 'Kelo v City of New London' (available at http://en.wikipedia.org/wiki/Kelo_v._City_of_New_London, accessed 3 September 2009).

39 Arkansas, Florida, Illinois, Kentucky, Maine, Montana, South Carolina and Washington: see more detail at Wikipedia, 'Kelo v City of New London' (available at http://en.wikipedia.org/wiki/Kelo_v._City_of_New_London, accessed 3 September 2009).

40 These prohibitions usually do not cover condemnations to rectify urban blight or slum conditions.

41 See Wikipedia, 'Kelo v City of New London' (available at http://en.wikipedia.org/wiki/Kelo_v._City_of_New_London, accessed 3 September 2009). See further S. Crow, 'Compulsory Purchase for Economic Development: An International Perspective' (2007) *JPEL* 1102, 1105. CE Cohen, 'Eminent Domain after *Kelo v City of New London*: An Argument for Banning Economic Development Takings' (2005–2006) 29 *Harvard JL & Public Policy* 491, 559–66 reviews the substance of state laws that ban takings for economic

Academic reaction has been mixed. While some academic commentators from the US defend the decision,[42] others describe it as a mistake and call for a ban on takings for development purposes, even if it requires amending the Constitution.[43] In the same spirit, UK commentators Gray and Gray argued that the *Kelo* decision could mean that '"real property" may have ceased to be "real" in the authentic, historic sense'[44] and that 'private property would have become simply a mush of social and economic resource to be reallocated at will by the state'.[45] In another context, Kevin Gray assessed the import of the *Kelo* decision in even stronger terms:

> The *Kelo* case brings together many of the features of the enduring American paradox. It concerns the limits of coercive state power in the land of the free. It exposes the unresolved tension between the sanctity of private property and the power of the mighty dollar. It highlights a confrontation between little people and big business, between individual claims of personal privacy and the collective American dream of wealth and prosperity. It marks a point at which the democratic ideal slides arguably into majoritarian tyranny.[46]

---

development and considers the problems experienced with different approaches in the legislation. A.W. Goodin, 'Rejecting the Return to Blight in Post-Kelo State Legislation' (2007) 82 *NYULR* 177, 192–207 also reviews the post-*Kelo* legislation and criticizes it for being either ineffectual or too caught up in the unhelpful rhetoric of blight. See further I. Somin, 'Post-*Kelo* America: Assessing the Progress of Eminent Domain Reform' (2007) (available at http://www.reason.com/news/show/119766.html, accessed 3 September 2009), who argues that the Executive Order is ineffectual in that it allows 'takings for private owners who promise to use the land for both private and "public" development', which is more or less the argument accepted in the *Kelo* decision.

42 A. Bell and G. Parchomovsky, 'The Uselessness of Public Use' (2006) 106 *Col LR* 1412, 1415 argue that 'Kelo was rightly decided and that criticisms of the decision are ill conceived and misguided.' They argue (at 1412), amongst other things, that the power of 'eminent domain is the government power least pernicious to property owners as it is the only one that guarantees them compensation.' D. Schultz, 'What's Yours can be Mine: Are there any Private Takings after *Kelo v City of New London*?' (2005–2006) 24 *UCLA Journal of Environmental Law & Policy* 195 argues that *Kelo* establishes a new test that is not entirely satisfactory but still in line with the public use requirement, based on the existence of a specific development plan, which provides the framework within which the power of eminent domain has to be exercised.

43 The most comprehensive case is made by C.E. Cohen, 'Eminent Domain after *Kelo v City of New London*: An Argument for Banning Economic Development Takings' (2005–2006) 29 *Harvard JL & Public Policy* 491.

44 K. Gray and S.F. Gray, *Elements of Land Law* (5th edn Oxford University Press, Oxford 2009) 11.2.9.

45 Ibid., 1.5.36.

46 K. Gray, 'Human Property Rights: The Politics of Expropriation' (2005) 16 *Stell LR* 398, 401.

However, the majority of academic commentators from the US reacted to the public outcry by pointing out that the *Kelo* decision did not create new law, nor did it signal a new departure in US constitutional jurisprudence.[47] At most, this decision underlined the deference with which the US Supreme Court has exercised its jurisdiction to apply the 'public use' requirement in the Fifth Amendment ever since the earlier, direction-giving decisions in *Berman v Parker*[48] *and Hawaii Housing Authority v Midkiff*.[49] In *Berman*, the US Supreme Court accepted that a taking of private land for resale to a private developer in terms of a general slum clearance and land development plan was in the public interest *because the authorising legislation declared it so*:

> Subject to specific constitutional limitations, when the legislature has spoken, the public interest has been declared in terms well-nigh conclusive. In such cases the legislature, not the judiciary, is the main guardian of the public needs to be served by social legislation.[50]

This deferential approach was continued in *Hawaii Housing Authority*,[51] albeit in a context where the purpose of the taking was not redevelopment of the land but rectification of what was seen as an unhealthy distribution of land.[52] In *Poletown*

47 D. Schultz, 'What's Yours can be Mine: Are there any Private Takings after *Kelo v City of New London*?' (2005–2006) 24 *UCLA Journal of Environmental Law & Policy* 195, 196, 218; T.W. Merrill, 'Six Myths about Kelo' (January–February 2006) 20 *Probate & Property* 19 ('Myth 1'); L.S. Underkuffler, '*Kelo's* Moral Failure' (2006) 15 *William & Mary Bill of Rights Journal* 377. If anything, the court's finding that 'the City [would not] be allowed to take property *under the mere pretext of a public purpose*, when its actual purpose was to bestow a private benefit' (*Kelo v City of New London* 545 US 469 (2005) 478, emphasis added) might indicate an interpretation of the public use requirement that would be more protective of homeowners' rights than *Hawaii Housing Authority v Midkiff* 467 US 229 (1984), where the court seemed to suggest that any conceivable public purpose would justify the taking. I am indebted to Eduardo Peñalver for pointing this potentially restrictive interpretation out to me.

48 348 US 26 (1954).

49 467 US 229 (1984).

50 *Berman v Parker* 348 US 26 (1954) 32–3.

51 The court confirmed in *Hawaii Housing Authority v Midkiff* 467 US 229 (1984) 240 that the public use requirement in the Takings Clause is 'coterminous with the scope of a sovereign's police powers'. See M. Taggart, 'Expropriation, Public Purpose and the Constitution' in C. Forsyth and I. Hare (eds), *The Golden Metwand and the Crooked Cord: Essays on Public Law in Honour of Sir William Wade QC* (Oxford University Press, Oxford 1998) 91–112, 99–100; D. Schultz, 'What's Yours can be Mine: Are there any Private Takings after *Kelo v City of New London*?' (2005–2006) 24 *UCLA Journal of Environmental Law & Policy* 195, 209–11; C.E. Cohen, 'Eminent Domain after *Kelo v City of New London*: An Argument for Banning Economic Development Takings' (2005–2006) 29 *Harvard JL & Public Policy* 491.

52 I return to this distinction below, arguing that it is a vital one that could insulate the decision in *Hawaii Housing Authority* against at least some of the criticism levelled against

Neighborhood Council v City of Detroit[53] the Michigan Supreme Court upheld the City of Detroit's taking decision that involved levelling a residential neighbourhood in Detroit and relocating 1,362 private households and more than 150 private businesses, so as to accommodate the General Motors Corporation's wish to build a new assembly plant. Despite objections from private homeowners and businesses, the state Supreme Court held that the taking was for public use under the state constitution, considering the severely depressed economic condition of parts of the city and the prospect of new industrial development and the economic boost that the development would bring about.[54]

There are indications that some state courts would decide taking for economic development cases differently, though. Twenty years after the *Poletown* decision, the Michigan Supreme Court overturned its own previous decision in *County of Wayne v Hatchcock*, arguing that its earlier view of the public use requirement was too wide.[55] Subsequent to the *Kelo* decision, the Ohio Supreme Court cited this reversal of the Michigan Supreme Court in overturning an earlier decision of the Ohio Court of Appeals in *City of Norwood v Horney*,[56] rejecting both the increasingly broad conception of public use that had inspired the US Supreme Court and state courts in holding that 'general economic development is a public use' and the 'artificial judicial deference' on which this wide notion of public use was based. Accordingly, the court held that economic development by itself does not satisfy the public use requirement in the Ohio Constitution.

Despite the public outcry and political criticism, the strong dissents and the subsequent deviations in state legislation and jurisprudence, the *Berman–Kelo* line of decisions confirms that the US Supreme Court will not test the public use requirement in takings of land for development at all vigorously, deferring as it does to the policy decision of the federal or state legislature that promulgated the relevant law or the executive authority that took the decision to expropriate. When Stevens J refused to apply the heightened standard of scrutiny favoured

---

Berman and *Kelo*.

53 304 NW2d 455 (Mich 1981), overruled in *County of Wayne v Hatchcock* 684 NW2d 765 (Mich 2004). On the *Poletown* decision see F. Michelman, 'Property as a Constitutional Right' (1981) 38 *Wash & Lee LR* 1097; D. Schultz, 'What's Yours can be Mine: Are there any Private Takings after *Kelo v City of New London*?' (2005–2006) 24 *UCLA Journal of Environmental Law & Policy* 195; L.S. Underkuffler, '*Kelo's* Moral Failure' (2006) 15 *William & Mary Bill of Rights Journal* 377.

54 *Poletown Neighborhood Council v City of Detroit* 304 NW2d 455 (Mich 1981) 459.

55 684 NW2d 765 (Mich 2004). In this case, the plan was to condemn private properties for the construction of a 1300 acre business and technology park intended to help revitalise the ailing economy of south-eastern Michigan. The Michigan Supreme Court decided that the taking was not for public use because Wayne County intended to transfer the condemned properties to private parties 'in a manner wholly inconsistent with the common understanding of "public use" at the time our Constitution was ratified.'

56 853 NE2d 1115 (Ohio 2006). See 'Recent Cases' (2006) 120 *Harvard LR* 643.

by the minority judges in *Kelo*, he was simply 'reflecting our [the US Supreme Court's] longstanding policy of deference to legislative judgments in this field.'[57] As Stevens J pointed out:

> For more than a century, our public use jurisprudence has wisely eschewed rigid formulas and intrusive scrutiny in favor of affording legislatures broad latitude in determining what public needs justify the use of the takings power.[58]

Accordingly, applying this long-standing policy to the facts, the result looks inevitable:

> Those who govern the City were not confronted with the need to remove blight in the Fort Trumbull area, but their determination that the area was sufficiently distressed to justify a program of economic rejuvenation *is entitled to our deference*.[59]

Smith & ors v Secretary of State for Trade and Industry

The English case of *Smith & ors v Secretary of State for Trade and Industry*[60] also involved a compulsory acquisition (expropriation) that resulted in people being evicted from their homes, albeit that the affected occupiers in this case were lessees rather than owners of the land. The situation in Smith was further complicated by the fact that the case involved specific groups of occupiers (Romani Gypsies and Irish Travellers) who, once evicted, would find it particularly difficult to find suitable alternative residential accommodation because of their identity and lifestyle.

In November 2005 the London Development Agency made a compulsory purchase order under s. 20(1) of the Regional Development Agencies Act 1998, authorising the compulsory purchase of 339 hectares of land in London. The compulsory purchase was made for purposes related to economic development and regeneration of the area, mostly involving provision of central facilities for the 2012 Olympic and Paralympics Games.[61] The land affected by the compulsory acquisition included sites in Newham and Hackney where the claimants lived with

57 *Kelo v City of New London* 545 US 469 (2005) 480.

58 Ibid. 483.

59 Ibid. 483 (emphasis added).

60 [2007] EWHC 1013 (Admin). Another case arising from the same set of facts is *Sole v Secretary of State for Trade and Industry and ors* [2007] EWHC 1527 (Admin). The claimant occupied premises in a communal housing scheme for single people in the area affected by the Olympics acquisition. The objection was similar to those in *Smith*, namely that the acquisition should not be finalised before a secure relocation strategy had been put in place. The court held, like the *Smith* court, that the decision not to make the compulsory acquisition order conditional on a relocation strategy was justified.

61 *Smith & ors v Secretary of State for Trade and Industry* [2007] EWHC 1013 (Admin) [5].

their families.[62] There were objections against the compulsory acquisition order and an inspector was appointed to hold a local public inquiry. The main thrust of the objections was 'to assert that no compulsory purchase order should be made unless and until alternative sites had been provided upon which the occupiers could pitch their caravans.'[63] The inspector reported that the area was indeed characterised by decay, neglect and social problems and that it needed redevelopment;[64] he also acknowledged that the regeneration promised by the preparations for the Olympic Games would provide the right sort of injection to salvage the area from complete degeneration.[65] There was no possibility that the Olympics development could proceed without the agency acquiring control of the sites occupied by the claimants before the due date.[66] However, the inspector nevertheless advised that the compulsory acquisition order should not be confirmed until the Secretary of State was satisfied that 'suitable relocation sites will be available to meet the reasonable needs of the Gypsies and the Travellers who would be displaced.'[67] The defendant considered the report but decided to confirm the order and to proceed with the compulsory acquisition before having secured guaranteed relocation to a suitable alternative site, and as a consequence the claimants instituted proceedings to ask for a court order to quash the decision to confirm the order in terms of s. 23 of the Acquisition of Land Act 1981.

The defendant had realised at an early stage that it would be necessary to find alternative sites to house those affected by compulsory acquisition of the two caravan sites. Enquiries had been made and possible sites had been identified, but at the time when the order was confirmed none of these sites had been secured for the relocation of the claimants.[68] The claimants challenged the decision to confirm the compulsory acquisition order before alternative relocation sites had been secured, relying on Article 8 of the ECHR to argue that the order unlawfully interfered with their right to respect for family life and home. The defendant did not deny that the order would constitute an interference, but argued that the interference with the claimants' family life and homes was 'in accordance with the domestic law and necessary in the interests of the economic wellbeing of the country.'[69]

---

62 The first claimant in *Smith*, a Romani gypsy, was a licensee of a plot in an authorised caravan site in Newham where she had lived in a caravan, with two children, for 20 years. The second claimant, an Irish Traveller, had lived in a caravan in an authorised caravan site in Hackney, together with her five children, for 13 years. The third claimant, also an Irish Traveller, lived in a caravan at the same site, with three children (two of whom were school-going age). She and one of her children suffered from significant disability. See *Smith & ors v Secretary of State for Trade and Industry* [2007] EWHC 1013 (Admin) [1]–[3].

63 Ibid. [7].

64 The details of the inspector's report on the area are set out in ibid. [14].

65 Ibid. [16], [17].

66 Ibid. [18].

67 Ibid. [8].

68 Ibid. [21].

69 Ibid. [28].

At this point the *Smith* case raised the same issues as the *Kelo* case, namely whether it is justified to allow state exercises of the power of eminent domain to achieve general or specific economic development goals, on the unspoken or explicit assumption that the development goal is of a higher order of public importance, when it is clear that individuals or communities will be evicted from their homes and that communities will be destroyed as a consequence of the expropriation, without there being any indication that those who are evicted will receive any benefit from the development. Unlike the *Kelo* case, the claimants in *Smith* were not home owners and they did not oppose the development or the relocation – their primary objection was security in the sense of certainty about being suitably accommodated elsewhere, which is a serious concern for Romani Gypsies, Irish Travellers and other communities who share their lifestyle. The court acknowledged the special requirements of these communities with reference to the leading decision of the European Court of Human Rights on the point, *Chapman v UK*,[70] where it was recognised that living in caravans was an essential part of the Gypsy lifestyle, that measures which affect the stationing of their caravans have a wider impact than respect for the home and that such measures also affect their ability to maintain their identity as Gypsies and to lead their lives according to that tradition. Accordingly, in the *Chapman* decision the court found that there is a positive obligation on the contracting ECHR states to facilitate the Gypsy lifestyle in accordance with Art. 8, both in the framing of legislation and in the taking of individual decisions under legislation that protects general public interests such as access to housing or the environment.[71]

The *Smith* court also confirmed that the interference with the claimants' rights in this particular instance was substantial[72] but decided that, since all those involved accepted that a convincing case had been made out for the acquisition, the issue of proportionality only affected the timing of confirmation of the compulsory acquisition order, that is, whether it should have been confirmed prior to securing alternative sites for relocation.[73] On this view it was unnecessary for the defendant to prove that the measure proposed was the least intrusive measure possible; the court nevertheless decided that the decision to confirm the compulsory acquisition order was indeed proportionate, as required by Article 8. The reason for this finding was that the defendant had established that the measure he proposed, namely to proceed with the compulsory acquisition order before alternative land had been secured, was the least intrusive measure possible *that would still achieve the important objective* of ensuring that a substantial proportion of the required

70 (App no 27238/94) [2001] 33 EHRR 399 [73]; see *Smith & ors v Secretary of State for Trade and Industry* [2007] EWHC 1013 (Admin) [29]. The decision in *Chapman* was confirmed in *Connors v UK* (App no 66746/01) (2005) 40 EHRR 9 [84].

71 (App no 27238/94) [2001] 33 EHRR 399 [96]; see *Smith & ors v Secretary of State for Trade and Industry* [2007] EWHC 1013 (Admin) [29].

72 Ibid. [49].

73 Ibid. [42].

land for the development (which included the caravan sites) was under the control of the defendant by mid 2007.[74] The deciding factor was therefore the overriding importance of the government objective in developing the land and not the effect that the dislocation would have on the affected individuals or communities. This places the *Smith* decision squarely in the same category as *Kelo*.

The power of compulsory acquisition is an important tool for the policy of urban regeneration in the UK.[75] As in the case of *Kelo* in the US, the *Smith* case was decided in the wake of earlier case law on the use of the power of compulsory acquisition for economic development purposes. In *Alliance Spring Co Ltd v the First Secretary of State*[76] the local authority wanted to use its power of compulsory acquisition to drive a comprehensive regeneration project in an area of north London. Objectors argued that the real reason behind the regeneration scheme was to obtain land for a new stadium for Arsenal Football Club, a development that the local authority supported but for which it could not obtain all the required land in the open market. Having considered the objections and the inspector's report,[77] the court acknowledged that owners of businesses to be dispossessed by the compulsory acquisition would clearly suffer an interference with their property rights under Article 1 of the First Protocol to the ECHR, but decided that any interference with those rights was proportionate. The court dismissed the claim that the compulsory acquisition was not for a public purpose but mainly for Arsenal's benefit, arguing that regeneration developments are often spearheaded by private enterprise.[78] In its finding that the decision of the secretary of state to proceed with the compulsory acquisition was lawful, even in the face of Article 8 of the ECHR, the court displayed a level of deference that is reminiscent of the

---

74 Ibid. [50]. T. Hickman, 'The Substance and Structure of Proportionality' [2008] *Public Law* 694, 704 argued that this narrow approach allowed the court to escape the difficult proportionality issues posed by Art. 8 ECHR and that this 'sidestep' by the court has the potential 'to rob the proportionality test of its function as a means for ensuring that there is a fair balance between individual rights and the desires of the general community at least in many cases.' At 706 Hickman adds that it is often difficult 'accurately to distil the objectives of a measure to the level of specificity' relied upon in the case.

75 See P. Winter and R. Lloyd, 'Regeneration, Compulsory Purchase Orders and Practical Related Issues' [2006] *Journal of Planning and Environmental Law* 781: 'This policy shift towards urban regeneration has led to a significant increase in the use of compulsory purchase powers to assemble sites for redevelopment in the interests of regeneration.'

76 [2005] EWHC 18 (Admin). See S. Crow, 'Compulsory Purchase for Economic Development: An International Perspective' [2007] *Journal of Planning and Environmental Law* 1102, 1108–10.

77 The inspector recommended that the compulsory acquisition order should not be confirmed: *Alliance Spring Co Ltd v the First Secretary of State* [2005] EWHC 18 (Admin) [7], [10] –[13].

78 S. Crow, 'Compulsory Purchase for Economic Development: An International Perspective' [2007] *Journal of Planning and Environmental Law* 1109.

US Supreme Court in *Berman* or in *Kelo*: 'Once [the secretary of state] decided that there was a compelling case that the CPO [compulsory purchase order] should be confirmed, that view was not only not erroneous but was manifestly correct.'[79] Similarly, in *Ainsdale Investments Ltd v First Secretary of State*[80] the High Court upheld a compulsory acquisition of property that was, in the eyes of the local authority, not making a proper contribution to the housing stock in the area.

However, English courts will not always simply defer to legislative or executive decision-making powers on compulsory acquisitions. There are indications that courts will scrutinise the power to acquire property compulsorily, based on the principle that compulsory acquisition has to serve a legitimate purpose and must be authorised by legislation.[81] In *Pascoe v First Secretary of State*[82] the objection was not against the compulsory acquisition of private land in a much decayed area of eastern Liverpool for redevelopment, but against the acquisition and destruction of parcels of land where the existing houses were not affected by decay or blight and arguably worthy of preservation for presenting a fine Victorian townscape.[83] In the end, the compulsory acquisition was quashed because the court judged that the secretary of state was wrong to accept the inspector's recommendation on the basis that the land concerned was 'predominantly under-used or ineffectively used'. This decision was inspired by the conclusion that s. 159(2)(c) of the *Leasehold Reform, Housing and Urban Development Act 1993*, which allows acquisition of 'land which is under-used or ineffectively used', requires that the land must be wholly, not 'predominantly', under-used or ineffectively used.[84]

A Note on German Case Law

It is not my intention to write extensively on German law in this context, but a brief note on German case law might be useful, as there are decisions that compare

---

79 *Alliance Spring Co Ltd v the First Secretary of State* [2005] EWHC 18 (Admin) [21].

80 [2004] EWHC 1010 (Admin). See K. Gray and S.F. Gray *Elements of Land Law* (5th edn Oxford University Press, Oxford 2009) 11.2.8, citing further examples from English law.

81 This principle is also recognised in German law, albeit that it is applied more strictly; see below, n. 84 and associated text.

82 [2006] EWHC 2356 (Admin). See S. Crow, 'Compulsory Purchase for Economic Development: An International Perspective' [2007] *Journal of Planning and Environmental Law* 1108.

83 *Pascoe v First Secretary of State* [2006] EWHC 2356 (Admin) [80]; see S. Crow, 'Compulsory Purchase for Economic Development: An International Perspective' [2007] *Journal of Planning and Environmental Law* 1108.

84 *Pascoe v First Secretary of State* [2006] EWHC 2356 (Admin) [38], [42], [44], [49]. See S. Crow, 'Compulsory Purchase for Economic Development: An International Perspective' [2007] *Journal of Planning and Environmental Law*, 1108; R. Harwood, 'Case Comment: Pascoe v First Secretary of State' [2007] *JPEL* 607, 641.

quite interestingly with the cases discussed so far. The most significant general principles in German law on the topic are that expropriation is always seen as a last resort, not to be undertaken lightly, and that expropriation must therefore always be justified by the public purpose for which it is undertaken – the fact that compensation is paid cannot in itself justify expropriation.[85] If the property is not used for the purpose for which it was expropriated, the affected person can claim the property back.[86] For these reasons, both the statutory authority and the public purpose for any given expropriation are always tested quite strictly in German law.[87] The German courts accept that expropriation undertaken for a legitimate public purpose might sometimes in fact benefit a private party, for example when it is necessary to expropriate property for the effective provision of a public utility such as electricity, under circumstances where provision of the utility has been outsourced to a private concern that will make profit from it.[88] Apart from the public utility cases, the German Federal Constitutional Court has handed down two decisions dealing specifically with expropriation for economic development.[89] In one perspective, the outcomes in these cases look disappointing because they appear to have been decided on narrow and rather formalist issues of statutory authority, but on closer scrutiny they prove to be very interesting.

In *Dürkheimer Gondelbahn*[90] the proposed expropriation for economic development would not have resulted in eviction, since the plan was to expropriate not land, but servitudes over private property for a cable car line that would link the inner city of Dürkheimer with the Teufelstein, a popular tourist destination outside the city. The court decided that the expropriations would have been unlawful because of a technical shortcoming in the expropriation powers of the local authority, and not directly with regard to the question whether the expropriation was for the public interest. Closer analysis shows that the issue was not simply a lack of authority to expropriate, but the quite technical finding that the authorising legislation must allow the local authority to promote the relevant public purpose (public transport) and to expropriate property in promoting it; in

85 See discussion above, n. 80 and associated text, demonstrating that a similar principle applies in English law.

86 *BVerfGE* 38, 175 [1974] 181ff (German Federal Constitutional Court); *BVerfGE* 56, 249 (*Dürkheimer Gondelbahn*) [1981] 260–1, 271 (German Federal Constitutional Court); *BVerfGE* 97, 89 [1997] 89 (German Federal Constitutional Court). See A.J. van der Walt, *Constitutional Property Clauses: A Comparative Analysis* (Juta, Cape Town 1999) 147–9.

87 See generally in this regard A.J. van der Walt, *Constitutional Property Law* (Juta, Cape Town 2005) 254–6.

88 *BVerfGE* 66, 248 [1984] (German Federal Constitutional Court).

89 *BVerfGE* 56, 249 (*Dürkheimer Gondelbahn*) [1981]; *BVerfGE* 74, 264 (*Boxberg*) [1986]. See A.J. van der Walt, *Constitutional Property Clauses: A Comparative Analysis* (Juta, Cape Town 1999) 147–9; A.J. van der Walt, *Constitutional Property Law* (Juta, Cape Town 2005) 257–8.

90 *BVerfGE* 56, 249 (*Dürkheimer Gondelbahn*) [1981].

this case, the real problem was a lack of statutory authority for this overlap of the two powers. The court was therefore required to scrutinise compliance with the public purpose requirement by checking very closely and technically whether the legislature had in fact contemplated and allowed expropriation for the specific purpose it is to be used for; if not, the authority to expropriate would be lacking. This meant that the court could scrutinise the authority to expropriate quite strictly without second-guessing the legislature's policy decisions concerning the wisdom or desirability of promoting the particular public purpose: once the legislature has clearly authorised the public purpose in question (for example, public transport) and the means to achieve it (expropriation) the judiciary will not interfere, but it will scrutinise very closely whether the necessary legislative authority for the expropriation is indeed present and sufficient.[91]

The decision in *Dürkheimer Gondelbahn* is also interesting because Böhmer J examined the public purpose requirement for expropriation in greater detail in a separate concurring judgment. The essence of his concurring opinion was that the public purpose requirement has to be interpreted strictly, with reference to strict scrutiny of the state's statutory power of expropriation (this was the basis of the majority decision); that the public purpose that is required for a legitimate expropriation is narrower than what may be simply in the public interest; and that what may be in the public interest is again narrower than what may be considered a public benefit. Accordingly, economic development that may well bring about a public benefit or that might even be in the public interest would not necessarily satisfy the public purpose requirement laid down in the constitutional provision. On this approach, the mere fact that an expropriation would benefit the public generally would cut no ice – the question is whether it serves a more specific public purpose, the promotion of which through expropriation is authorised by legislation.

In *Boxberg*[92] the facts were very similar to those of the US *Poletown* case, in that the two local authorities involved in the German case also intended to use their power of expropriation to acquire land to enable the Daimler-Benz motor company to establish a testing ground. The idea was that the testing ground would help improve the poor economic and unemployment situation in the area. As in the *Dürkheimer* case, the court again decided that the expropriation was not authorised by the relevant

91 As was pointed out earlier, this judicial attitude resembles the approach of the English courts, with the significant difference that German law is based on the principle of constitutional review and not parliamentary sovereignty. The test is thus whether the necessary legislative authorisation for state action that infringes a constitutional right indeed exists. Unlike the approach of the US Supreme Court, this test for legislative authority is applied strictly, perhaps even more strictly than in the English courts. Somewhat like the English courts in terms of Art. 8 ECHR, the German courts also apply a proportionality test to measure the legislative decision against Art. 14 of the Basic Law, with the significant difference that the notion of a 'wide margin of appreciation' that insulates domestic decision making against ECHR controls is absent in German constitutional review.

92 *BVerfGE* 74, 264 (*Boxberg*) [1986].

legislation or by the statutory powers of the local authorities in terms of the planning laws they relied on. The decision confirmed that expropriation would not necessarily be invalid just because it is carried out in favour of a private party, especially if the private concern carries out a public duty for the public benefit and in the public interest, but it again emphasised that the expropriation should be necessary for a public purpose and that it should be authorised by legislation for that purpose. In this case the court decided that the expected general economic benefit of establishing the testing ground was insufficient to justify the expropriation in favour of a private company, and consequently the expropriation was invalid for being in conflict with the public purpose requirement in Art. 14.3 of the Basic Law.

Four useful perspectives emerge from this brief overview of German case law. The first is that expropriation is an extraordinary power, not to be used lightly and always to be regarded as the only available solution, the last resort for accomplishing a legitimate public purpose. This principle means that the payment of compensation does not in itself justify expropriation; it must be justified before compensation becomes an issue. Similarly, if the property is not used for the purpose for which it was expropriated, the affected person can claim the property back. The second perspective is that expropriation can serve a legitimate public purpose even when it benefits a private person, provided that it is necessary for a public purpose that is undertaken for the public by that private person, such as providing a public utility. The third point is more directly relevant to the topic under discussion: in deciding whether an expropriation for the sake of economic development satisfies the public purpose requirement, the German courts start out from the legislation that authorises expropriation in general or the promotion of the relevant public purpose (for example, town planning) in particular, requiring that both the expropriation and the purpose served by it should be authorised and justified clearly and more or less directly by the legislation. Concretely, expropriation for the sake of stimulating economic regeneration would be possible only if the authority in question is authorised by legislation to promote economic regeneration *and* to use expropriation for that purpose. The legislation would also have to set out the framework within which compensation has to be calculated and laid for expropriation in cases of that kind. The fourth perspective is that public purpose, as a consideration that legitimises expropriation of private property, is narrower than public interest and even narrower than public benefit – this indicates that the German courts apply a much stricter level of scrutiny when interpreting this requirement than the US courts do.

Assessment of Taking-for-economic-development Cases

There is a clear principle in English law, US law and German law that expropriation for an improper purpose or purely for private benefit is illegitimate, regardless of whether the expropriated owner receives adequate compensation.[93] Not one of these systems or South African law will allow expropriations that are manifestly for an improper or purely private purpose. However, having said that, in assessing the impact and validity of cases where eviction from people's homes was allowed in the wake of expropriation for the sake of economic development, one should be aware of the systemic differences between US, English, German and South African law.

One important difference is the fact that property is protected constitutionally in US, German and South African law, whereas the 'constitution-like' protection of property in the UK (via the Human Rights Act 1998 and the ECHR) is at least more tangential. The same holds for the constitutional protection, in so far as it exists, of a right to security of tenure in, or 'respect for' one's home.[94] A second significant difference is the role of parliamentary sovereignty (which is strong in England) compared to constitutional supremacy and review (which is strong in the US, Germany and South Africa). Obviously, one could expect a stronger tendency to defer to legislative decisions in a system characterised by parliamentary sovereignty, while one might perhaps expect less deference under a sovereign constitution. At the same time one should be aware of the fact that one of these approaches is not necessarily better than the other; parliamentary sovereignty in the English system is balanced out with a strong tradition of robust parliamentary debate and controls over the granting and exercise of legislative powers, which arguably reduces the need for constitutional review. These differences have a marked effect on the way in which legislation is made and in how it is tested against constitution-like norms and standards and can therefore have an effect on the outcome of the case law discussed here.

Although the deferential attitude adopted in *Smith* resembles the deference with which the US Supreme Court has applied the public use requirement since *Berman*, the two systems and the reasons for adopting the respective judicial attitudes in these cases are different in important ways. In English law there are strong constitutional reasons (the principle of parliamentary sovereignty) for leaving the decision whether legislation could or should authorise compulsory acquisition to the legislature, while the principle of constitutional review suggests that the US courts might test legislative decisions of that kind more strictly against constitutional requirements. When the US Supreme Court defers to legislative

---

93 See K. Gray and S.F. Gray, *Elements of Land Law* (5th edn Oxford University Press, Oxford 2009) 11.2.4, citing the Supreme Court of Queensland in *Prentice v Brisbane City Council* [1966] Qd R 394, 406. Compare *James v UK* (App no 8795/79) [1986] 8 EHRR 123 [40]. On German law compare A.J. van der Walt, *Constitutional Property Law* (Juta, Cape Town 2005) 254–6.

94 As is argued below, this right is strong in South African law because of ss 25 and 26 of the Constitution and in England because of Art. 8 of the ECHR, but in Germany a similar right is construed on the basis of Art. 14 of the Basic Law: *BVerfGE* 89, 1 (*Besitzrecht des Mieters*) [1993] (German Federal Constitutional Court). The ECHR is of course also applicable in Germany as a member state.

decisions on taking private property for public use, it is placing a limit or a restraint upon the power of constitutional review, whereas the English courts are acting in accordance with the principle of parliamentary sovereignty when they refrain from getting mixed up in policy decisions. Similarly, the superficial similarities between the German cases and the seemingly strict review in the English *Pascoe* case should be seen against the backdrop of the differences between the systems: the English court was testing for statutory authority because that would bring the principle of parliamentary sovereignty into play; the German courts are testing for proper authority as a matter of constitutional review, because expropriation interferes with a constitutionally guaranteed right.

A further point that emerges from the overview of case law on expropriation for economic development is that these cases (and their treatment of the public purpose requirement in third party transfers) should be distinguished clearly from two categories that look similar, namely expropriation for the sake of a private party that provides a public utility; and expropriation for the sake of a third party transfer that serves some other public purpose than economic development pure and simple. The first of these categories has been mentioned already – it seems relatively simple to accept that the public purpose requirement should be applied more leniently when the expropriation benefits a private party who needs the expropriation because it is providing a public utility or another kind of public service on behalf of the state. Of course there will be borderline cases in this category that might be difficult to judge, but as a general rule this category does not cause too much trouble with the public purpose requirement and I do not discuss it further here.

The second category distinguished above is expropriation for the benefit of a private party for a public purpose that is neither related to delivery of a public utility or another public service, nor connected with economic development as such. In *Hawaii Housing Authority*,[95] private land was taken for redistribution to other private owners in order to break up a traditional, feudal and economically unhealthy pattern of land holdings and to replace it with a more equitable and open system of land holdings. The distinction between this case and the economic development cases discussed earlier is immediately apparent – both involved taking of private land and giving it to other private persons, but in *Hawaii Housing Authority* the redistribution served what looks like a more easily justifiable state or public function, namely reform of the system of land holding. In this instance, the private beneficiary of the scheme is almost incidental to the overall redistribution project, the public purpose of which is relatively easily established as state regulatory control over a healthy, vibrant and equitable distribution of land holdings. The case of *James v UK*[96] also belongs in this category. What distinguishes cases like *Hawaii Housing Authority* and *James* from cases like *Kelo* and *Smith* is the fact that in the former category expropriation is justified by a public purpose related to

95 *Hawaii Housing Authority v Midkiff* 467 US 229 (1984).

96 (App no 8795/79) [1986] 8 EHRR 123.

the general public interest in (morally or constitutionally) legitimate land reform that should broadly speaking improve access to and security of land holdings, while the latter involves expropriation that serves the broader purpose of allowing or promoting or facilitating economic development or redevelopment that might or might not serve the specific interests of the very group whose home rights are negatively affected. Both could result in people being evicted from their homes, but as the *James* case shows, eviction is not inevitable in the expropriation for redistribution cases, since the idea might often be exactly the opposite, namely to secure the security of tenure of those who in fact occupy the property.[97]

The logic of eviction from and protection of the home interest suggests that expropriation for general economic development might be more difficult to justify than expropriation for redistribution (including provision of housing). In the language of human rights, one might think that the home interest should always or mostly trump the power to expropriate and evict people for the sake of economic development, while it may often actually be served by expropriation for redistribution. Expropriation for the sake of slum clearance and regeneration probably features uncomfortably somewhere in between these two categories, depending upon the severity of the prevailing blight conditions and the general tenor and impact of the regeneration and redevelopment plans. If slum clearance and redevelopment involves clearing areas that inadequately house people who would otherwise have been homeless and making the land available for development of upmarket economic use, without providing housing for those who have been evicted, the effect might be towards the *Kelo* end of the continuum, where the overall impression is one of potential for exploitation and unequal treatment. If the redevelopment is primarily aimed at providing more and better housing, which could also benefit those who had been displaced by it, the effect might be towards the *James* end, where one tends to feel more comfortable with what looks like a temporary displacement rather than eviction and exploitation, even when private investors and entrepreneurs benefit or make a profit from the redevelopment.

Impact on the Home Interest

The City of New London's decision to use its power of eminent domain to implement its urban redevelopment plan not only took Susette Kelo's house away from her but also brought about a serious disruption in her life and in the life of

97 In that sense the recent decision of the High Court of Ireland in *John E Shirley v AO Gorman* [2006] IEHC 27 perhaps also belongs in this category, as would other residential right to buy schemes. The Irish Landlord and Tenant (Amendment) Act 1984 provides a mechanism to fix the purchase price against which tenants who qualify under the Act can acquire the fee simple interest held by their landlords by paying a prescribed percentage of the current value of the lease (as defined in the Act). The reforms brought about by the Act do not involve compulsory acquisition by the state, but nevertheless improve the position of tenants.

her erstwhile Fort Trumbull community, economically in decline as it might have been. Even though her house had been rebuilt on another plot, the neighbourhood and the community had been broken up irreversibly. As Lorna Fox has reminded us, homes consist of far more than just plots with building structures on them – even when a displaced person receives alternative accommodation, that does not automatically restore the community and the sense of belonging and security that it affords, especially in less affluent neighbourhoods. In the *Kelo* case, expropriation for the sake of economic development had dispossessed Ms Susette Kelo of her house, displaced her out of her neighbourhood and destroyed the community that constituted it.

It has been pointed out that people reacted negatively against the *Kelo* decision for diverging reasons – libertarians and free marketeers primarily criticise what they regard as the unjustified or inefficient state interference with private property, while other negative reactions to the excessive deference with which the courts approach these matters might be inspired by different political or doctrinal considerations.[98] For present purposes I am especially interested in those commentators who criticise decisions like *Kelo* for the destructive effect that it has on the neighbourhood, the home interest of those living in it and the community that is destroyed by it. The destructive effect that evictions have on the home interest of residential occupiers has been pointed out and developed in property and human rights literature on housing rights,[99] but in the wake of decisions like *Kelo* and *Smith*, similar questions should be and are now asked about the effect of state exercises of the power of eminent domain. In a commentary on *Kelo*, John Fee[100] describes the areas in which the law now attaches a heightened status to

98 L.S. Underkuffler, '*Kelo's* Moral Failure' (2006) 15 *William & Mary Bill of Rights Journal* 377. As has been pointed out earlier, not everyone is against expropriation for development, even if it affects home interests. See n. 41 above.

99 As I have stated earlier, I do not intend to reiterate Lorna Fox's work on home here, given the context and the venue of the seminar for which the essay was written. However, it should be mentioned that she made a telling contribution to the literature on this topic by explaining the ways in which home is more than just a house; see for example, L. Fox, 'The Meaning of Home: A Chimerical Concept or a Legal Challenge?' (2002) 9 *Journal of Law & Society* 580. In particular, Fox points out that the notion of home involves several aspects besides the physical structure, including the territory where the home is situated, the role that it plays in forming and upholding identity, and the social and cultural aspects. I am indebted to Gustav Muller for reminding me that a similar perception of the home interest found expression in the South African Constitutional Court decision in *Government of the Republic of SA v Grootboom* 2001 (1) SA 46 (CC) para. 35 and in the UN Committee on Economic, Social and Cultural Rights, 'General Comment No 4' (13 December 1991) UN Doc E/1992/23 para. 8 on the right to housing in Art. 11(1) of the International Covenant on Economic, Social and Cultural Rights (adopted 16 December 1966, entered into force 3 January 1976) 993 UNTS 3 (ICESCR).

100 J. Fee, 'Eminent Domain and the Sanctity of Home' (2006) 81 *Notre Dame LR* 783.

people's homes and investigates the strategies that could be employed to protect the home against the government's power of eminent domain. Fee dismisses alternative strategies, such as completely prohibiting economic-development expropriation of people's homes and employing stricter judicial scrutiny to ensure that the state does not abuse its power of eminent domain when homes are at stake, as inadequate. Instead, he opts for a third strategy, namely making the state pay a higher level of compensation (described as a premium) for expropriation of homes, to the extent that the measure of compensation should deter the government from using expropriation in all cases where the expropriation is not inspired by genuine public necessity.[101] Fee argued that the law recognises the heightened status of home in some areas, but points out that this awareness has not yet penetrated into the law of eminent domain,[102] which suggests that requiring a higher level of compensation for expropriation of a home might restore the current imbalance in government decision making.

In a somewhat similar spirit, Peñalver[103] considers the effect of *Kelo* on the metaphorical notion of one's home as your castle, but then with emphasis on the inherent dignity of homeownership rather than the tired old idea of ownership as 'despotic dominion'. In this perspective, Peñalver argues,[104] the idea of the home as a castle demands that the state should, when exercising its power of eminent domain, do so with due respect for and recognition of the importance of the

101 Ibid. 785–6, 803–17. Fee argues at 797 that the public-use solution, which would restrict expropriation to cases where the land is required for actual public use, is over-inclusive in that it would prevent the expropriation of private land for private redevelopment, even when the owner holds the land purely for economic value. It is also under-inclusive in that it would still leave homes vulnerable for traditional public-use expropriations, without any special consideration for their home value. An absolute ban on expropriation of homes would prevent the state from condemning land even for really legitimate and urgent public necessities (at 800–801), while stricter scrutiny suffers from the drawback that its protection relies on the imprecise standards of judicial review (at 802). In this respect Fee perhaps underestimates the German version of stricter scrutiny set out above. C.E. Cohen, 'Eminent Domain after *Kelo v City of New London*: An Argument for Banning Economic Development Takings' (2005–2006) 29 *Harvard JL & Public Policy* 491 favours a ban on economic development takings.

102 J. Fee, 'Eminent Domain and the Sanctity of Home' (2006) 81 *Notre Dame LR* 794–5.

103 E.M. Peñalver, 'Property Metaphors and Kelo v New London: Two Views of the Castle' (2006) 74 *Fordham LR* 2971. The reference in the article's title is of course to the famous article of G. Calabresi and A.D. Melamed, 'Property Rules, Liability Rules, and Inalienability: One View of the Cathedral' (1972) 85 *Harvard LR* 1089. Recent articles by Eduardo Peñalver and Gregory Alexander that explore the moral or social-obligation element of property point in the same direction as the other sources I cite here; see e.g. G.S. Alexander, 'The Social-Obligation Norm in American Property Law' (2009) 94 *Cornell LR* 745; E.M. Peñalver, 'Land Virtues' (2009) 94 *Cornell LR* 821.

104 E.M. Peñalver, 'Property Metaphors and Kelo v New London: Two Views of the Castle' (2006) 74 *Fordham LR* 2971.

property in the lives of the people who are displaced by expropriation. This can be done in two ways, first by refraining from using the power of expropriation at all to acquire residential property compulsorily, except when it is really necessary for an important public purpose and, secondly, by paying adequate compensation when expropriation of residential properties does take place. In cases like this, simple market value does not as a rule indicate adequate compensation. In a sense, Peñalver therefore combines a preliminary strategy of heightened scrutiny with a final fallback, when expropriation of a home cannot be avoided despite strict scrutiny, onto requiring a premium in compensation for destroying a home.

Commentators like Fee and Peñalver, who favour restricting the power of eminent domain when it results in eviction and displacement and therefore dispossesses people not only of property but of a home, are in effect extending the influence of human rights based theory on what has become known as the home interest in eviction law to the sphere of eminent domain law. Through their argument, the theory of home interest that was developed by Lorna Fox[105] and others in the general area of eviction acquires useful currency in the wider area of expropriation law. The fact that Article 8 of the ECHR was considered in a case like *Smith* indicates that the notion of a home interest already finds wider application in English law than merely in the conventional eviction cases not involving expropriation, such as *Harrow LBC v Qazi*,[106] *Connors v UK*,[107] *Kay and Another v London Borough of Lambeth and ors; Leeds City Council v Price and ors*[108] *or McCann v UK*.[109] The fact that the proportionality analysis prescribed by Article 8 of the ECHR is employed in English case law to assess the legitimacy of evictions in general and also of evictions resulting from exercises of the power of compulsory acquisition looks like a positive sign, indicating that the home-protection effect of human rights learning has found a stronger foothold in English law than in other jurisdictions, where the effects of human rights standards may have influenced eviction law in general but not expropriation law. However, it is worrying that cases like *Smith* could still be decided against the occupiers, despite the proportionality analysis, which suggests that the effect of home-interest reasoning might in fact be weaker in English law than one might have thought possible or desirable.[110] Having said that, one would rather see courts applying

105 L. Fox, *Conceptualising Home: Theories, Laws and Policies* (Hart Publishing, Oxford 2007), particularly ch. 10. Compare n. 98 above.

106 [2004] 1 AC 983 (HL).

107 (App no 66746/01) (2004) 40 EHRR 189.

108 [2006] UKHL 10.

109 (App no 19009/04) (2008) 47 EHRR 40. On these decisions see L. Fox, *Conceptualising Home: Theories, Laws and Policies* (Hart Publishing, Oxford 2007) 481–518; K. Gray and S.F. Gray, *Elements of Land Law* (5th edition Oxford University Press, Oxford 2009) 1.6; S. Bright, *Landlord and Tenant Law in Context* (Hart Publishing, Oxford 2007) 281–4, 610–13.

110 To a certain extent, see the tenor of the criticism that commentators such as Fox, Bright and Gray have against some of the eviction decisions; see the references, ibid.

Article 8 proportionality language to cases where expropriation results in eviction than having them not pay attention to the effect of the expropriation on the home interest at all – in this sense, recent English case law represents a step in the right direction. It would acquire real impact if the level of scrutiny could be heightened on account of the home interest that is at stake.

The potential impact of the idea of home and its potentially restricting effect, not only on eviction in general but particularly in the context of expropriation, is underlined even more clearly by the like-minded but slightly different line of argument developed by Frank Michelman[111] and Laura Underkuffler.[112] With an appeal to the earlier work of Michelman, Underkuffler argues that 'the selective disregard for community' displayed in expropriation actions such as *Kelo* 'violates the principle of equally respected participation'.[113] In Michelman's terms, if constitutionally protected property is understood purely in terms of reliance-based and expectation-based interests, decisions such as *Poletown* or *Kelo* would look correct and fair as long as the owners received just compensation, but when the political reliance interests of the residents – their rights to political participation – are taken into account, things might look different.[114] In addition to the personal financial interests usually emphasised by the courts and the personal, affective and social interests described by Fox, Michelman and Underkuffler focus specifically on socio-political interests. To gauge the effect of economic development takings on the right to equal political participation, it becomes necessary to take cognisance of the 'social and political significance of property in human lives',[115] and then the physical locality of property appears as the 'material foundation'[116] for social and political expression and self-determination.[117] 'When seen in this light,' Laura Underkuffler concludes,

111 F Michelman, 'Property as a Constitutional Right' (1981) 38 *Wash & Lee LR* 1097, commenting on *Poletown Neighbourhood Council v City of Detroit* 304 NW2d 455 (Mich 1981), overruled in *County of Wayne v Hatchcock* 684 NW2d 765 (Mich 2004).

112 L.S. Underkuffler, '*Kelo's* Moral Failure' (2006) 15 *William & Mary Bill of Rights Journal* 377, commenting on both *Poletown Neighborhood Council v City of Detroit* 304 NW2d 455 (Mich 1981) and *Kelo v City of New London* 545 US 469 (2005).

113 Ibid. 380.

114 This is a different formulation of the German constitutional principle that compensation alone cannot justify an expropriation; it is a necessary result of but not an adequate justification for the taking. See n. 84 and associated text.

115 L.S. Underkuffler, '*Kelo's* Moral Failure' (2006) 15 *William & Mary Bill of Rights Journal* 383.

116 F. Michelman, 'Property as a Constitutional Right' (1981) 38 *Wash & Lee LR* 1097, 1113. This aspect is also emphasised by L. Fox; see L. Fox, 'The Meaning of Home: A Chimerical Concept or a Legal Challenge?' (2002) 9 *Journal of Law & Society* 580.

117 L.S. Underkuffler, '*Kelo's* Moral Failure' (2006) 15 *William & Mary Bill of Rights Journal* 384. Although she places more emphasis on personal identity and social interaction than on political participation, L. Fox, 'The Meaning of Home: A Chimerical Concept or a Legal Challenge?' (2002) 9 *JL & Society* 580 includes this aspect in her analysis of the home interest.

'the destruction of neighbourhoods for economic redevelopment purposes has clear and severe consequences for the residents' continued, fair, and effective political participation.'[118] This consideration, Underkuffler argues, cannot automatically trump every public development project that destroys a thriving community, but the interests of the residents and citizens and its role in the political system 'must weigh very heavily in the calculation'.[119] Another consideration that would also weigh very heavily in the calculation, which Underkuffler describes as the 'certain knowledge of selective risk',[120] is the almost certainty that the poor and socially and politically weak are more likely to have their homes destroyed for economic redevelopment projects than the rich and powerful; a consideration that strengthens the impression of selective exclusion inherent in these exercises of the power of eminent domain.

The important point emerging from the arguments of Michelman and Underkuffler, supported by Fox, is that even paying a higher premium for the expropriation of a home[121] cannot compensate the loss of a home and the displacement that accompanies it adequately. It is hard to place a money value on the affective and personal attachment of an individual to her home and of a family or group to their community, but it is even more difficult or impossible to place such a value on the social and political cohesion and freedoms that are lost when a residential community is destroyed. This is especially true under circumstances where it appears likely that the destruction always targets those who are too weak or marginal to avoid it or to defend themselves and their interests.

Both Underkuffler and Fee point out that this consideration does not imply that the home interest or the existence of a settled community will always trump the state's desire to acquire property compulsorily – it merely underlines the principle that expropriation should not be used lightly and that it should be used even more sparingly when residential property is at risk. In cases where exercises of the power of eminent domain will or may result in people being evicted from their homes and displaced, the principle should be that the expropriation is only justified when the public purpose it serves is really necessary and in the interests of the public at large.[122] Generally speaking, expropriation for purposes of economic development should only be allowed to trump individual and community home interests when the redevelopment is a matter of public necessity and when the

---

118 L.S. Underkuffler, '*Kelo's* Moral Failure' (2006) 15 *William & Mary Bill of Rights Journal* 384.

119 Ibid. 384.

120 Ibid. 386.

121 As proposed by J. Fee, 'Eminent Domain and the Sanctity of Home' (2006) 81 *Notre Dame LR* 783.

122 It was pointed out at the text to n. 84 above that German constitutional theory generally accepts the principle that expropriation is always seen as a last resort solution to any problem, only to be used when it is properly authorised by legislation and in itself justified by the public purpose it is supposed to serve. The payment of compensation cannot justify the expropriation; it only follows when the expropriation is justified by the public purpose it serves.

affected individuals and community will also benefit from the development, for example by acquiring fair access to new or improved homes in the development. If the development is likely to bring general economic benefit for the community at large but will exclude the residents most closely affected by it, it should not be justified easily. All this indicates that a heightened standard of scrutiny is required when adjudicating eviction cases that result from exercises of the state's power to expropriate or to regulate the use of land. Stated in this form, the importance of the home interest in eviction brings to mind the South African case law concerning eviction for the sake of freeing land up for the building of more or better social housing.

(3) Eviction and Sharing in Development of Social Housing

Introduction

The question considered in this section is whether there is a way in which the effect of human rights thinking in eviction law could be extended to cases where the eviction was caused by expropriation of land for a supposedly stronger or higher public interest in economic redevelopment of the land, without losing the force that home-interest thinking has apparently acquired in eviction law generally. Three eviction cases decided by the South African Constitutional Court, namely *Port Elizabeth Municipality v Various Occupiers*,[123] *Occupiers of 51 Olivia Road, Berea Township, and 197 Main Street, Johannesburg v City of Johannesburg and ors*[124] and *Residents of Joe Slovo Community, Western Cape v Thubelisha Homes and ors (Centre on Housing Rights and Evictions and Community Law Centre, University of the Western Cape, amici curiae)*,[125] provide a useful starting point for this discussion.[126]

It is necessary to highlight the differences between the South African cases and the US and UK case law discussed earlier. Although some of the properties involved in the South African cases were owned privately, none of these cases involved expropriation – eviction resulted from state regulatory action in the process of land-use control and provision of housing. Perhaps somewhat surprisingly, the new South African government has used its power of expropriation sparingly,

123 *Port Elizabeth Municipality v Various Occupiers* 2005 (1) SA 217 (CC).

124 *Occupiers of 51 Olivia Road, Berea Township, and 197 Main Street, Johannesburg v City of Johannesburg and ors* 2008 (3) SA 208 (CC).

125 *Residents of Joe Slovo Community, Western Cape v Thubelisha Homes and ors (Centre on Housing Rights and Evictions and Community Law Centre, University of the Western Cape,* amici curiae*)* [2009] JOL 23711 (CC).

126 The following discussion is based on extracts from A.J. van der Walt, *Property in the Margins* (Hart Publishing, Oxford 2009) 153–9, where the decisions in *Port Elizabeth Municipality v Various Occupiers* 2005 (1) SA 217 (CC) are also discussed.

even in promoting land reform, and consequently there are no expropriation for development cases to compare with the US and UK decisions discussed earlier. However, despite these differences, in all the South African cases reviewed here eviction was aimed at clearing the land for redevelopment; in the last two cases development was specifically aimed at providing new and better social housing. The comparative value of these cases is therefore to be found in their promotion of a supposedly higher or more important state purpose, namely land development, at the cost of the home interests of individuals or communities who have to be evicted and displaced to realise the development plan.

South African Cases

In *Port Elizabeth Municipality v Various Occupiers*[127] the occupiers had been living on vacant privately owned land for between two and eight years, in shacks that they had erected without permission. They had not applied for housing under the municipality's housing development programme, but indicated that they were prepared to move if alternative land were provided for them. The High Court granted an eviction order against them, which was overturned by the Supreme Court of Appeal. In a further appeal, the Constitutional Court confirmed that the courts exercise a judicial discretion in deciding whether it is just and equitable to grant an eviction order in terms of the Prevention of Illegal Eviction from and Unlawful Occupation of Land Act 19 of 1998.[128] Secondly, the court pointed out that land reform laws can only be interpreted and applied for the sake of transformation when they are explicitly and purposively understood in their historical framework (the role of evictions and forced removals under apartheid) and their constitutional framework (the transformative purpose of the Constitution and the land reform laws).[129] Section 26(3) of the Constitution and anti-eviction legislation promulgated in terms of it are intended to rectify eviction abuses of the apartheid past and to prevent their recurrence.[130] In the historical and constitutional context of these provisions it is necessary to establish an appropriate constitutional relationship between the protection of property rights (s. 25) and the protection of access to housing (s. 26).[131] The Constitution challenges the courts to avoid the traditional hierarchical view of property and housing rights and to reconcile them in as just a manner as possible, taking into account all the interests involved and paying proper attention to the circumstances of each case.[132] In some instances,

127 *Port Elizabeth Municipality v Various Occupiers* 2005 (1) SA 217 (CC).

128 Ibid. paras 31–2.

129 Ibid. paras 8–23.

130 Ibid. paras 11, 14.

131 Ibid. para. 19. The contextual approach was reiterated in *Mphela and ors v Haakdoornbult Boerdery CC and ors* 2008 (4) SA 488 (CC).

132 *Port Elizabeth Municipality v Various Occupiers* 2005 (1) SA 217 (CC) para. 23.

such a contextual analysis could imply that a landowner might not be able to obtain or enforce an eviction order, even though she is able to satisfy the common law and statutory requirements, simply because the court deems eviction unjustified in view of the general socio-economic and the particular personal circumstances of the unlawful occupiers. However, the court also made it clear that the anti-eviction measures do not imply that it becomes impossible for a landowner to evict unwanted and unlawful occupiers of her land – in cases where it is justified, an eviction order will still be granted, even if it means that people would lose their home. The court emphasised that the decision whether to allow eviction is a highly case-specific one that has to be taken anew in every individual case, taking into account all the circumstances.[133]

In *Occupiers of 51 Olivia Road, Berea Township, and 197 Main Street, Johannesburg v City of Johannesburg and ors*[134] a local authority attempted to evict unlawful occupiers from inner city premises using its powers to promote public health and safety, as part of a programme designed to reverse inner city decay and eradicate dangerous and unhealthy living conditions.[135] The High Court, following the approach of the Constitutional Court in *Port Elizabeth Municipality*, emphasised that eviction is fundamentally a political matter and that eviction cases therefore have to be decided according to the historical and contextual approach set out by the Constitutional Court. Even when the post-apartheid democratic state legitimately exercises its police power to protect public health and safety it must reconcile that duty with its constitutional duty towards the housing needs of the poor and the destitute.[136] Accordingly, the personal circumstances of occupiers have to be considered before an eviction can be granted, both when a landowner applies for eviction to enforce her property rights and when a local authority

133 Ibid. para. 31. The court indicated that it would ordinarily not be just and equitable to grant an eviction order unless proper discussions and, where suitable, mediation had been attempted to settle the matter: para. 43. In *Occupiers of 51 Olivia Road, Berea Township, and 197 Main Street, Johannesburg v City of Johannesburg and ors* 2008 (3) SA 208 (CC) this proved to be a central aspect of the court's approach to evictions in general.

134 *Occupiers of 51 Olivia Road, Berea Township, and 197 Main Street, Johannesburg v City of Johannesburg and ors* 2008 (3) SA 208 (CC). The City of Johannesburg, relying on its Inner City Regeneration Strategy, wanted to evict the occupiers from three premises in the Johannesburg municipal area. The properties involved were privately owned, but in some cases they had been abandoned by the owners. Some occupiers were tenants, some were former tenants, some were unlawful squatters. The premises in question were said to present dangerous living conditions, including health and fire hazards, and the city claimed that it would promote public health and safety to 'evacuate' the premises as part of the process of reversing inner city decay. In certain instances the eviction notices were accompanied by notices directing the owners to demolish, alter or 'evacuate' the buildings.

135 Relying on its powers in the National Building Regulations and Building Standards Act 103 of 1977, the Health Act 63 of 1977 and local fire by-laws.

136 *City of Johannesburg v Rand Properties (Pty) Ltd and ors* 2007 (1) SA 78 (W) paras 26, 28.

applies for eviction to protect public health and safety. The mere fact that premises appear to be unsafe or unhealthy does not automatically or mechanically justify eviction by the local authority — the degree of desperation of the people living under those circumstances and the length of time of their occupancy have to be considered as well.[137] The Constitution requires that the state should ensure that everyone has access to affordable and acceptable housing; among other things this means not destroying existing access to housing unless it can be justified with reference to constitutional requirements and values.[138]

This decision was overturned by the Supreme Court of Appeal[139] but later confirmed by the Constitutional Court.[140] The court issued an interim order, based on s. 26 of the Constitution and the approach adopted in its earlier decisions,[141] to ensure that the city and occupiers 'would engage with each other meaningfully' on certain issues involved in the eviction.[142] This order was explained with reference to the fact that a city (local authority) has constitutional obligations towards the occupants of residential property in its jurisdiction, including the obligation to respect, protect, promote and fulfil the rights in the Bill of Rights, the most important of which are the rights to dignity and life. In view of these obligations, a municipality that evicts people from their homes without first meaningfully engaging with them to search for a solution 'acts in a manner that is broadly at odds with the spirit and purpose of the constitutional obligations'.[143] The duty to engage with people who may be rendered homeless by eviction is also 'squarely grounded' in the state's constitutional obligation (s. 26(2)) to take reasonable measures, within its available resources, to achieve the progressive realisation of the right of access to housing.[144] Meaningful engagement between a municipality and people who may be rendered homeless by eviction is a two-way process with an open-ended list of objectives, including determining what the consequences of eviction might be; whether the city could help to alleviate dire consequences of eviction; whether it is possible to render unsafe or unhealthy buildings relatively safe and conducive to health for an interim period; whether the city had any obligations towards the occupiers in

137 Ibid. para. 29.

138 Ibid. paras 50, 52.

139 *City of Johannesburg v Rand Properties (Pty) Ltd and ors* 2007 (6) SA 417 (SCA). The SCA granted the eviction orders and combined them with an order that the local authority should provide temporary accommodation for certain occupiers.

140 *Occupiers of 51 Olivia Road, Berea Township, and 197 Main Street, Johannesburg v City of Johannesburg and ors* 2008 (3) SA 208 (CC).

141 Particularly *Government of the Republic of SA and ors v Grootboom and ors* 2001 (1) SA 46 (CC) and *Port Elizabeth Municipality v Various Occupiers* 2005 (1) SA 217 (CC).

142 *Occupiers of 51 Olivia Road, Berea Township, and 197 Main Street, Johannesburg v City of Johannesburg and ors* 2008 (3) SA 208 (CC) paras 9–23.

143 Ibid. para.16.

144 Ibid. paras 17, 18.

the prevailing circumstances and when and how the city could or would fulfil those obligations. Engaging in meaningful discussion about these issues might be a burdensome task but is by no means impossible for the local authority; at the same time, the occupiers must cooperate and not engage in intransigent and unreasonable attitudes.[145]

The Constitutional Court subsequently explained that it had issued the interim order:

> because it was not appropriate to grant any eviction order against the occupiers, in the circumstances of this case, unless there had at least been some effort at meaningful engagement…The ejectment of a resident by a municipality in circumstances where the resident would possibly become homeless should ordinarily take place only after meaningful engagement.[146]

Accordingly, the court emphasised, meaningful engagement should in cases like this take place prior to litigation unless it is impossible for some compelling reason.[147] The court confirmed the so-called 'post-engagement agreement' reached by the parties, in terms of which the evictions were postponed and some buildings were rendered safe for occupation, while alternative accommodation was provided for occupiers of other buildings. In its decision, the Constitutional Court rejected the idea that the municipality could simply rely on its statutory powers to evict people from unsafe buildings and ignore the effect of eviction on the occupier.[148] The city must simultaneously take responsibility for safe and healthy buildings and for the welfare of its residents; it cannot just carry out the one obligation and ignore the other.[149]

In the decision[150] in *Residents of Joe Slovo Community, Western Cape v Thubelisha Homes and ors (Centre on Housing Rights and Evictions and Community Law Centre, University of the Western Cape*, amici curiae*)*[151] the Constitutional Court's evolving approach to eviction cases culminated in a decision that illustrates the issues in this essay very nicely. The case involved the relocation of 4,386 households (around 20,000 residents) from an informal settlement known as Joe Slovo, about 10 kilometres to the east of Cape Town, in order to facilitate the development of better quality housing than the existing informal housing. The residents of Joe Slovo were to be relocated to an area known as Delft, about

145 Ibid. paras 14, 19, 20.

146 Ibid. para. 22.

147 Ibid. para. 30.

148 Ibid. para. 43.

149 Ibid. para. 44.

150 Decision of 10 June 2009.

151 *Residents of Joe Slovo Community, Western Cape v Thubelisha Homes and ors (Centre on Housing Rights and Evictions and Community Law Centre, University of the Western Cape,* amici curiae*)* [2009] JOL 23711 (CC).

15 kilometres away. The undeveloped land where the Joe Slovo settlement was situated[152] belonged to the City of Cape Town. There was a dispute on the facts about the question whether the residents ever had real or constructive permission to occupy the land, especially since the city had provided the residents with certain facilities and infrastructure,[153] but the court decided unanimously that the residents were unlawfully occupying the land by the time the relocation application was brought. The majority of the Constitutional Court[154] held that the residents did have constructive permission at some point, but decided that the permission was revoked when the city began making preparations to clear the land for development of formal housing.

The eviction order for the relocation of the community was brought by the body charged with development of Joe Slovo, Thubelisha Homes and the provincial and national housing ministers. The High Court[155] granted the order as applied for, directing the residents of Joe Slovo to vacate the area, to move to Delft according to a prescribed relocation schedule, where necessary with assistance from the applicants, and not to return to Joe Slovo or to erect informal structures there again. This decision was taken on appeal to the Constitutional Court.

The planned redevelopment of Joe Slovo forms part of the N2 Gateway Housing Project, which is intended to eradicate all informal developments and structures in the Cape Peninsula, and which is itself a part of the national Breaking New Ground policy to replace informal housing structures with formal housing all

152 The land had been settled since about 1990 and residents were regularly subjected to forced removals and destruction of their properties: ibid. para. 20.

153 Ibid. para. 21.

154 Moseneke DCJ, Ngcobo J, O'Regan J, Sachs J and Mokgoro J. Five judgments were delivered. The whole court concurred in the order. Yacoob J disagreed with the majority on just one point, namely whether the residents ever had permission to occupy the premises in Joe Slovo. According to his minority judgment, they never had either explicit or constructive permission. Langa CJ and Van der Westhuizen J concurred in the judgment of Yacoob J. The majority held that the residents did have constructive permission at one stage, but that their permission was revoked when the city started to clear the land for redevelopment in 2004. Four judgments were written in support of this finding: Moseneke DCJ, Ngcobo J, O'Regan J and Sachs J. Sachs J concurred in the judgment of Moseneke DCJ. Moseneke DCJ and Sachs J concurred in the judgment of Ngcobo J. Moseneke DCJ and Mokgoro J concurred in the judgment of Sachs J. See *Residents of Joe Slovo Community, Western Cape v Thubelisha Homes and ors (Centre on Housing Rights and Evictions and Community Law Centre, University of the Western Cape,* amici curiae*)* [2009] JOL 23711 (CC) para. 4.

155 Previously the Cape High Court, changed to the Western Cape High Court, Cape Town by the Renaming of High Courts Act 30 of 2008, which commenced on 1 March 2009.

through South Africa.[156] According to the development plan for Joe Slovo, housing would be provided in three phases, each consisting of housing made available to poor people at minimal rentals, housing available at higher rentals, as well as credit-linked housing for people who could afford it, on the basis of privately obtained loans secured by mortgages.[157] During the already completed Phase 1 and the current Phase 2 promises had already been broken in that no housing was provided for the poorest and that the rental housing was made available at much higher prices, but the applicants assured the court that this would change in Phase 3. There were also concerns about the earlier promises that 70 per cent of the new housing would be made available to former residents from Joe Slovo, as opposed to people from other surrounding informal settlements. In the event the Constitutional Court granted the eviction and relocation order, but made it explicitly subject to the condition that 70 per cent of the new housing would be made available to former residents from Joe Slovo.[158] The court further specified the quality of the temporary accommodation in which the occupiers will be housed after the eviction and required an ongoing process of engagement between the residents and the respondents concerning the relocation process, to ensure that the negative impact of the relocation on the community was alleviated as far as possible.[159] In justifying its decision that the relocation was a reasonable strategy in the state's effort to comply with its housing obligations under the Constitution, the court recognised the hardship that relocation would cause, but held that causing the hardship in this case was justified by the purpose of the relocation and ameliorated by the special conditions placed on the relocation order:

> It is true, as is emphasised by the amici, that this relocation would entail immense hardship. I have considerable sympathy with the applicants, but there are circumstances in which this Court and all involved have no choice but to face the fact that hardship can only be mitigated but can never be avoided altogether. The human price to be paid for this relocation and reconstruction is

156 Yacoob J discusses the N2 Gateway Project in *Residents of Joe Slovo Community, Western Cape v Thubelisha Homes and ors (Centre on Housing Rights and Evictions and Community Law Centre, University of the Western Cape,* amici curiae*)* [2009] JOL 23711 (CC) para. 29 ff.

157 *Residents of Joe Slovo Community, Western Cape v Thubelisha Homes and ors (Centre on Housing Rights and Evictions and Community Law Centre, University of the Western Cape,* amici curiae*)* [2009] JOL 23711 (CC) para. 30.

158 The reason why 70 per cent rather than 100 per cent of the new housing is reserved for former residents is the apparently generally accepted fact that the new housing would be less dense than the current informal settlement, where the density of the shacks prevent provision of proper services and roads and access for emergency vehicles.

159 See the summary of the order in *Residents of Joe Slovo Community, Western Cape v Thubelisha Homes and ors (Centre on Housing Rights and Evictions and Community Law Centre, University of the Western Cape,* amici curiae*)* [2009] JOL 23711 (CC) para. 5 and the order in para. 7.

> immeasurable. Nonetheless it is not possible to say that the conclusion of the City of Cape Town, to the effect that infrastructural development is essential in the area and that the relocation of people is necessary, is unreasonable. There are circumstances in which there is no choice but to undergo traumatic experiences so that we can be better off later. Significantly, they are ameliorated by the state undertaking to provide transport and to ensure that schooling is available to children and that people moved to Delft can get to work.[160]

This aspect of the decision, on which the court was unanimous, emphasises an important point that is sometimes overlooked in the expropriation and/or eviction for development cases, namely that it is possible or at least easier to justify what might otherwise be an impossibly unfair eviction (and, in some instances, the expropriation that gives rise to the eviction), if those who are displaced by it also stand to profit from or share in the advantages of the redevelopment. In cases where development takes place at the cost of people and communities that lose their homes, this not only means that the development should at least also provide new housing to replace the homes that were lost, but also that the same people and communities should get secure and preferential access to the housing provided in the new development. In the absence of such a guarantee of access to the benefits of the development, the eviction (and possibly the expropriation) might well be impossible to justify.

This problem was at the heart of the *Smith* case and was also, to judge from subsequent developments, a crucial aspect of local resistance to the *Kelo* displacement. If the objectors in *Smith* and *Kelo* were assured of secure and preferential access to suitable replacement housing in the respective new developments, neither might have ended in litigation. This point also underlines the significance of the distinction I made earlier between cases like *Kelo* and *Smith* on the one hand and *Hawaii Housing* and *James* on the other, in the sense that it seems at least arguable that the dispossession and displacement that took place in the latter group of cases might be easier to justify because the aim was to improve the currently inequitable land distribution.

Moseneke DCJ makes it abundantly clear that he regarded the assurance of access to housing in the development as a crucial factor in the decision:

> I must emphasise that, on the facts of this case, I would have had great difficulty in holding that it is just and equitable to forcibly evict the residents of Joe Slovo and to relocate them far from their homes and modest comfort zones in order to give way to the construction of new subsidised homes in circumstances where the evicted residents would have had no reasonable prospects of satisfying their own dire need to access adequate housing. That eviction and relocation order would

160 *Residents of Joe Slovo Community, Western Cape v Thubelisha Homes and ors (Centre on Housing Rights and Evictions and Community Law Centre, University of the Western Cape,* amici curiae*)* [2009] JOL 23711 (CC) para. 107 (Yacoob J).

> have made the residents of Joe Slovo sacrificial lambs to the grandiose national scheme to end informal settlements when the residents themselves stood to benefit nothing by way of permanent and adequate housing for themselves.[161]

The Constitutional Court decision in *Residents of Joe Slovo* is also significant for the purposes of this article because it interestingly demonstrates the change of thinking that is required if we were to rethink the worrying aspects of expropriations and evictions for economic development. One of the most important aspects of the idea of home that Lorna Fox emphasised in her work[162] is the effect that legal doctrine, and particularly rights doctrine, has on the way in which we see and treat people's homes as legal objects or commodities. Within the framework of rights and commodities, the legal label we attach to the interest that a person can prove in her home largely determines whether she can successfully defend that interest against the exercise of state powers such as compulsory acquisition and forced relocation. As long as we focus exclusively on rights and legal powers and entitlements, it is difficult to defend what may look like a nebulous home interest against seemingly legitimate exercises of state power or of private rights. Within this context it is fascinating to observe the subdued[163] but vitally important[164] difference of opinion between Constitutional Court judges who wanted to approach the issue from the perspective of legal doctrine and those who rejected such an approach.

In his minority judgment,[165] Yacoob J refused to accept that the residents could ever have had permission to occupy the land, arguing that 'occupation is either lawful or unlawful',[166] that tacit consent can only be construed as 'tacit voluntary

161 *Residents of Joe Slovo Community, Western Cape v Thubelisha Homes and ors (Centre on Housing Rights and Evictions and Community Law Centre, University of the Western Cape,* amici curiae*)* [2009] JOL 23711 (CC) para. 138 (Moseneke DCJ).

162 L. Fox, *Conceptualising Home: Theories, Laws and Policies* (2007) ch. 6, where she refers to the 'commoditisation of home' and 'property for personhood'.

163 I describe it as subdued because the difference has no impact in the decision, all judges concurring that the residents' occupation had become unlawful by the time when the relocation application was brought.

164 I qualify it as vitally important because it signifies a crucial difference of approach to legal questions of this nature. Sachs J in *Residents of Joe Slovo Community, Western Cape v Thubelisha Homes and ors (Centre on Housing Rights and Evictions and Community Law Centre, University of the Western Cape,* amici curiae*)* [2009] JOL 23711 (CC) para. 329 states that 'important jurisprudential issues are raised that affect the status, and in my view, the dignity, of a vast number of people throughout the country living in informal settlements.'

165 Yacoob J discusses this aspect in *Residents of Joe Slovo Community, Western Cape v Thubelisha Homes and ors (Centre on Housing Rights and Evictions and Community Law Centre, University of the Western Cape,* amici curiae*)* [2009] JOL 23711 (CC) paras 36–82.

166 Ibid. para. 52.

agreement',[167] that there is no reason why the Prevention of Illegal Eviction from and Unlawful Occupation of Land Act 19 of 1998 (PIE) should require a wider interpretation of the notion of consent,[168] and that there was no cogent evidence to suggest that the city had ever given its consent to the occupiers to remain on the land as of right.[169] However, some of the other judges baulked at the prospect of even labelling the residents of Joe Slovo unlawful occupiers.[170] The majority decided that the notion of consent in PIE had to be construed generously[171] and that, on the facts, the residents of Joe Slovo had constructive or tacit consent to occupy the premises during the late 1990s.[172] Until the point when consent was cancelled when the city started making its intention clear to go ahead with the relocation and redevelopment, they were therefore lawful occupiers of the settlement.

However, even more interesting than this accommodating but ultimately technical decision on the facts are the clear indications that some judges considered the traditional label of unlawfulness simply inappropriate for the case, considering the socio-economic[173] and personal circumstances of the residents and the constitutional and legal obligations of the state as owner of the land and as provider of housing. Although he agreed with his colleagues on the outcome of the case and the order, Ngcobo J refused to be drawn into deciding whether the residents were unlawful occupiers.[174] Arguing that the state acts in accordance with its constitutional duties by not simply evicting homeless people who may find themselves to occupy land without permission and that such tolerance should not

167 Ibid. para. 57.

168 Ibid. para. 68.

169 Ibid. paras 72–82.

170 In ibid. para. 141 Moseneke DCJ refers to what he describes as 'a constitutional matter that has caused me considerable agony. And that is whether landless people who have no access to adequate housing and who as a result erect homes and live on vacant public land with the knowledge and prolonged support of its owner, a government body, should be regarded as no more than unlawful occupiers'. In ibid. para. 291 O'Regan J accepted that it was unfortunate to label the residents of Joe Slovo unlawful occupiers, but pointed out that doing so brought them under the protective umbrella of PIE, which provides them with significant protection.

171 Ibid. paras 142–8 (Moseneke DCJ); paras 341–52 (Sachs J).

172 Ibid. paras 149–56 (Moseneke DCJ); paras 274–8 (O'Regan J); paras 353–8 (Sachs J).

173 Following the example of Sachs J in *Port Elizabeth Municipality v Various Occupiers* 2005 (1) SA 217 (CC) paras 8–13, Ngcobo J reviews the historical background of the housing crisis in *Residents of Joe Slovo Community, Western Cape v Thubelisha Homes and ors (Centre on Housing Rights and Evictions and Community Law Centre, University of the Western Cape,* amici curiae*)* [2009] JOL 23711 (CC) paras 191–8.

174 *Residents of Joe Slovo Community, Western Cape v Thubelisha Homes and ors (Centre on Housing Rights and Evictions and Community Law Centre, University of the Western Cape,* amici curiae*)* [2009] JOL 23711 (CC) paras 178–233.

be read as granting consent or occupation rights,[175] Ngcobo J preferred to approach the matter from the point of view that, where people are:

> to be relocated in order to pave the way for the implementation of a government programme aimed at providing residents with adequate housing, the proper question to ask is not whether the residents are unlawful occupiers, but whether it is in the public interest and thus just and equitable to relocate them for that purpose.[176]

Sachs J, pointing out that '[t]his is not a matter in which formal legal logic alone can solve the conundrum of how to do justice to the one side without imposing a measure of injustice on the other',[177] argued that the court had to avoid attempting to distinguish right from wrong and adopt the 'intellectually more modest role of managing tensions between competing legitimate claims'.[178] Placing the case squarely within the framework of earlier Constitutional Court decisions mentioned above,[179] Sachs J pointed out three significant elements of the *Joe Slovo* case: firstly, the state authorities were not seeking the evictions on behalf of 'private landowners seeking vacant possession of land they own or are about to acquire', but to 'secure governmental interests'. Secondly, the community was relatively settled and had been on the land for long periods up to 15 years. Thirdly, the eviction was not sought 'to secure vacant possession' to enable the owner to do with it as it pleases or to 'open the way to private entrepreneurial activity', but to 'secure the improvement of the housing conditions' of the occupiers themselves, who are thus not to be removed from the land permanently.[180] Against this backdrop, Sachs J, whose approach resembled that of Ngcobo J closely on this point, aimed at what he refered to as a 'transformative approach to section 26',[181] according to which the question of the lawfulness of the occupation of state land:

175 Ibid. paras 211, 214.

176 Ibid. para. 217. In para. 218 Ngcobo J added that asking whether homeless people were unlawful occupiers was 'inimical to the foundational values of human dignity as evidenced by the provisions of ss 26 and 25 of the Constitution' and that it 'would be more consonant with human dignity of landless people' to approach the matter as described above.

177 Ibid. para. 331.

178 Ibid. para. 333.

179 Ibid. paras 335–8; *Government of the Republic of SA and ors v Grootboom and ors* 2001 (1) SA 46 (CC); *Port Elizabeth Municipality v Various Occupiers* 2005 (1) SA 217 (CC); *Occupiers of 51 Olivia Road, Berea Township, and 197 Main Street, Johannesburg v City of Johannesburg and ors* 2008 (3) SA 208 (CC).

180 *Residents of Joe Slovo Community, Western Cape v Thubelisha Homes and ors (Centre on Housing Rights and Evictions and Community Law Centre, University of the Western Cape,* amici curiae*)* [2009] JOL 23711 (CC) para. 339.

181 Ibid. para. 344.

> by homeless families must be located not in the framework of the common law rights of landowners, but in the context of the special cluster of legal relationships between the council and the occupants established by the Constitution and the Housing Act.[182]

Following on this approach, the relationship between the parties cannot be determined purely according to the logic of private law rights, but rather by 'an articulation of public responsibilities in relation to the achievement of guaranteed social and economic rights'.[183] Therefore, the lawfulness of the residents' occupation of land in the Joe Slovo settlement must be determined with reference to the relevant constitutional and statutory housing framework and not according to the precepts of private law.[184]

The approach followed by Ngcobo and Sachs JJ highlights perhaps the two most significant aspects of the decision in *Joe Slovo*. Firstly, both judges attempt to extract what is for them a difficult and painful decision from the normal logic of both private law rights and public law powers used for the promotion of private interests. Instead, they try and insert the decision into a completely different logic of state responsibility towards the provision of housing, thereby indirectly acknowledging the importance of what Lorna Fox calls the home interest for all eviction cases, albeit within the perhaps unique framework of post-apartheid South African housing policy and legislation. The correct context for this and other, similar decisions, they emphasise, is the matrix of constitutional and statutory provisions that set out the obligations of the state with regard to provision of housing. Secondly, especially Ngcobo J makes it abundantly clear that he would not have countenanced the order allowing the relocation to proceed if it were not for the assurance that the redevelopment would provide the Joe Slovo community direct and guaranteed access to the new housing stock.[185]

(4) Assessment

The South African *Port Elizabeth Municipality*, *City of Johannesburg* and *Joe Slovo* decisions are both similar to and different from the US *Kelo* and English *Smith* cases discussed earlier, and it is important in evaluating these decisions to recognise the similarities and differences. The cases are similar in the significant

182 Ibid. para. 344

183 Ibid. para. 343.

184 Ibid. para. 351. In paras 287–89 O'Regan J agreed that the private-law principles that apply to prior notice in cases of *precarium* cannot apply unchanged in this case, since the landowner is a state organ with special obligations to provide access to housing, but stated that she nevertheless considered the private-law principles of ownership relevant.

185 Sachs J arguably made the same point when he mentioned this as one of the three distinguishing features of the case: ibid. para. 339.

respect that they all involved eviction of individual residents from their homes on the initiative of a local authority acting in terms of one of its statutory powers (expropriation or land-use control).[186] In some cases, namely *Kelo*, *Smith*, *City of Johannesburg* and *Joe Slovo*, the local authorities were explicitly exercising their powers to evacuate private land with a view to redevelopment.[187] In *Kelo* the properties were not necessarily blighted, but the area was in economic decline and it was foreseen that development would improve the whole area. In *Smith* the area was seriously neglected and in need of development; in *City of Johannesburg* at least some of the properties were considered health and safety risks. In *Joe Slovo* the area was prone to fires and in need of redevelopment. Development promised general improvement and economic progress in all cases, but it was not foreseen in all of them that the affected previous occupiers would benefit from the improvements directly or indirectly, at least not in the sense of acquiring rights in the newly developed area. In that respect, *Joe Slovo* is unique in explicitly requiring that the development should benefit the occupiers.

The most obvious difference between the cases is that *Kelo* and *Smith* were expropriation cases, where eviction and displacement resulted from compulsory state acquisition of the land for the sake of economic development. In *Port Elizabeth Municipality* the land remained in private hands and the eviction was merely aimed at clearing unlawful occupiers off the property. In *City of Johannesburg* the land also remained in private hands and the local authority used its public health and safety regulatory powers to clear the land for economic development. In *Joe Slovo* the land belonged to the local authority and relocation was explicitly intended to enable the building of social housing. In *Port Elizabeth Municipality* and *City of Johannesburg* the land was privately owned and the local authority could theoretically have used its power of expropriation to obtain the land for state housing development but ironically, in view of the South African government's strong constitutional duty to provide access to housing,[188] the post-1994 South African government has been extremely cautious in using this power to acquire land for redistributive purposes or to expropriate large areas of residential land for more or less any purpose. As a consequence, there are no big expropriation for development cases to compare with the US or UK decisions discussed earlier.

The most significant difference between the cases discussed earlier is the explicit focus on redevelopment for housing purposes in the South African

186 The local authority did not participate in the eviction in *Residents of Joe Slovo Community*, but the provincial and national authorities did.

187 It was not entirely clear from the facts that redevelopment was the ultimate aim in *Port Elizabeth Municipality v Various Occupiers* 2005 (1) SA 217 (CC), but one can safely assume that the squatters were preventing the private owners from developing their land economically.

188 S 26(1)–(2) of the 1996 Constitution: '(1) Everyone has the right to have access to adequate housing. (2) The State must take reasonable legislative and other measures, within its available resources, to achieve the progressive realisation of this right.'

cases and the courts' recent insistence that those who are displaced by such a development should also benefit from it. The *Joe Slovo* decision has now made it clear that relocation of a settled community would probably only be tolerated if the same community also benefits from the development. Economic development could in these cases not exclude the evictees from its benefits. In that sense, the *City of Johannesburg* and *Joe Slovo* cases resemble cases like *James v UK*[189] or *Hawaii Housing Authority*[190] more closely than they do *Kelo* or *Smith*, where the redevelopment was aimed at upmarket uses and users and not at the kind of residents initially evicted from the property.[191]

Another glaring difference between the cases is of course the reformist or transformative context within which one has to read the South African cases. In the first place it is necessary, as Sachs J reminds one in *Port Elizabeth Municipality*, to read the South African land and housing legislation and case law in its historical and constitutional context: access to land and housing was distorted seriously by the discriminatory land laws and practices of apartheid, and the tenor of the post-1994 legislation and case law is inevitably affected by efforts to redress the resulting imbalances and injustices. Whatever one chooses to think about the US Supreme Court's deferential approach to eminent domain condemnations or about the legitimacy of economic development expropriations generally, the South African historical and constitutional context is unique and has to be taken into account when comparing the legislation or case law referred to above. Moreover, it has to be kept in mind that legislation has long been in place, in some cases extensively (Germany and the UK), to provide for some of the housing goals now set out in the South African Constitution, even though these countries did not have the same historical baggage to deal with.

Given these similarities and differences, the most significant inference to be drawn from the comparative analysis of these cases is that the human rights inspired advances that have been made over the past decade or so in the recognition and protection of the home interest in general eviction law may well be rendered empty unless the legal and logical strategies that were developed in 'normal' eviction cases are extended to cases where eviction results from relocations for the sake of economic development. In this context, we should recognise a special interplay developing between the common law, legislation and constitutional or human rights principles. Whenever expropriation and land-use regulation aimed at economic or general redevelopment causes dispossession and displacement from people's homes, heightened judicial scrutiny is called for. In redevelopment cases, the legitimacy of both the expropriation (if there is one) and the relocation should be tested in terms of the matrix of constitutional and statutory measures that describe state responsibility with regard to housing and that directly or indirectly protect home interests in most modern countries, and not purely according to the logic of

189 (App no 8795/79) [1986] 8 EHRR 123.

190 *Hawaii Housing Authority v Midkiff* 467 US 229 (1984).

191 See the evaluation at text to nn. 92–6 above.

private rights (including the right to compensation) or state powers (including the power of eminent domain). Protection of the home interest cannot always trump the power to expropriate private property for a public purpose, but when homes and communities are destroyed for a public purpose the expropriation should actually serve a real and serious public purpose, and when the public purpose relates to economic development the affected residents and community should benefit from it. Unless the residents who are evicted to facilitate economic development benefit from direct and secure access to new and better housing in the new development, both as individuals and as a community, it should be very hard, in all but the most exceptional cases of real and serious public necessity, to justify either the taking of individual property or the resulting eviction that destroys the community.

Chapter 5

The Displacement and Dispossession of Asylum Seekers: Recalibrating the Legal Perspective

James A. Sweeney and Lorna Fox O'Mahony[1]

(1) Introduction

Asylum seekers have been rightly described as 'among the most legally and socially disadvantaged people in western societies'.[2] Amongst immigrants, and as a product of their *forced* migration, asylum seekers are especially vulnerable to suffering from limited access to social housing. Immigration and social housing already sit on a precarious axis. Two recent contrasting media headlines on a 2009 report by the UK's Equality and Human Rights Commission illustrate this aptly.

The report, entitled *Social Housing Allocation and Immigrant Communities*, was designed specifically to look at the facts behind '[w]idespread media reports [which] suggest that migrants receive priority in the allocation of social housing, and in doing so displace non-migrants'.[3] The report found quite clearly that less than two per cent of all social housing residents are people who have moved to the UK in the last five years and that nine out of ten people who live in social housing were born in the UK.[4] Equipped with the report, Housing Minister John Healy attempted to counter claims that social housing favours immigrants at the expense of the indigenous population, stating that he 'wanted to "nail the myth" that certain groups were losing out in terms of housing allocation. [...] It is largely a problem of perception [...]. The report shows there is a belief, a wrong belief, that there is a bias in the system.' The BBC covered the report and the minister's comments under the headline, 'Housing "not favouring migrants"'.[5] Tabloid newspaper the

1 lorna.fox@durham.ac.uk/j.a.sweeney@durham.ac.uk.

2 S. Castles and A. Davidson, *Citizenship and Migration: Globalisation and the Politics of Belonging* (Macmillan, London 2000), 73.

3 Equality and Human Rights Commission, *Social Housing Allocation and Immigrant Communities* (EHRC, London 2009), vii.

4 Ibid, viii and 19.

5 BBC, 'Housing "Not Favouring Migrants"' (available at http://news.bbc.co.uk/1/hi/uk_politics/8137408.stm, accessed 18 February 2010).

Daily Mail took a rather different interpretation, carrying the headline 'One in ten state-subsidised homes goes to an immigrant family'.[6]

In this example one idea of home has been set up in opposition to another, and a tension created between protecting (and defending) the indigenous population's sense of home, on the one hand and making *home* – at both the state and housing levels – available to 'others' who may have been displaced and dispossessed from elsewhere on the other. Indeed, this has been regarded as a deliberate effect of the 'domopolitics' which constructs these images of 'them and us' in an effort: 'to contain citizenship, to uphold a certain statist conception of citizenship in the face of social forces that are tracing out other cultural and political possibilities [through]…the assertion of a right to settle as "illegal" and "dangerous".'[7]

This chapter draws upon the recent emergence of 'home' as a subject of legal analysis,[8] and particularly on the proposition that the occupied home is a distinct type of property, due to its central role in our lived experiences as humans,[9] to reconsider the relationships between 'housing' and 'home' for human rights. There are obvious but implicit synergies across the three conceptual fields of shelter, housing and home as they influence human rights laws and norms. As Kenna has recently noted: '[h]ousing addresses the basic need for human shelter, but also facilitates the essential human requirement for a home.'[10] This chapter seeks to make explicit those relationships in the context of asylum seekers, and considers

6 Steve Doughty, 'One in Ten State-subsidised Homes goes to an Immigrant Family' *Daily Mail* (London 9 July 2009; available at http://www.dailymail.co.uk/news/article-1198016/One-state-subsidised-homes-goes-immigrant-family.html?ITO=1490, accessed 18 February 2010).

7 W. Walters, 'Secure Borders, Safe Haven, Domopolitics' (2004) 8 *Citizenship Studies* 237 at 256.

8 See, for example, L. Fox, *Conceptualising Home: Theories, Laws and Policies* (Hart Publishing, Oxford 2006); D.B. Barros, 'Home as a Legal Concept' (2006) 46 *Santa Clara Law Review* 255; M.J. Ballard, 'Legal Protections for Home Dwellers: Caulking the Cracks to Preserve Occupancy' (2006) 56 *Syracuse Law Review* 277; A. Margalit, 'The Value of Home Ownership' (2006) 7 *Theoretical Inquiries in Law* 7; T. Inglesias, 'Our Pluralist Housing Ethics and the Struggle for Affordability' (2007) 42 *Wake Forest Law Review* 511; T.H. Wu, 'The Legal Representation of the Singaporean Home and the Influence of the Common Law' (2007) 37 *Hong Kong Law Journal* 81; A. Buyse, 'Strings Attached: the Concept of "Home" in the Case Law of the European Court of Human Rights' (2006) *European Human Rights Law Review* 294.

9 The legal concept of home has emerged our of cross-disciplinary and interdisciplinary 'home' scholarship, building on empirical studies and theoretical analyses of the lived experience of home, the meanings which home represents for occupiers, and the experience of losing one's home; see generally L. Fox, *Conceptualising Home: Theories, Laws and Policies* (Hart Publishing, Oxford 2006) n. 9, especially ch. 4.

10 P. Kenna, 'Globalization and Housing Rights' (2008) 15 *Indiana Journal of Global Legal Studies* 397.

how a clearer articulation of this triad could usefully inform legal analysis and policy debates concerning asylum seekers and failed asylum seekers.

Displaced from their state of origin, and easily displaced again from their precarious claim to housing in the UK, the 'double displacement' of asylum seekers highlights how law and policy effectively coerces behaviour through the promise or denial of housing with little reference to human rights or notions of 'home'. In exploring 'double displacement', two key features characterise our approach, both of which are drawn from an emphasis on the displaced or dispossessed human person who is the subject of the discussion. Firstly, we argue that the dominating or hegemonic discourse of legal and policy approaches to asylum seekers[11] produces a minimalist 'shelter' approach to questions of housing and home for asylum seekers. This chapter seeks to consider how human rights approaches might create possibilities for developing new thinking on this subject from a person-centred and problem-solving perspective rooted in analysis of how the asylum seeker experiences the absence of 'adequate housing' and the absence of 'home'.[12]

Secondly, and consequent on this approach, the paper considers the relationships between home, housing and human rights within the broader panoply of international and European human rights law. The importance of viewing housing within the broader framework of human rights – as a 'gateway' right – was emphasised by the UN Committee on Economic, Social and Cultural Rights when it recognised that:

> the right to housing is integrally linked to other human rights and to the fundamental principles upon which the [International Covenant on Economic, Social and Cultural Rights] is premised. Thus 'the inherent dignity of the human person' from which the rights in the Covenant are said to derive requires that the term 'housing' be interpreted so as to take account of a variety of other considerations, most importantly that the right to housing should be ensured to all persons irrespective of income or access to economic resources.[13]

The Committee also noted that: 'the indivisibility and interdependence of civil and political rights and economic, social and cultural rights [as] fundamental tenets of international human rights law…has been repeatedly reaffirmed, most recently at

---

11 For a more detailed discussion of the human experience of displacement and dispossession for asylum seekers, see L. Fox O'Mahony and J.A. Sweeney, 'The Exclusion of (Failed) Asylum Seekers from Housing and Home: Towards an Oppositional Discourse' (2010) *Journal of Law and Society* 285–314. .

12 For further discussion of this approach, see H. van der Horst, 'Living in a Reception Centre: the Search for Home in an Institutional Setting' (2004) 21 *Housing, Theory and Society* 36 at 37.

13 See UN Committee on Economic, Social and Cultural Rights, 'General Comment No. 4', 'The Right to Adequate Housing (Art.11 (1))' (1991) UN Doc HRI/GEN/1/Rev.7.

the World Conference on Human Rights in 1993.'[14] For example, without a secure base in housing in which the person can be based, the realisation of civil and political rights – while perhaps theoretically available – is practically more difficult.

The chapter explores the importance of 'home' to being human and, in turn, to human rights laws, both when 'housing' is available, in relation to the location and quality of accommodation provided to asylum seekers, and in relation to policies and practices that limit access to such accommodation, so that no shelter is provided. With regard to the latter, three case studies are undertaken to demonstrate that home and human rights thinking are absent from policies which exclude asylum seekers and failed asylum seekers from any claim to home, housing or shelter: the situation of people with a (medical) need for 'care and attention', late-applying asylum seekers and failed asylum seekers themselves. We demonstrate that the policies embodied in the relevant UK statutes, while arguably 'compliant' with international obligations, inadequately address the home needs of asylum seekers and failed asylum seekers, who must rely on the activism of individual judges to ameliorate their situation. Yet, without a statutory framework and a broader legal discourse that recognises the importance of home to the human needs of asylum seekers, the extent to which judicial responses can temper the harsh consequences of exclusion from housing and home is necessarily limited. The final section of the chapter argues against a 'minimal compliance' approach to human rights as externally imposed international obligations, in favour of an approach that sees human rights norms as a platform on which to build domestic policy solutions.

(2) Home, Exile and Alienation: 'Double Displacement'

The central importance of themes of home, exile and alienation for the human experience has long been recognised in philosophical writing.[15] We all exist in a relationship with place, whether positive or negative, whether with a meaningful

14 UNGA Res 32/130 (16 December 1977) UN Doc A/Res/32/130 also asserted, in paragraph 1, that (a) All human rights and fundamental freedoms are indivisible and interdependent; equal attention and urgent consideration should be given to the implementation, promotion and protection of both civil and political, and economic, social and cultural rights; (b) The full realization of civil and political rights without the enjoyment of economic, social and cultural rights is impossible; the achievement of lasting progress in the implementation of human rights is dependent upon sound and effective national and international policies of economic and social development, as recognized by the Proclamation of Teheran of 1968.

15 See, for example, D. Cooper, *The Measure of Things* (Oxford University Press, Oxford 2002) for a philosophical account of what it might mean to 'be at home in the world'. Levinas described the *home* as a precondition for existence, since: '[m]an abides in the world as having come from a private domain, from being at home with himself, to which at each moment he can retire'; E. Levinas, *Totality and Infinity* (Martinus Nijhoff, The Hague 1969) 152.

connection to *home*, or – without such connections – in a state of alienation resulting from displacement and/or dispossession from a home-place.[16] In *Being and Time*,[17] Heidegger's ontological argument was that people cannot 'be' without having some connection to a particular place:

> The way in which you are and I am, the manner in which we humans *are* on the earth, is *Buan*, dwelling. To be a human being means to be on the earth as a mortal. It means to dwell…man *is* insofar as he *dwells*.[18]

When man loses the ability to dwell – for example, the exile or asylum seeker, who is displaced from, and/or dispossessed of their dwelling place and so has lost their place in the world – and, further, is rendered unable to recover a home-place elsewhere, whether in the sense of a dwelling, or a sense of place in the new region or homeland, this constitutes a threat to his human being. In contrast to voluntary migration, 'exile' can be read as 'enforced displacement and dislocation':[19] in the case of refugees and asylum seekers, the significance of *home*, in the sense of both displacement and dispossession from one's home, and the need to establish a new home, is evident.[20] Blunt and Dowling have indicated that:

> Notions of home are central in these migrations. Movement may necessitate or be precipitated by a disruption to a sense of home, as people leave or in some cases flee one home for another. These international movements are also processes of establishing home, as senses of belonging and identity move over space and are created in new places.[21]

The problem, however, is that some asylum seekers are prevented from creating a new sense of belonging or identity in the new place. Casey has noted that: '[n]ot only may the former place be lost but a new place in which to settle may not be

---

16 M. Heidegger, 'Bauen, Wohnen, Denken' (1951) ['Building Dwelling Thinking'] and the 1951 lecture '…dichterisch wohnet der Mensch' ['…Poetically man dwells…'] in A. Hofstadter (trans.), *Poetry, Language, Thought* (Harper Colophon Books, New York 1971).

17 M. Heidegger, *Sein und Zeit* (1927); J. Macquarrie and E. Robinson (trans.), *Being and Time* (Blackwell Publishers Ltd, Oxford 1962).

18 M. Heidegger, 'Bauen, Wohnen, Denken' (1951) ['Building Dwelling Thinking'] in A. Hofstadter (trans.), *Poetry, Language, Thought* (Harper Colophon Books, New York 1971) n. 17, part I.

19 H.K. Bhabha, 'Preface' in H. Naficy (ed.) *Home, Exile, Homeland: Film, Media, and the Politics of Place* (Routledge, New York 1999), xii.

20 For a more detailed discussion of the human experience of displacement and dispossession for asylum seekers see L. Fox O'Mahony and J.A. Sweeney, 'The Exclusion of (Failed) Asylum Seekers from Housing and Home: Towards an Oppositional Discourse' (2010) *Journal of Law and Society* 285–314.

21 A. Blunt and R. Dowling, *Home* (Routledge, London 2006), 2.

found…[the exile faces] the risk of having no proper or lasting place, no place to be or remain.'[22] This is the essence of our notion of 'double displacement'.

Yet, the impact of double displacement is not reflected in the laws and policies which govern access to housing and home for asylum seekers in the UK. The following sections demonstrate how the 'double displacement' of asylum seekers is excluded from legal reasoning, whether in relation to legislative policies towards asylum seekers and failed asylum seekers, or in the judicial application of international human rights standards to their predicament. The purpose of this analysis is to highlight the disjuncture between human experiences of displacement and dispossession from home on the one hand, and the limitations of human rights law in formulating responses which value these experiences, on the other. Finally, we move on to consider alternative methods of framing 'human rights' which might allow greater scope for recognising and responding to the double displacement of asylum seekers.

(3) Asylum and Destitution in the UK

We now turn to an exploration of the very real predicament of asylum seekers, as the paradigm of double displacement: displaced from their home state and dispossessed from 'home in housing'. Rather than responding to the adverse human consequences of displacement and dispossession, successive policies pursued by the UK government have actually heightened asylum seekers' vulnerability and sense of dislocation by adding conditions to and restrictions upon their right to, and ability to, access and participate in the labour market and to obtain social housing.

Pervasive amongst these policies is the attempt to use denial of housing as a means of coercing certain behaviour from (failed) asylum seekers. From the outset the paradox embodied by these policies must be acknowledged: while these policies typically give very little weight to the human cost of asylum seekers' inability to re-establish 'home', it is the universally acknowledged human need for 'home', and the deleterious effects of denying access to a meaningful home experience, that underpins their power to coerce.[23]

The following sections sketch the legal context of asylum seekers' home experiences, and show some potential legal solutions to their predicament based on European and international human rights law. However, we note that since these current approaches are rooted in the fairly blunt tools of existing law, and depend to a large extent on the activism of judicial interpretation, the vision of

22 E.S. Casey, *Getting Bank into Place – Toward a Renewed Understanding of the Place-World* (Indiana University Press, Bloomington 1993), preface, xii.

23 See further L. Fox O'Mahony and J.A. Sweeney, 'The Exclusion of (Failed) Asylum Seekers from Housing and Home: Towards an Oppositional Discourse' (2010) *Journal of Law and Society* 285–314.

'home' that they reveal is, at best, an atrophied vision that does little to ameliorate the risk of double displacement.

(4) Sketching the Legal Context: Asylum Seekers' Diminishing Rights to Housing

The UN Refugee Convention specifies some economic, social and cultural rights for persons recognised as refugees. However, whilst the person is still an asylum seeker awaiting the determination of their claim to be a refugee, the rights derived from the Refugee Convention generally do not apply.[24] States may choose to assimilate welfare support and social housing for asylum seekers with the national population, to separate it entirely, or to hold asylum seekers in detention. The exclusion of asylum seekers from the Refugee Convention leaves them vulnerable to political trends at the domestic level, and may result in only the barest of provision. Furthermore, even where domestic policies entitle asylum seekers to receive some shelter from the state, it is clear that merely providing a roof overhead does not suffice to satisfy even the most basic housing needs to enable a person to function in society.

The provision of support to asylum seekers in the domestic law of the UK was described by the Joint Committee on Human Rights in 2007 as 'a confusing mess'.[25] We pick up the story in the 1990s when, in a policy trajectory spanning the transition from Conservative to Labour governments, the rights of asylum seekers to social security benefits were progressively extinguished. When combined with a general prohibition upon the right of asylum seekers to work, the vulnerability and exposure that this engendered was clear.[26] Yet, a striking feature of the policies outlined below is that they rest on the premise that it is legitimate (indeed 'normal')

24 See *R v Secretary of State for Social Security, ex parte Joint Council for the Welfare of Immigrants and ex parte B* [1996] 4 All ER 385 (CA); [1997] 1 WLR 275, 292 (Simon Brown LJ noting that 'no obligation arises under Art 24 [Refugee Convention] until asylum seekers are recognized as refugees. […] Not for one moment would I suggest that prior to that time their rights are remotely the same'); R. Cholewinksi, 'Enforced Destitution of Asylum Seekers in the UK' (1998) 10 *IJLR* 462, 477; R. Cholewinski, 'Economic and Social Rights of Refugees and Asylum Seekers in Europe' (2000) 14 *Georgetown Immigration Law Journal* 709, 711; C. Sawyer and P. Turpin, 'Neither Here Nor There: Temporary Admission to the UK' (2005) 17 *IJLR Law* 688.

25 Joint Committee on Human Rights, 'The Treatment of Asylum Seekers' HL (2006–2007) 81-I; HC (2006–2007) 60-I, 110.

26 After one year an asylum seeker may apply for permission to work (but not to become self-employed or to engage in a business or professional activity), and only then if they can demonstrate that they are not responsible for the delay: Immigration Rule 360. Immigration Rule 360A provides that any permission to work will expire when a claim is 'fully determined', thus excluding failed asylum seekers from working. In *Tekle v Secretary of State for the Home Department* [2009] 2 All ER 193 the High Court held that the one year

to base the extent to which asylum seekers should 'benefit' from social housing and other elements of the welfare state on political policy-making. The later stages of this chapter demonstrate the cost of failing to recognise the impact of these policies on asylum seekers' rights to housing and home as human rights.

In 1996 delegated legislation[27] attempted to remove the entitlement to social security benefits of asylum seekers who did not claim asylum at the point of entry into the UK. The role of judicial responses in ameliorating the plight of destitute asylum seekers was demonstrated when the Regulations were successfully challenged in *R v Secretary of State for Social Security Ex p. Joint Council for the Welfare of Immigrants*.[28] In the conclusion of his judgment, Neill LJ noted that the Asylum and Immigration Appeals Act 1993 had provided 'fuller rights' to asylum seekers than they had previously enjoyed, particularly in relation to appeals against negative decisions. However, the court went on to note that the Regulations would either render these fuller rights useless by encouraging potential refugees to leave the UK before concluding their appeals, or the Regulations must:

> necessarily contemplate for some a life so destitute that to my mind no civilised nation can tolerate it. So basic are the human rights here at issue that it cannot be necessary to resort to the European Convention on Human Rights to take note of their violation…[29]

In a powerful indictment of the impact of the regulations in practice, Neill LJ went on to claim that he:

> would hold it unlawful to alter the benefit regime so drastically as must inevitably not merely prejudice, but on occasion defeat, the statutory right of asylum seekers to claim refugee status…I for my part regard the Regulations now in force as so uncompromisingly draconian in effect that they must indeed be held ultra vires.[30]

In upholding the asylum seekers' challenge to the Regulations, Neill LJ recognised the adverse human consequences of destitution when he reasoned that:

> Parliament cannot have intended a significant number of genuine asylum seekers to be impaled on the horns of so intolerable a dilemma: the need either

---

period also applies where a hitherto failed asylum seeker presents a fresh claim for asylum (so on the expiry of a further year, they would be able to apply for permission to work).

27 Social Security (Persons from Abroad) Miscellaneous Amendment Regulations 1996.

28 *R v Secretary of State for Social Security Ex p. Joint Council for the Welfare of Immigrants* [1997] 1 WLR 275.

29 Ibid., 292 (Neill LJ).

30 Ibid., 293 (Neill LJ).

> to abandon their claims to refugee status or alternatively to maintain them as best they can but in a state of utter destitution. Primary legislation alone could in my judgment achieve that sorry state of affairs.[31]

Unfortunately this comment proved to be prophetic, and the 'sorry state of affairs' envisaged by Neill LJ was achieved when the Conservative government introduced, and Parliament passed, the Asylum and Immigration Act 1996 in order to more securely achieve the aims of the impugned Regulations.

Faced with destitution, asylum seekers began to assert rights under the residual safety net of the UK's welfare state provided by the National Assistance Act 1948.[32] In *R. v Hammersmith and Fulham London Borough Council, Ex parte M*[33] the Court of Appeal held that asylum seekers who were sleeping rough and going without food were covered by section 21(1)(a) of the NAA 1948, which imposes upon every local council a duty to provide residential accommodation 'for persons who by reason of age, infirmity or any other circumstances are in need of care and attention which is not otherwise available to them'. One of the most significant elements of this development is that it transferred primary responsibility for housing those asylum seekers who qualified for NAA support on to local authorities. The incoming Labour government identified this issue in the White Paper *Fairer, Faster and Firmer: A Modern Approach to Immigration and Asylum*, which in turn informed the Immigration and Asylum Act 1999. Rather than reinstating asylum seekers' eligibility for mainstream social security benefits, the 1999 Act created an alternative to the residual NAA 1948 right to housing in the form of a separate national system of support for asylum seekers to be administered by a new National Asylum Support Service (NASS).

Under section 95 of the Immigration and Asylum Act 1999 the Secretary of State may provide support to asylum seekers 'who appear to the Secretary of State to be destitute or to be likely to become destitute'. In addition to accommodation, a single adult asylum seeker may receive £35.13 per week in cash. Different rates apply to parents and children.[34] Under section 4 of the same Act, the Secretary of State may also provide support to failed asylum seekers, as long as they cooperate with efforts to remove them from the UK.[35] If the failed asylum seeker does *not* comply with removal directions then, under section 54 IAA 1999 and Schedule

---

31 Ibid., 293 (Neill LJ).

32 The history of s. 21 NAA 1948 is summarised in *R. (on the application of M) v Slough BC* [2008] 1 WLR 1808 [7] (Baroness Hale), discussed further below.

33 *R. v Hammersmith and Fulham London Borough Council, Ex parte M* (1997) 30 HLR 10.

34 Asylum Support (Amendment) (No. 2) Regulations 2009; see http://www.bia.homeoffice.gov.uk/asylum/support/cashsupport/currentsupportamounts/ (accessed 8 January 2010).

35 The criteria are set out in Regulation 3 of the Asylum (Provision of Accommodation to Failed Asylum Seekers) Regulations 2005.

3 NIAA 2002, they become ineligible either for NASS 'hard case' support or for local authority 'destitution plus' provision.[36] Under section 9 of the Asylum and Immigration (Treatment of Claimants) Act 2004, even failed asylum seekers with children may have their support removed in this way.

The section 4 scheme, known as 'hard case' support, is designed for failed asylum seekers who are unable to leave the UK immediately due to reasons beyond their control. Unlike section 95 support, this does not result in cash payments, but consists of accommodation plus £35 per week in vouchers. Significantly, the use of vouchers rather than cash may exacerbate the stigmatisation of failed asylum seekers and also limits their choice as to where they purchase goods to meet their essential needs.[37] Thus, the use of vouchers in this way compounds the lack of autonomy which renders accommodation for asylum seekers 'unhomely'. However, as we shall see below, the section 4 regime is hugely problematic, not least of all because it is estimated that only four per cent of failed asylum seekers in the UK are in receipt of it,[38] thus leaving the vast majority unsupported.

(5) The Location and Quality of Asylum Accommodation: Shelter, Housing and Home

Even where asylum seekers are able to secure shelter from the state, the adequacy of provision in supporting housing and home has been criticised. Two key issues have emerged in reports scrutinising the accommodation provided when an asylum seeker is eligible under the national system set out in section 95 of the Immigration and Asylum Act 1999: the location and the quality of the accommodation provided. The emergence of these issues underscores the state's perception of its role as providing 'shelter' rather than housing or home as they might be understood in the context of the 'right to housing' or the 'right to respect for home'. Indeed the approach of the UK to *sheltering* asylum seekers might deliberately undermine meanings of housing and home. For example the issue of location is rooted in the policy of dispersal, which has come under criticism from the UK's House of Commons Public Accounts Committee. The primary criterion in this process, which disperses asylum seekers around the UK, is the availability of accommodation, which the PAC has recognised 'can result in individuals becoming isolated.'[39] This reflects Diken's observation that refugee spaces (whether 'open' spaces, such

36 Schedule 3 also comprehensively excludes support under other non-asylum-seeker-specific welfare provisions.

37 Joint Committee on Human Rights, 'The Treatment of Asylum Seekers' HL (2006–2007) 81-I; HC (2006–2007) 60-I [110].

38 Independent Asylum Commission, Second Report of Conclusions and Recommendations, 'Safe Return' (Independent Asylum Commission, London 2008), 31.

39 Public Accounts Committee, 'Management of Asylum Applications' HC (2008–2009) 325, 6.

as accommodation centres or reception centres, or closed spaces e.g. detention centres) are often deliberately located 'outside cities, in suburbia or in rural areas, as a rule in demonstrably peripheral sites';[40] away from amenities and facilities, and 'characterised by a sterilised, mono-functional enclosure: contact with the outer world is physically minimised behind the fences, which yield no permission to touch the outer world resulting in the complete isolation of the refugee from public life.'[41]

The second, and perhaps more even more pressing issue is the quality of accommodation. The UK's Joint Committee on Human Rights argued in its 2007 report on 'The Treatment of Asylum Seekers' that in some cases the quality and terms of accommodation provided to asylum seekers is so woeful as to constitute a failure to respect home and family life under Article 8 ECHR and the right to adequate housing under Article 11 ICESCR,[42] discussed further below. Nevertheless, the government maintains that it 'has agreed standards and contracts' which ensure there is no breach of international obligations.[43]

Against this background, and the likelihood that the asylum seeker already, by virtue of their displacement from (and probably also dispossession in) their home state, is experiencing 'a sense of powerlessness and dependence...frequently mixed with an acute anxiety about their new circumstances and strong feelings of homelessness';[44] the impact of further displacement in respect of asylum seekers' precarious claim to housing (and by extension to re-establish *home*) is significant. Thus we are not just concerned with 'homelessness' in the sense of being without shelter, but with the argument that although asylum seekers may be provided with a roof over their heads, the evidence clearly indicates that the provision of shelter in this respect cannot necessarily be described as 'housing', and is not likely to be conducive to feelings of home.

The distinction between being without shelter and being homeless was recognised by the UN in its definition of homelessness as 'a condition of detachment from

---

40 B. Diken, 'From Refugee Camps to Gated Communities: Biopolitics and the End of the City' (2004) 8 *Citizenship Studies* 83, 91.

41 Ibid.

42 These comments related specifically to accommodation provided under s. 95 IAA 1999, discussed further below. See also Joint Committee on Human Rights, 'The Treatment of Asylum Seekers' HL (2006–2007) 81-I; HC (2006–2007) 60-I [104]; note that according to the High Court in *R (Baiai & another) v Secretary of State for the Home Department* [2006] EWHC Admin 823, in so far as JCHR reports express opinions on matters of law, they have only persuasive value; see generally J. Hiebert, 'Parliament and the Human Rights Act: Can the JCHR help Facilitate a Culture of Rights?' (2006) 4 *International Journal of Constitutional Law* 38.

43 Joint Committee on Human Rights, 'Government Response to the Committee's Tenth Report of this Session: The Treatment of Asylum Seekers', HL (2006–2007) 134; HC (2006–2007) 790 [9].

44 C. Kinnvall, 'Globalisation and Religious Nationalism: Self, Identity, and the Search for Ontological Security' (2004) 25 *Political Psychology* 741, 747.

society characterised by the lack of affiliative bonds…[that] carries implications of belonging nowhere rather than having nowhere to sleep.'[45] As 'non-citizens', exiles, refugees and asylum seekers are already marked out as not belonging, and as subject to explicit policies which seek to ensure that they are not enabled in developing a sense of belonging, or coming to feel 'at home'. The negative impacts of homelessness on individual well-being are well-established in research literature:

> Coping without a home is a stressful, time-consuming occupation. Every single day, homeless people are faced with the task of securing food, shelter, and other necessities of life. Frequently they are obliged to negotiate complex bureaucratic systems, endure alienating and dehumanising service-delivery routines, and risk arrest or jail. They live with the physical and psychological consequences of poor diet, inadequate rest, and lack of health care.[46]

The absence of home is also associated with alienation from the practical and psychological benefits (particularly in relation to ontological security and identity) that flow from having an opportunity to establish a home, for example, the potential to develop social, cultural or community capital in a particular location. While Bourdieu recognised the importance of durable networks for the acquisition of social capital,[47] Putnam linked social capital to effective democracy,[48] and for individual and community engagement in civil society.[49]

---

45 UNCHS/Habitat, *Strategies to Combat Homelessness* (UN Centre for Human Settlements, Nairobi 2000), xiii.

46 J. Wolch and M. Dear, *Malign Neglect: Homelessness in an American City* (Jossey-Bass Publishers, San Francisco 1993), 246; quoted in A. Blunt and R. Dowling, *Home* (Routledge, London 2006) 127.

47 Defined as: 'the aggregate of the actual or potential resources which are linked to possession of a durable network of more or less institutionalized relationships of mutual acquaintance and recognition' (P. Bourdieu, 'The Forms of Capital' in J Richardson (ed.) *Handbook of Theory and Research for the Sociology of Education* (Greenwood, New York 1986), 241–58; while sense of belonging and place attachment have not been central to the meta-theories of social capital, the role and relevance of place for social capital particularly amongst young people is emphasised by Schaefer-McDaniel, who argues that social capital must be grounded in the physical environment. See N.J. Schaefer-McDaniel, 'Conceptualizing Social Capital among Young People: Towards a New Theory' (2004) 14 *Children, Youth and Environments* 140 (available online at http://www.colorado.edu/journals/cye/14_1/articles/article6full.htm, accessed 17 September 2010); the role of the 'sense of belonging' in social capital is also noted in D. Narayan and M.F. Cassidy 'A Dimensional Approach to Measuring Social Capital: Development and Validation of a Social Capital Inventory' (2001) 49(2) *Current Sociology* 59–102.

48 See R.D. Putnam, *Making Democracy Work: Civic Traditions in Modern Italy* (Princeton University Press, Princeton 1993).

49 See R.D. Putnam, *Bowling Alone: America's Declining Social Capital* (John Hopkins University Press, Baltimore 1996).

Viewed from another perspective, the absence of housing and home can be viewed not merely as a material hardship but as the denial of opportunity, for example, to participate in civil society,[50] and – recognising housing as a gateway right – to realise civil and political rights. Considering the similarly marginalised position of the poor in a society, Haworth noted that:

> One is poor not because he has no money, but because, possibly owing to lack of money, he lacks also access to the social instrumentalities that make humanly significant action possible. In part, it is a simple matter of not having the price of admission…[51]

Furthermore, where the population who are excluded from such actions are not randomly distributed but belong to a particular group – for example, asylum seekers – this arguably raises a question about discriminatory infringement of civil and political rights.

Of course, to make such a claim legally enforceable, it would be necessary to establish a causal link between the exclusion from housing and home and the inability to exercise particular civil and political rights to which the asylum seeker is entitled, and we do not currently claim to be in a position to make that link explicit. It is, however, possible to begin to map out some of the steps. The need for displaced persons to re-establish some sense of home for their mental and physical wellbeing was emphasised in van der Horst's Dutch study of asylum seekers living in reception centres.[52] Van der Horst noted that, while policy discourse concerning accommodation for asylum seekers tends to focus on efficiency, functionality and the provision of shelter, when discussing their lives in the centre the residents used home discourses to describe their experiences, including their frustration at not having 'even the most basic attributes of home'.[53] Yet, she argued, this perspective 'is hardly represented in the dominant discourse.'[54]

> Talk about the right to a home is very marginal when the people involved are not legal residents, as is the case with asylum seekers. The centres are hardly aimed at providing a home. The concern is with giving a shelter and making the procedure run smoothly. Functionality within the aims of the

50 See for example, F. Michelman, 'On Protecting the Poor through the Fourteenth Amendment' (1959–70) 83 *Harvard Law Review* 7.

51 Haworth, 'Deprivation and the Good City' in W. Bloomberg and H. Schmandt (eds), *Power, Poverty, and Urban Policy* (Sage, Beverly Hills 1968), 27.

52 H. van der Horst, 'Living in a Reception Centre: the Search for Home in an Institutional Setting' (2004) 21 *Housing, Theory and Society* 36.

53 Ibid.

54 Ibid.

> asylum procedure is top priority…it is a discourse of temporality, insecurity and authority…[55]

The home meanings most often missed by the residents of the reception centre in van der Horst's case study were autonomy (for example, the ability to choose what you eat and to prepare it) and the possibility to live your life in accordance with your cultural customs.[56]

It would therefore appear that there is a strong conceptual basis for arguing that 'housing as home' considerations – that is, considerations that go beyond concern with mere shelter – should be better represented in legal and policy discourse on housing for asylum seekers. Yet, as the following sections will demonstrate, there remain considerable challenges to the development of legal strategies that can effectively represent the asylum seeker's interest in securing accommodation which can function as a home, against the state's expressed interest in avoiding the establishment of home attachments in the UK during the asylum process. These are brought to the fore in three case studies in which the (failed) asylum seeker's limited rights to housing and home are challenged. Without mainstream acceptance of the importance of 'home' in legal and political discourse generally, or immigration and asylum law in particular, the extent to which asylum seekers in the UK 'enjoy' access to meaningful home has depended upon the judicial interpretation of domestic legislation that only indirectly addresses the idea of 'home'.

(6) Case Study 1: Asylum Seekers in Need of 'Care and Attention'

To coincide with the introduction of the national system of support for asylum seekers, section 116 of the Immigration and Asylum Act 1999 attempted to remove their access to local authority support under section 21(1)(a) NAA 1948 by inserting a new section 21(1A). The new section 21(1A) NAA 1948 excludes the provision of section 21(1)(a) support to persons subject to immigration control where their need for care and attention arises 'solely' because of destitution or the physical effects of destitution upon them. It was judicial activism, once again, which sought to ameliorate the impact of the legislation when in *R. v Wandsworth London Borough Council, Ex parte O* and *R. v Leicester City Council, Ex parte Bhikha*,[57] the Court of Appeal dampened the effect of the new section 21(1A) by indicating that virtually any infirmity would mean that the need for care and attention was not 'solely' because of destitution. In an evocative passage, Simon Brown LJ said, 'If

55 Ibid., 41.

56 Residents mentioned, for example, the absence of men and women's spaces, and cultural norms on suitable relations between family members.

57 *R. v Wandsworth London Borough Council, Ex parte O* and *R. v Leicester City Council, Ex parte Bhikha* [2000] 1 WLR 2539.

there are to be immigrant beggars on our streets, then let them at least not be old, ill or disabled.'[58] Significantly, even failed asylum seekers may continue to benefit from section 21(1)(a) support under this line of cases.[59]

In her judgment in *R. (on the application of M) v Slough Borough Council*, discussed below, Baroness Hale revealed that, following the *Wandsworth* case, it had been expected by the senior judiciary that only those asylum seekers with the sort of care needs which could only be met in specialised accommodation, and people who fell outside the asylum scheme altogether, would continue to fall under section 21(1)(a) NAA 1948 and thus be supported by local authorities, with others supported through the national system.[60] But, highlighting again the tensions which have been evident between the judiciary – who are routinely faced with the human and personal stories of the people who are seeking housing through this route – and national policy-makers, she added, '[T]his was wrong. The Secretary of State was determined that the national scheme would indeed be a last resort.'[61] If support was available from the local authority, then it would not be provided through the national system, even where the mere provision of accommodation could have met the asylum seeker's further needs arising from infirmity.

This has created difficulties where particular local authorities, in places like Slough in the south-east of England, have come under pressure to provide support to (failed) asylum seekers in need of care and attention. At a political level, it is perhaps understandable that the local authorities resent footing the bill for asylum seekers since matters relating to immigration are quintessentially national government issues. However, the consequence has been a series of cases where local and national government have been in dispute as to who is responsible for providing accommodation support for particular asylum seekers,[62] giving rise to what Sweeney has described as: 'an inverted and unseemly turf war between local and central government.'[63]

In the recent *Slough*[64] case the House of Lords, citing Sweeney, has shifted some of the responsibility back on to national government by narrowing the scope of eligibility under the National Assistance Act 1948. In *Slough* the House of Lords examined the predicament of 'M', an HIV-positive Zimbabwean 'overstayer' (i.e. someone who had stayed beyond the amount of time permitted on their visa). His

58 Ibid., 2548.

59 See J.A. Sweeney, 'The Human Rights of Failed Asylum Seekers in the UK' (2008) *PL* 277 and C. Lewis 'Asylum Support Brief – Part Three: Failed Asylum Seekers' (2006) 156 *NLJ* 1246.

60 *R. (on the application of M) v Slough BC* [2008] 1 WLR 1808 [27].

61 Ibid.

62 Discussed in C. Sawyer and P. Turpin, 'Neither Here Nor There: Temporary Admission to the UK' (2005) 17 *IJLR Law* 710.

63 J.A. Sweeney, 'The Human Rights of Failed Asylum Seekers in the UK' (2008) *PL* 277 and C. Lewis 'Asylum Support Brief – Part Three: Failed Asylum Seekers' (2006) 156 *NLJ* 285.

64 *R. (on the application of M) v Slough BC* [2008] 1 WLR 1808.

immediate need was for medication and a refrigerator in which to keep it. The House of Lords put forward a narrower reading of section 21(1)(a) NAA 1948 with the effect of upholding the local authority's decision to refuse accommodation. The court held that the 'need for care and attention' required to trigger the duty to provide residential accommodation must mean something more than a mere need for 'accommodation': the ordinary meaning of 'care and attention' was 'looking after',[65] and as M did not need 'looking after',[66] he therefore did not have a need of care and attention.

In *Slough* the House of Lords thus cut back on the eligibility of asylum seekers to local authority housing, suggesting that, henceforth, 'destitution plus' cases – in which the local government obligation to provide residential accommodation under the NAA will apply – will be limited to those persons whose need does not arise solely from destitution but who also, in some sense, need 'looking after'. The immediate effect of the *Slough* judgment is that local authorities are now within their rights to re-examine the circumstances of the persons to whom they are providing accommodation under section 21(1)(a) and to cease support for those who do not meet the stricter conditions set out in the *Slough* case. In theory, asylum seekers now have, in its place, extant rights to support under the national system administered by NASS. The reality, however, is that these people will likely face administrative delays, complex application processes, and, ultimately, barriers in accessing housing which is capable of functioning as *home*.

The House of Lords in *Slough* was silent on the potentially very serious implications of the judgment for 'M' himself, but in the introduction to her leading judgment Baroness Hale noted that since he had now made an application to remain in the UK on the ground that he feared breaches of his Article 3 ECHR rights on being returned to Zimbabwe, he would be entitled henceforth to NASS accommodation irrespective of the outcome of the case (at least for the duration of that application). The wider impact of the judgment is that by restricting access to local authority support under the NAA 1948 to people who need 'looking after', the House of Lords rendered *more* people eligible for national support by NASS. Thus the judgment put an end to the surprisingly restrictive approach to gaining access to accommodation theoretically provided at a national level. However, the judgment of the House of Lords, necessarily pinned to the facts and the legislation before it, could not address the central concern of this chapter: the importance of 'home' as central element of 'being human' and, thus, of human rights law. Indeed this case study is marked instead by its concern with the allocation of financial responsibility between branches of government and its immunity to concerns about the particular vulnerability of asylum seekers, and others subject to immigration control, to double displacement.

---

65 Ibid. [33] (Baroness Hale).

66 As Baroness Hale put it, M did not need looking after as, '[P]eople with the virus can now live normal lives for many years.' Ibid. [36] (Baroness Hale).

(7) Case Study 2: Late-applying Asylum Seekers

In 2002 primary legislation was passed that attempted to exclude late-applying asylum seekers from NASS accommodation and support. Section 55(1) of the Nationality, Immigration and Asylum Act 2002 (NIAA) places the Home Secretary under a duty to exclude asylum seekers who do not make their application for asylum 'as soon as reasonably practicable'. However, a 'safety net' under section 55(5) NIAA 2002 does 'not prevent' the Home Secretary exercising a power to support late-applying asylum seekers to the extent necessary for the purpose of avoiding a breach of the European Convention on Human Rights, so preventing the Act from requiring the Home Secretary to act in such a way as to conflict with section 6(1) of the Human Rights Act (HRA) 1998.[67] Yet, in what appears to be a spirit of minimal compliance, the Home Secretary has seemed at times reluctant to exercise this power, even in the face of considerable hardship.

An example of the judiciary forcing the use of the safety net can be seen in the case of *Adam, Limbuela and Tesema*,[68] where each applicant had been excluded from access to support by virtue of section 55(1), and the power under section 55(5) had not been exercised by the Home Secretary. The facts presented to the House of Lords indicated that the applicants had each experienced real hardship, including sleeping rough, and the House of Lords went on to hold that the Home Secretary's failure to exercise the power under section 55(5) NIAA 2002 amounted to a violation of their right to freedom from inhuman and degrading treatment under Article 3 ECHR. The House of Lords found that because the statutory framework combined the exclusion from support and accommodation with a prohibition on work, it was a positive act by the state against asylum seekers.[69] It was therefore caught by Article 3's prohibition upon inflicting inhuman and degrading treatment, rather than a positive obligation to protect the applicants from experiencing inhuman and degrading conditions.

It is significant to note that this case was adjudicated on the basis of Article 3 ECHR, which at one level provides a welcome recognition that homelessness and destitution strike at the heart of what it means to be human: that they can constitute inhuman and degrading treatment. However, it might seem counterintuitive to base any 'home' rights available to asylum seekers on Article 3 rather than the right to respect for home, family and private life in Article 8 ECHR. As well as reserving protection only to those cases with the most extreme adverse facts, as the discussion below will demonstrate, this can also be viewed as an acknowledgement of the particularly contingent nature of the right to respect for home under Article

---

67 s. 6(1) HRA 1998 renders it unlawful for a public authority to act in a way that is incompatible with a Convention right.

68 *R. v Secretary of State for the Home Department ex parte Adam, Limbuela and Tesema* [2005] UKHL 66; [2006] 1 AC 396.

69 Ibid. [7] (Lord Bingham); [56] (Lord Hope); [77] (Baroness Hale).

8 ECHR as well as the right to adequate housing in the International Convention on Economic, Social and Cultural Rights.

(8) Case Study 3: 'Failed' Asylum Seekers

At the end of the asylum process, a failed asylum seeker may be 'removed' from the UK. However, it is recognised that making a successful forced removal is challenging. Indeed a 2009 report of the UK Public Accounts Committee on this issue has observed that since its previous report removals of failed asylum seekers have actually decreased.[70] Therefore, in returning failed asylum seekers to their state of origin, much depends on their willingness to make a 'voluntary' departure from the UK.

Restricting entitlements to social assistance including housing is one means of encouraging failed asylum seekers' voluntary departure, although some refugee groups, for example, the European Council on Refugees and Exiles, have argued that departure from the UK in these circumstances should not be described as 'voluntary' at all. Where consent to return has been coerced, it is argued, it cannot be said that the person has 'freely chosen' to return so that this practice should be classified as 'mandatory return'.[71] Colm O'Cinneide has observed in this regard that it is 'highly questionable' to justify state inflicted destitution based on failed asylum seekers' choice because, 'this ignores the complex reality of their situation and permits the state to deny any responsibility to protect an extremely vulnerable and dependent group against destitution'.[72]

In the case of *Adam, Limbuela and Tesema*, discussed above, the Article 3 claim was successful because the House of Lords accepted that the government was 'directly responsible' for the destitution of the applicants. However, applying this logic to the experiences of failed asylum seekers who are not in receipt of section 4 'hard case' support is particularly problematic because the courts have generally taken the approach that where *failed* asylum seekers become destitute then it is their own fault since, unlike asylum seekers with pending applications or extant rights of appeal, there is nothing to prevent them leaving the UK; consequently, the state is not 'directly responsible'. We shall return to authority for this disappointing orthodoxy shortly.

---

70 Public Accounts Committee, 'Management of Asylum Applications' HC (2008–2009) 325, 6.

71 See ECRE, *The Return of Asylum Seekers whose Applications have been Rejected in Europe* (ECRE 2005; available at http://www.ecre.org/files/return.pdf, accessed 17 September 2010).

72 C. O'Cinneide, 'A Modest Proposal: Destitution, State Responsibility and the European Convention on Human Rights (2008) *European Human Rights Law Review* 583, 604.

There are, however, a number of possible arguments that might be raised against the orthodoxy. For example, Sweeney has argued that the causal link between the statutory framework and the destitution of failed asylum seekers is not broken by their refusal to leave the UK: rather, he argued, the government remains 'directly responsible', so that Article 3 ECHR is engaged, and the power under paragraph 3, Schedule 3 NIAA 2002 should be exercised in favour of destitute failed asylum seekers.[73] This argument was based on the observation that the successful applicants in *Adam, Limbuela and Tesema* had 'chosen' not to apply for asylum as soon as reasonably practicable, and so the 'choice' exercised by failed asylum seekers should not be regarded as a complete barrier to the engagement of the state's direct responsibility.[74]

It is also arguable that human rights law imposes some duties on the state to protect individuals from their unwise or illogical choices. For example in *Uçar v Turkey*[75] the European Court of Human Rights articulated the protective duty owed to a suicidal or self-harming detainee under Article 2 ECHR. The court held that if the state was aware that a detainee posed a 'real and immediate risk' of suicide, it would be under a positive obligation to do all that could reasonably be expected to prevent that risk from materialising.[76] The detainee's apparent 'choice' to inflict harm upon their own person does not displace the state's responsibility to attempt to prevent the harm.[77]

A further set of arguments that might be made relates to the weakness of the section 4 scheme, described by the Joint Committee on Human Rights as 'inhumane and inefficient', and the government's acquiescence to the fact of mass homelessness amongst failed asylum seekers. As noted above, the Independent Asylum Commission found that in 2007 less than four per cent of failed asylum seekers who were still in the UK received support under the section 4 scheme (9,365 out of 283,500 people).[78] Thus it would seem indisputable that the legislative framework leaves large numbers of people destitute, and that the government must be aware of this. Furthermore, the European Court of Human Rights judgment in *Chahal v UK*,[79] recently reaffirmed in *Saadi v Italy*, makes it clear that suffering of the type covered by Article 3 ECHR can never be justified on wider policy grounds, as 'the prohibition of torture and of inhuman or degrading treatment or

73 J.A. Sweeney, 'The Human Rights of Failed Asylum Seekers in the UK' (2008) *PL* 277 and C. Lewis 'Asylum Support Brief – Part Three: Failed Asylum Seekers' (2006) 156 *NLJ* 1246, 294.

74 Ibid.

75 *Uçar v Turkey* [2006] ECHR 390.

76 Ibid. [86]. The European Court found that in this case the Respondent State had in fact fulfilled its duty.

77 Ibid. [83] *et seq*; *Akdoğdu v Turkey* [2005] ECHR 932 [44] (only available in French); *Tanribilir v Turkey* [2000] ECHR 612 [70–1] (also only available in French).

78 Independent Asylum Commission, Second Report of Conclusions and Recommendations, 'Safe Return' (Independent Asylum Commission, London 2008), 31.

79 *Chahal v UK* (1997) 23 EHRR 413.

punishment is absolute, irrespective of the victim's conduct'.[80] In the light of this principle, it is reasonable to assert that if the statutory framework leads to the fact of mass destitution amongst failed asylum seekers, the observation that such destitution may pursue the policy of deterring unmeritorious applicants from ever seeking to come to the UK is irrelevant.

The UK government has strongly refuted[81] the JCHR's finding that the government 'has indeed been practising a deliberate policy of destitution' of asylum seekers and failed asylum seekers.[82] However, in apparent contradiction of this the Court of Appeal has recently stated that the objective of the exclusions contained in Schedule 3 of the NIAA 2002 can be 'readily inferred' from its content:

> It is to discourage from coming to, remaining in and consuming the resources of the United Kingdom certain classes of person who can reasonably be expected to look to other countries for their livelihood.[83]

The 'discouraging' effect of Schedule 3 is rooted in the threat of street homelessness: that having arrived in the UK, the asylum seeker will not (unless and until an application for asylum has been successfully processed) be allowed an opportunity to establish a home in this country, either in the sense of an adopted homeland or in the sense of obtaining housing as home. As we have seen, in some cases this goes beyond questions of adequacy of housing and home, to the basic denial of shelter.

In such cases it is helpful to bear in mind that in *Adam, Limbuela and Tesema*,[84] Lord Brown noted that an intention to cause street homelessness could 'readily be characterised' as involving 'degrading treatment' and would be enough to engage the direct responsibility of the state.[85] Thus if the government can be taken to know about the mass destitution of failed asylum seekers, resulting from the poor administration of, and tough eligibility criteria for, section 4 support, then

---

80 *Saadi v Italy* (2009) 49 EHRR 30 [127]. The question was whether expulsion of a terrorist suspect to a state where he might suffer torture, inhuman or degrading treatment was justifiable. The full quotation is, 'As the prohibition of torture and of inhuman or degrading treatment or punishment is absolute, irrespective of the victim's conduct [see *Chahal v UK* (1997) 23 EHRR 413, § 79], the nature of the offence allegedly committed by the applicant is therefore irrelevant for the purposes of Article 3 […].'

81 Joint Committee on Human Rights, 'Government Response to the Committee's Tenth Report of this Session: The Treatment of Asylum Seekers', HL (2006–2007) 134; HC (2006–2007) 790, 14.

82 Joint Committee on Human Rights, 'The Treatment of Asylum Seekers' HL (2006–2007) 81-I; HC (2006–2007) 60-I, 110 (emphasis added).

83 *R. (Kimani) v Lambeth London Borough Council* [2003] EWCA Civ 1150 [24] (Lord Phillips MR).

84 *R. v Secretary of State for the Home Department ex parte Adam, Limbuela and Tesema* [2005] UKHL 66; [2006] 1 AC 396.

85 Ibid. [101] (Lord Brown).

it would seem that the government is directly responsible for the deliberately 'discouraging' conditions resulting from the ensuing denial of housing rights amounting to inhuman and degrading treatment. This opens up the possibility for a significant advance under Article 3 in respect of asylum seekers and failed asylum seekers facing street homelessness, particularly since, following *Chahal*, if the statutory framework gives rise to destitution amounting to inhuman and degrading treatment,[86] it cannot be justified or balanced against other policy aims.

The recent High Court decision in *R. on the Application of N v Coventry City Council*[87] has, unfortunately, confirmed that the courts have not yet adopted this reasoning, but appear to be continuing to pursue a 'minimal compliance' approach to their ECHR obligations in respect of housing asylum seekers. Mr Garnham QC (sitting as a deputy High Court judge) examined whether the Coventry City Council's cessation of section 21(1)(a) NAA 1948 support to an HIV-positive failed asylum seeker suffering from tuberculosis, TB meningitis, syphilis and cognitive disturbance would trigger the human rights safeguard of paragraph 3, Schedule 3 of the NIAA 2002. The judgment found that the cessation of local authority support would not be a breach of the ECHR:

> because it would be open to the claimant to return to his home country of South Africa…If he chooses to stay in the United Kingdom, the degradation he may suffer is a consequence of that decision, not the cessation of Coventry's support.[88]

The Article 3 argument is an important element of the overall approach to questions of shelter, housing and home for asylum seekers. It is a potentially powerful argument since, as the decision in *Chahal* has indicated, as an absolute right it is not subject to qualification, so that the court cannot justify an interference with Article 3 rights based on the balance of the individual's right against other policy aims. On the other hand, the Article 3 right is inherently limited in that it is likely to apply only in the most extreme cases of destitution, where a failed asylum seeker is facing street homelessness. As such, it goes to lack of shelter, rather than questions of the adequacy of housing or the home experience. In addition, as the discussion in this section has demonstrated, to date the UK courts have adopted a minimal compliance approach which undermines the applicability of Article 3 even in cases of extreme destitution.

Nevertheless, and despite having not yet been taken on board by the judiciary, the Article 3 approach outlined here offers the strongest compliance or legal enforcement based argument in this context. The following sections show that while the International Covenant on Economic Social and Cultural Rights

86 By prohibiting work, denying support, and failing to arrange genuinely voluntary departure or facilitate efficient forced removals.

87 [2008] EWHC 2786 (Admin).

88 Ibid. [51].

(ICESCR) sets out a right to housing, and Article 8 of the European Convention on Human Rights contains the right to respect for home, the legal frameworks for the enforcement of these rights are structurally weaker than Article 3 so far as any compliance-based approach is concerned.

(9) The ICESCR Argument: the Right to Housing

The right to housing in international law has its origins in Article 25(1) of the 1948 Universal Declaration of Human Rights. The 1966 International Covenant on Economic, Social, and Cultural Rights (ICESCR) is now the most significant international human rights law applicable in this field. Under Article 2(2) ICESCR States Parties agree to guarantee the rights contained within without discrimination on, amongst other grounds, 'national and social origin'. Thus, under this Covenant, states must guarantee the rights of non-nationals such as refugees and asylum seekers. Article 11 of the ICESCR requires that states recognise:

> the right of everyone to an adequate standard of living for himself and his family, including adequate food, clothing and housing, and to the continuous improvement of living conditions

This article is included within the rights owed to 'aliens generally' under Article 21 of the 1951 UN Refugee Convention, and has been used to ensure that refugee accommodation is, for example, habitable and not impracticably remote.[89]

The weakness of housing rights for refugees and asylum seekers derived from the ICESCR lies within the nature of the obligation that the Covenant places upon states. The notion of economic, social and cultural rights is controversial in some quarters because they may be understood as insufficiently precise in scope and requiring an unrealistic amount of state expenditure.[90] In the light of this, under Article 2(1) ICESCR each State Party undertakes 'to take steps…to the maximum of its available resources…with a view to achieving progressively the full realisation of the rights recognised…'

The UN Committee on Economic, Social and Cultural Rights has expressed its view of the obligations arising under the Covenant in its 'General Comment No. 3: The Nature of States Parties Obligations'.[91] It has argued that under Article 2(1) ICESCR States Parties are under an immediate duty to take steps to secure the

89 See J.C. Hathaway, *The Rights of Refugees Under International Law* (Cambridge University Press, Cambridge 2005), 826, discussing UN Committee on Economic, Social and Cultural Rights, 'General Comment No. 4', 'The Right to Adequate Housing (Art.11 (1))' (1991) UN Doc HRI/GEN/1/Rev.7.

90 See generally, H. Steiner, P. Alston and J. Goodman, *International Human Rights in Context* (3rd edn Oxford University Press, Oxford 2008), 263 *et seq*.

91 UN Doc E/1991/23.

rights contained in the Covenant,[92] unless they can demonstrate that they do not have the resources to comply with even a 'minimum core obligation'.[93] Moreover, in carrying out any actions relative to the right to housing, states are bound by the overarching principle of non-discrimination.[94]

It has discussed the issue of housing specifically in its 'General Comment No. 4: The Right to Adequate Housing', which has taken a broad interpretation of Article 11 ICESCR so that it encompasses not merely the provision of shelter, but 'the right to live somewhere in security, peace and dignity.'[95] The content of the right to housing, in respect of both practical issues such as location and quality, and in relation to the human need to establish a home, has been extensively scrutinised by Kenna,[96] who has emphasised the inter-relationships between shelter, housing and home.[97]

In addition to its inherent value, it has also been recognised that the 'right to housing' under ICESCR has instrumental value, since it facilitates the protection of other rights. As the discussion in the opening section of this chapter has highlighted, the UN Committee on Economic, Social and Cultural Rights has emphasised the importance of viewing housing within the broader framework of human rights, as 'integrally linked to other human rights',[98] and as indivisible and interdependent with civil and political rights.[99] The potential for adopting a legal strategy which relates the right to housing – with all the barriers to enforcement as a positive obligation that economic, social and cultural rights carry – to civil and political rights – inherently more enforceable as 'absolute rights' – must lie in the argument that housing and home can function as a gateway to civil and political rights.

This proposition can be viewed as echoing Hegel's argument in *Elements of the Philosophy of Right*,[100] where the institution of private property was justified on the basis that it provided a gateway to the property owner's engagement in civil society.[101] In fact, Hegel claimed that the function of private property as a means

---

92 Ibid. [2].

93 Ibid. [10].

94 Ibid. [1].

95 See S. Breau, 'The International Law Rights to Home and Homeland' in this volume.

96 P. Kenna, 'Globalization and Housing Rights' (2008) 15 *Indiana Journal of Global Legal Studies* 397.

97 See P. Kenna, 'Can International Housing Rights Based on Public International Law Really Impact on Contemporary Housing Systems?' in this volume.

98 See UN Committee on Economic, Social and Cultural Rights, 'General Comment No. 4', 'The Right to Adequate Housing (Art.11 (1))' (1991) UN Doc HRI/GEN/1/Rev.7.

99 See UNGA Res 32/130 (16 December 1977) UN Doc A/Res/32/130.

100 G.W.F. Hegel, *Elements of the Philosophy of Right* A.W. Wood (ed.), H.B. Nisbet (trans.) (Cambridge University Press, Cambridge 1991) 73–102.

101 Hegel argued that in order for human beings to live fully developed, conscious lives, it was necessary that they should be capable of acquiring property.

of establishing personhood took precedence over the function of private property as a means of satisfying a person's material needs, since property was fundamental to the existence of the *person*: thus, Hegel asserted that '[n]ot until he has property does the person exist as Reason.'[102] For Hegel, the essential basis of property for the existence of the *person* was derived from the function of private property as a medium through which individuals could exhibit their will. The approach is also reflected in Radin's theory of 'property for personhood', which posited that 'that to achieve proper self-development – to be a *person* – an individual needs some control over resources in the external environment.'[103] A crucial further step for Hegelian philosophy, however, was the idea that people needed to be made secure in their control over parcels of the material world in order to be capable of developing as persons within the wider material and social world, and so to function within civil society. Thus:

> That all human beings should have their livelihood to meet their needs is, on the one hand, a moral *wish*; and when it is expressed in this indeterminate manner, it is indeed well intentioned, but like everything that is merely well intentioned, it has no objective being. On the other hand, a livelihood is something other than *possession* and belongs to another sphere, that of civil society.[104]

While Hegel was primarily concerned with property *ownership*, the analogy to the opportunity to establish housing as home, so enabling the asylum seeker to acquire some degree of control over their environment in a context in which they have been stripped of autonomy and their identity has been disrupted is not difficult to make.

The possibility of applying Hegel's comments concerning *property ownership* more broadly is recognised by Ryan when he noted that:

> the point of there being property rights is to be seen in a variety of ways in which people anchor themselves and their purposes in the world. There is no suggestion that each and every person can or should have certain sorts of property in order to be at home in the world…No particular property rights seem essential – though rights certainly are.[105]

---

102 G.W.F. Hegel, *Elements of the Philosophy of Right* A.W. Wood (ed.), H.B. Nisbet (trans.) (Cambridge University Press, Cambridge 1991) 73 (s. 41).

103 See M.J. Radin, 'Property and Personhood' [1982] 34 *Stanford Law Review* 957.

104 G.W.F. Hegel, *Elements of the Philosophy of Right* A.W. Wood (ed.), H.B. Nisbet (trans.) (Cambridge University Press, Cambridge 1991) 80 (s. 49).

105 See G.W.F. Hegel, *Elements of the Philosophy of Right* A.W. Wood (ed.), H.B. Nisbet (trans.) (Cambridge University Press, Cambridge 1991) (s. 33); A. Ryan, *Property and Political Theory* (Blackwell, Oxford 1984), 124.

Thus, in Radin's terminology, 'object-relations' is identified as 'the first step on [the] road from abstract autonomy to full development of the individual in the context of the family and the state.'[106] This development, in turn, can be seen as a necessary precursor to the individual's ability to exercise civil and political rights, so enabling the position of the right to housing as a gateway right to civil and political rights to be delineated. This is also reflected in the proposition that: '[n]ot being able to call any place "home" is implicitly considered to be a handicap for being a complete human being.'[107] The consequence of various legal frameworks which exclude asylum seekers from rights to secure shelter, housing and home, can thus be seen to have consequences beyond housing *per se*, which spill over into exclusion from civil and political life, as 'the refugee is not simply excluded from the law in an indifferent manner but rather abandoned by it.'[108]

(10) Article 8, ECHR: the Right to Respect for Home

The idea of an enforceable 'right to respect for home' is similarly not one which sits easily within English law. Historically, references to respect for home have tended to revolve around the idea of *privacy* at home, and particularly with the extent to which the state can lawfully impinge upon a citizen's private dwelling.[109] While Article 8(1) of the European Convention on Human Rights states that 'Everyone shall have the right to respect for his private and family life, his home and his correspondence', the reference to 'respect for home' in this paragraph is clearly embedded in the overall context of Article 8. For example, in *London Borough of Harrow v Qazi*,[110] the first landmark decision of the House of Lords on the right to respect for home, Lord Hope noted that: '[m]ost international human rights instruments recognise a right to privacy. That is the concept which underlies Article 8 of the Convention.'[111] Thus, the references in Article 8 to the right to respect for family life, for home and for correspondence are often viewed conjunctively, as aspects of the right to private life,[112] and the right to respect for

---

106 M.J. Radin, 'Property and Personhood' [1982] 34 *Stanford Law Review* 957, 45.

107 H. van der Horst, 'Living in a Reception Centre: the Search for Home in an Institutional Setting' (2004) 21 *Housing, Theory and Society* 36.

108 B. Diken, 'From Refugee Camps to Gated Communities: Biopolitics and the End of the City' (2004) 8 *Citizenship Studies* 89.

109 *Entick v Carrington* (1765)19 St Tr 1030; *Malone v Commissioner of Police for the Metropolis (No 2)* [1979] Ch 344.

110 [2003] UKHL 43.

111 Ibid. [49].

112 Van Dijk and van Hoof have noted that: '[a]s a collection noun designating the rights involved in Article 8, the 'right to privacy' is often used nowadays.'; P. van Dijk and G.J.H. van Hoof, *Theory and Practice of the European Convention on Human Rights* (3rd edn Kluwer, The Hague 1998) 489 [8.1].

home in Article 8 has tended to be narrowly interpreted as meaning the right to *privacy* from the state's gaze within one's home.[113]

A first important point of note in relation to Article 8 of the Convention is that it is directed at protecting citizens against interferences with their established home; Article 8 does *not* provide for a *right to a home*. This was clearly established shortly after the Convention was adopted, in the decision of the European Commission on Human Rights in *X v Germany*.[114] The Commission, which ruled on the admissibility of claims brought under the Convention, rejected the argument that Article 8(1) imposed a duty on the state to provide citizens with a home.[115] Indeed, in several subsequent cases, the European Court of Human Rights has repeatedly confirmed that Article 8 does not give the right to be provided with a home, nor does it give a right to have one's housing problem solved by the state.[116] Rather, Article 8 is concerned with protecting citizens against interferences with their *existing* homes. When applying this to the case of asylum seekers, the limitations are clear: for those without existing homes, there is a fundamental difficulty in identifying the node of enforceability. Indeed, the explicit policy of the UK government to prevent asylum seekers from establishing homes might be seen to exclude any application of Article 8.

However, even in such cases where the asylum seeker has secured (temporary) accommodation, the strength of Article 8 in enabling that position to be defended is – so far as enforceable rights are concerned – likely to be weak. Any entitlement which an occupier might have to respect for home under Article 8 is qualified, as even when an interference with an Article 8 right has been established, that interference may be justified under Article 8(2), if it can be shown to be:

> in accordance with law and necessary in a democratic society in the interests of national security, public safety or the economic well-being of the country, for the prevention of disorder or crime, for the protection of health or morals, or for the protection of the rights and freedoms of others.

113 For example, work to develop more robust criminal and civil responses to domestic violence within the home in England had to overcome the additional challenges associated with policing offences with the private space of the home; see for example S.S.M. Edwards, *Policing 'Domestic' Violence: Women, the Law and the State* (Sage, London 1989).

114 (1956)1 Yearbook 202.

115 The Commission held that the right to an adequate standard of living and the right to suitable accommodation were not in principle among the rights and freedoms safeguarded by the Convention. See, for example, A.H. Robertson (ed.), *Privacy and Human Rights* (Manchester University Press, Manchester 1973) [79].

116 *Chapman v United Kingdom* (2001)33 EHRR 399, 427 [99]; *Marzari v Italy* (1999)28 EHRR CD 175, 179; *O'Rourke v United Kingdom* (26 June 2001, Application No 39022/97).

In a series of recent cases,[117] the House of Lords has sought to set the bar for minimal compliance with Article 8 in relation to UK nationals so that it would not be necessary to consider whether any interference was justified where the occupier had no contractual or proprietary right to remain in occupation;[118] or so that any such interference could be presumed to be justified where Parliament had already struck a balance between the competing interests.[119] More recently, in *Doherty v Birmingham City Council*,[120] the House of Lords allowed for the possibility of some review of the *process* by which a local authority made a decision to evict, although the procedural nature of this review is emphasised by the decision to allow this through a (HRA-informed) judicial review process, rather than a 'proportionality review', such as that expected by the European Court of Human Rights in discussing the right to respect for home in *Connors v UK*,[121] and *McCann v UK*.[122]

Thus, while the decision in *Doherty* has extended the applicability of Article 8 to eviction cases by allowing for a judicial review process which can scrutinise the reasons behind the local authority's decision to evict, the applicability of this article to asylum seekers is limited in two key respects. Firstly, as a qualified right, any assertion of the right to respect for home is subject to balance against competing policy aims which, in the case of failed asylum seekers, have been very clearly articulated in the shape of the policy of return. However, beyond this, it is also significant that as a qualified right, the state is entitled in considering claims under Article 8 to make a distinction between citizens and non-citizens, so that even the weakly enforceable rights available to UK citizens against eviction can be denied to asylum seekers.

(11) Conclusion: Human Rights as Policy Goals, not Legal 'Minima'

The manipulation of (failed) asylum seekers' vulnerable grasp on 'home' connections has led us to explore the quality and location of asylum accommodation, and policies aimed at restricting access to such accommodation and support as they have been mediated through the lens of legal interpretation. However, the existing legal tools for giving effect to home interests are crude, and often ineffective, and it is therefore a bare, atrophied vision of home that is glimpsed through them. The

117 *London Borough of Harrow v Qazi* [2003] UKHL 43; *London Borough of Lambeth v Kay; Leeds City Council v Price* (*Kay & Price*) [2006] UKHL 10; and *Doherty v Birmingham City Council* [2008] UKHL 57.

118 *London Borough of Harrow v Qazi* [2003] UKHL 43.

119 *London Borough of Lambeth v Kay; Leeds City Council v Price* (*Kay & Price*) [2006] UKHL 10.

120 *Doherty v Birmingham City Council* [2008] UKHL 57.

121 Application No 66746; judgment, 27 May 2004.

122 Application No 19909/04; judgment, 13 May 2008.

right to housing is inherently weak as a socio-economic right, and the English courts have applied a restrictive interpretation to the (qualified) right to respect for home in Article 8 ECHR. Even the protection afforded by Article 3 ECHR in the *Limbuela* case hinged upon applicants being able to show that they their situation exposed them to an 'imminent prospect' of inhuman and degrading conditions,[123] which is a desperate and fearful state and, thus, assistance at this stage comes too late and too infrequently to constitute a reliable legal recourse. Yet, despite the apparent weakness of arguments that rely on the enforcement of strict legal rights under human rights law to secure housing and home for asylum seekers, we would argue that the notion of home as a core element of being human, and thus of human rights, can still help us to rework our understanding of (failed) asylum seekers' destitution, and to support legislative interventions that are not dependent on the generosity of sympathetic and activist judges to mitigate its worst effects.

There is some evidence that an approach to asylum seekers that recognises the importance of home is realistic. For example the obsession with failed or late applying asylum seekers' 'choice' to be homeless is not mirrored within domestic housing policy. Part 7 of the Housing Act 1996 recognises a category of person who is 'intentionally homeless' but is also 'in priority need', and who must be provided temporary accommodation for such a period as would given them a reasonable opportunity to find accommodation for themselves. For this category of person, it would seem that at a policy level (i.e. rather than by compulsion from Article 3 ECHR) it has been deemed appropriate that local authorities must provide support, notwithstanding the 'choice' of the applicant.

A second set of examples that demonstrate how respect for 'home' might influence the legislative process can be seen in recent debates about the treatment of failed asylum seekers. During the parliamentary debates on the UK Borders Act 2007, to which reference was made briefly above, an alliance of refugee organisations lobbied in favour of an amendment which would have allowed failed asylum seekers access to support and accommodation until they left the UK or were removed. The amendment was opposed by both the government and the opposition, and it was rejected.[124] A striking feature of the debates was that the issue of human rights, let alone the importance of 'home' to being human, was largely absent from the discussions.[125]

Similar legislative suggestions have, however, been put forward in relation to the proposals of the European Commission for reforms to the Common European Asylum System, and in relation to which the connection to human rights has

123 *R. v Secretary of State for the Home Department ex parte Adam, Limbuela and Tesema* [2005] UKHL 66; [2006] 1 AC 396.

124 The passage of the Act, and the arguments about this amendment are covered in more detail in J.A. Sweeney, 'The Human Rights of Failed Asylum Seekers in the UK' (2008) *PL* 277 and C. Lewis 'Asylum Support Brief – Part Three: Failed Asylum Seekers' (2006) 156 *NLJ* 1246, 277 *et seq.*

125 Ibid., 280.

been more explicit (although, as we shall see, the UK Home Office remains rather sceptical). The European Union is in the process of reforming its Common European Asylum System. In European parlance, issues such the housing rights of asylum seekers would be termed as involving their 'material reception conditions'. One of the key legislative proposals is to recast the current Reception Directive,[126] the legal instrument that specifies minimum levels of treatment for people claiming asylum in the EU.

The thinking of the UK Home Office under the outgoing Labour government was indicated in the form of an Explanatory Memorandum dated 23 December 2008, and signed by Phil Woolas, then Minister of State for Borders and Immigration.[127] The general theme of the memorandum is that many of the proposals reflect existing practice in the UK, and are therefore not necessary. This applies, for example, to the proposal to unify the procedure for considering 'pure' asylum claims and claims for subsidiary protection (e.g. fears of more general human rights abuses falling short of the refugee definition) in a single process, which the UK already does.[128] It also applies to proposals to enhance protection for detained people[129] and people with special needs,[130] and to improve standards of living for asylum seekers.[131] The Home Office has, however, expressed concern over the proposal to allow asylum seekers to gain access to the labour market after they have been in the UK for six months.[132]

The approach to human rights is, however, rather telling. In an early section of memorandum headed 'legal and procedural issues' the memorandum presents an assessment of the compatibility of the European Commission proposals with human rights norms, and concludes that the proposals respect fundamental rights.[133] En route to this conclusion the memorandum notes that the European Commission proposals state that to ensure higher and more equal standards of reception will have 'an overall strong positive impact from a fundamental rights point of view'.[134] The memorandum, however, continues by stating that, '[W]e [the Home Office] believe that these proposals would grant entitlements that go substantially beyond *the minima guaranteed by those rights*'.[135]

126 Council Directive (EC) 2003/9 laying down minimum standards for the reception of asylum seekers [2003] OJ L31/18; the reform proposals are set out in Commission (EC), 'Proposal for a Directive of the European Parliament and of Council Laying Down Minimum Standards for the Reception of Asylum Seekers' COM (2008) 815 final, 3 December 2008.

127 Explanatory Memorandum on file with the authors.

128 Ibid. [14].

129 Ibid. [15–17].

130 Ibid. [23–27].

131 Ibid. [21–22].

132 Ibid. [18–20].

133 Ibid. [8].

134 Ibid.

135 Ibid., emphasis added.

When this general approach is coupled with the previously noted concerns about improving the standard of living for asylum seekers and their access to the labour market, it would seem to have led to the avoidance of human rights thinking as a mobilising force for responding to double displacement on the part of the Home Office. The treatment of human rights in the memorandum implies, as the heading also suggests, that human rights law constitutes a legal and procedural hurdle to be overcome, rather than human rights norms acting as a goal or aspiration to be progressively realised. Yet this is not the only way to view the role of human rights thinking in the legislative process. Indeed the Committee of the Regions of the European Union issued its own formal Opinion on Commission Proposals, which adopted a human rights oriented approach and went further in its attempts to avoid double displacement, with proposals on failed asylum seekers that can be described as particularly humane.

The Committee of the Regions was established in 1994, following the Maastricht Treaty of 1992, to give a voice to sub-national bodies in the European legislative process. It is by no means equal in its influence to the core 'institutional triangle' of the European Commission, Council and Parliament, but its views are sought on topics that concern its membership. It is presently comprised of 344 members, who are all local politicians across the 27 member states of the EU.[136] Since local authorities are closely involved in the reception of asylum seekers and the integration of refugees, the Opinion of the Committee of Regions is particularly significant in this context.

At its 81st Plenary Session on 7 October 2009, the Committee of the Regions voted to adopt its Opinion on the CEAS reforms.[137] In it, the Committee broadly welcomed the Commission's proposals, including those relating to access to the labour market,[138] but then, taking inspiration from Article 3 ECHR,[139] proposed an amendment to the recast Reception Directive that would greatly enhance the situation of failed asylum seekers. The proposal merits quotation in full:

> Article 20(6). Member States shall not withdraw or reduce material reception conditions from refused applicants for international protection until plans for their removal or voluntary return are in place.
>
> Article 20(7). Forced destitution, or the threat of it, shall never be used in order to coerce refused applicants to return to their state of origin.

---

136 See www.coe.europa.eu, accessed 6 January 2010.

137 Committee of the Regions (EU), 'Opinion of the Committee of the Regions on The Future of the Common European Asylum System II' (Opinion) CdR (09) 90 final, 5–7 October 2009. James A. Sweeney acted as expert advisor to the Committee of the Regions during this process.

138 The Committee noted that access after six months is a controversial proposal for some member states, but that it could benefit both the asylum seeker and the member state: ibid. [18].

139 The rationale is explained in the text accompanying the proposed amendment.

Article 20(8). Refusal of primary healthcare, or the threat of such, shall never be used in order to coerce refused applicants to return to their state of origin.

These clear statements (which still acknowledge that failed asylum seekers must nevertheless depart the state in which they claimed asylum) would, if they were incorporated in the Directive, do much to ameliorate the situation of the *people* who are labelled 'failed asylum seekers'. It would also recognise that these people, whether they have a legal right to remain in the host state or not, still possess human rights.

Most importantly, and as argued in the first part of this paper, these proposals recognise that protection of 'home' is not a second order human right, deserving of protection only when its denial amounts to inhuman and degrading treatment within Article 3 ECHR, but it is, rather, a crucial element of the distinctively human experience. While there is little indication at present that this type of argument is likely to be recognised by the UK courts as giving rise to any enforceable right on the part of the asylum seeker, it is appropriate to remember that the 'minimal compliance' approach (which we have also recognised in relation to Article 3) is not the only route to realising human rights norms within UK law. As a matter of international human rights law, and in conformance with the principle of subsidiarity underpinning the ECHR, it is permissible for the UK to go further than the strict requirements of the ECHR, one element of which is reflected in Article 53 where it is stated that: 'Nothing in [the] Convention shall be construed as limiting or derogating from any of the human rights and fundamental freedoms which may be ensured under the laws of any High Contracting Party or under any other agreement to which it is a Party.' The logical corollary of this provision is that a Contracting Party is free to choose a non-minimalist approach to the protection of human rights,[140] rooted not in the relatively weak enforceability of the right to housing, but in a wish to develop good practice based on human rights norms.

To suggest that such development should be curtailed because it goes beyond the international minima is to fundamentally misunderstand the relationship between human rights norms at large and the provisions of international human rights treaties. Morality, including human rights norms, begins with richness and complexity, rooted in particular societies. It is only in times of stress that complex moral positions need to be reduced to universally identifiable statements such as 'No one shall be subjected to torture or to inhuman or degrading treatment or punishment.' Such universal principles are human rights norms at their most intense, but they derive from, rather than lead to, human rights norms expressed

140 Herbert Petzold noted this with respect to the pre-Protocol 11 Convention: 'The Convention and the Principle of Subsidiarity' in R. St J. Macdonald, F. Matscher, and H. Petzold (eds), *The European System for the Protection of Human Rights* (Martinus Nijhof, Dordrecht 1993), 49–59.

by particular societies.[141] Thus, the idea of the right to housing as home, which has been seen to resonate strongly with experiential evidence relating to asylum seekers, can be seen to have considerable critical potential. Human rights norms can help inculcate political willingness to act responsibly in contentious areas such as the relationship between immigration and social housing.

To achieve this potential, however, the discourse on 'home' must shift from a focus on the judicial enforceability of existing human rights norms via the circuitous routes detailed above, to the applicability of human rights norms in the formulation of legislative solutions to the needs of asylum seekers, who are at risk of double displacement. Human rights, including home rights, should not be seen as legal minima, but rather as policy goals that legislation should seek to achieve.

141 On this point see J.A. Sweeney, 'Margins of Appreciation: Cultural Relativity and the European Court of Human Rights in the Post-Cold War Era' (2005) 54 *ICLQ* 459, 470, discussing M. Walzer, *Thick and Thin: Moral Argument at Home and Abroad* (University of Notre Dame Press, Notre Dame 1994).

Chapter 6
Can International Housing Rights Based on Public International Law Really Impact on Contemporary Housing Systems?

Padraic Kenna

(1) Introduction

The concept of home advances a new basis for evaluating housing rights, emphasising their human and personal benefits. Housing rights address, at a national, regional and global level, displacement and dispossession, as well as access to home for all. These rights are forging a new discourse and jurisprudence across the world, largely based on public international law instruments. However, the legal liberalist approach and framework of such housing rights discourse needs to engage with housing systems at the *macro*, *meso* and *micro* levels. There is a particular and urgent challenge in addressing the structural and institutional elements of housing systems, such as housing finance, infrastructure, ownership and exchange of housing and regulation of housing systems and sub-systems. Ultimately, this could ensure that the contemporary revival of global housing finance regulation can incorporate a housing rights perspective.

(2) The Concept of Home

The concept of home is widely viewed as central to housing and housing rights – a critical element of the basic physiological needs of food, clothing and shelter, established by Maslow, and in contemporary societies often relating to the safety, love/belonging, esteem and self-actualisation needs.[1] Housing and home are connected to health, child development, poverty and opportunity in general. The emotional and symbolic significance of housing and home relate to the sense

---

1 See A.H. Maslow, 'Theory of Human Motivation'. Originally published in *Psychological Review* (1943) 50 370–96. See also A.B. Trigg, 'Deriving the Engel Curve: Pierre Bourdieu and the Social Critique of Maslow's Hierarchy of Needs' (2004) 62 (3) *Review of Social Economy* 393, 406.

of permanence and security, as well as fixing a person's place in society and community.[2]

Of course, the idea of house is usually central in the legal treatment of home, but there is also a further set of factors which distinguishes the home from a physical structure providing shelter. Fox suggests that home needs to be conceptualised as house plus an 'x factor'. This 'x factor' represents the social, psychological, and cultural values which a physical structure acquires through use as a home.[3] Thus, 'home' can be seen as a physical structure, a territory implying security, control and rootedness, as identity, and as a social and cultural phenomenon or a base for relationships. It also acts as a geographical space from where a person or household can access other services, and amenities.

In a valuable and innovative examination of the way the home is treated in English common law, Fox finds that it variously encompasses a physical space, an object of investment and ownership, a social and cultural unit, a 'family home', a 'women's place', a place for children and a human right.[4] While housing usually involves the provision of a physical structure, 'home' involves housing plus the experiential elements of home. These include: as a valued territory, as a signifier and constituent of self and social identity, as a part of the social and cultural environment associated with a person's way of life and participation in society and as a base for family and children. Indeed, the concept of home has been widely researched in many disciplines, and there is hardly a more emotionally loaded word, since it epitomises situations of family, affection, love and other human experiences.

The women's or feminist perspective on home is clearly absent from the English common-law contemporary conceptual framework, and indeed, most legal systems across the world. The home has been correlated with a site of hierarchical relations and a place of oppression for women, a base of domestic violence, a forced workplace for cooking cleaning, nurturing and childrearing, inherently denying women access to wider societal participation.[5]

For some people, the notion of home as involving only a physical structure carries little or no significance. For nomads, children, some people with disabilities, many older people and others, the need and expectation for support, care, communal assistance and trusting relationships usually surpasses the requirements of a distinct physical location. Unless there are proper safeguards in place, there

2 See R.G. Bratt, M.E. Stone and C. Hartman, *A Right to Housing; Foundation for a New Social Agenda* (Temple University Press, Philadelphia 2006).

3 L. Fox, 'The Meaning of Home: A Chimerical Concept or a Legal Challenge?' (2002) 29(4) *Journal of Law and Society* 580.

4 L. Fox, *Conceptualising Home: Theories, Laws and Policies* (Hart, Oxford 2007).

5 See for example, M. Eagleton (ed.) *A Concise Companion to Feminist Theory* (Blackwell, Oxford 2003); M.L. Adams, 'There's No Place Like Home: On the Place of Identity in Feminist Politics' (1989) 31(22) *Feminist Review* 33.

is a danger that even the most well-intended homes provided by organisations can become a 'facility' rather than a 'real home.'[6]

At another level, and drawing on the definitional shift in the concept in the US over the past 100 years, Retsinas traces the different but changing American image of home. Early immigrants to America saw home as an anchor in a safe harbour. The definition of home was more a state of mind rather than a physical structure. Retsinas decribes the US and developed states phenomenon where the home has become a vehicle for enforced savings, a hedge against inflation and in more recent times a fungible investment, only to return to the 'home as anchor', in the current turbulent economic times. However, Retsinas also highlights the huge disparity in this concept between rich and poor in the US.

Poor-to-middle-class Americans rarely owned, much less hoped to own, such homes. They could not afford them – banks wrote five-year loans and demanded 50 per cent down payments. The wealthy owned mansions, but a peripatetic class that summered in Newport, Rhode Island, wintered in Manhattan and toured Europe in between did not want anchors. Ironically, while replete with a number of houses the privileged of that era were 'home-less'.[7]

Contemporary common law, with its feudal and legal liberalist roots has been unable to relate to the variety of relations people have with home, which are complex and changing, positive and negative. Fox points out that:

> Home provides the backdrop for our lives, and is often the scene or the subject of legal disputes...while the authenticity of home as a social, psychological, cultural and emotional phenomenon has been recognised in other disciplines, it has not penetrated the legal domain, where the proposition that home can encapsulate meanings beyond the physical structure of the house, or the capital value it represents, continues to present conceptual difficulties.[8]

(3) Displacement

Displacement from home constitutes a particular violation of housing rights. Displacement means compelling a person to leave their usual place of home, country etc, and possibly their replacement by others. Many are displaced within

---

6 M. Kendrick 'The Choice between a Real Home and a Program' (1993) 2 *Progress* 1. The Commonwealth of Massachusetts, Department of Mental Retardation, sets out 14 points for consumers, families and staff striving towards building a proper and rich sense of 'home' for people with disabilities. The oppressive institutionalisation of people with disabilities probably represents the greatest violations of housing rights today.

7 N.P. Retsinas, 'Definitional Shifts in a Place Called Home' (November/December 2008) *Urban Land*.

8 L. Fox, *Conceptualising Home: Theories, Laws and Policies* (Hart, Oxford 2007).

their own countries, and are known as internally displaced persons (IDPs), estimated to number over 35 million people.

The UN *Guiding Principles on Internal Displacement* points out that IDPs or groups of persons who have been forced or obliged to flee or to leave their homes or places of habitual residence, in particular as a result of or in order to avoid the effects of armed conflict, situations of generalised violence, violations of human rights or natural or human-made disasters, and who have not crossed an internationally recognised state border.[9]

Of course, the reasons behind such compulsion can be economic, with survival as the imperative.[10] The term 'forced migrant', or internally displaced person, distinguishes this group of people from others who move across state borders, such as refugees.[11] A refugee is defined in the Geneva Convention as a person who owing to well-founded fear of being persecuted for reasons of race, religion, nationality, membership of a particular social group or political opinion is outside the country of his nationality and is unable, or owing to such fear, is unwilling to avail himself of the protection of that country.[12]

9 'Guiding Principles on Internal Displacement' (11 February 1998) UN Doc E/CN.4/1998/53/Add.2.

10 *The UNDP Human Development Report 2009* points out that there are some 741 million internal migrants and 124 million international migrants, with migration within Asia accounting for nearly 20 per cent of all migration.

11 There are an estimated 10.4 million refugees and as many as 25 million uprooted civilians in their own countries, so-called internally displaced persons. See UNHCR: The U.N. Refugee Agency, http://www.unhcr.ch/ (accessed 3 April 2009). See also Centre on Housing Rights and Evictions, *Forced Evictions in Bangladesh* (COHRE, Geneva 2001); *Housing and Property Restitution for Refugees and Internally Displaced Persons* (COHRE, Geneva 2002); *Violence – the Impact of Forced Evictions on Women in Palestine, India and Nigeria, Forced Evictions – Violations of Human Rights* (COHRE, Geneva 2003).

12 The UN Convention Relating to the Status of Refugees (adopted 28 July 1951, entered into force 22 April 1954) 189 UNTS 137 defines a refugee as a person who 'owing to well-founded fear of being persecuted for reasons of race, religion, nationality, membership of a particular social group or political opinion, is outside the country of his nationality and is unable, or owing to such fear, is unwilling to avail himself of the protection of that country; or who, not having a nationality and being outside the country of his former habitual residence as a result of such events, is unable or, owing to such fear, is unwilling to return to it'. See http://www.unhchr.ch/html/menu3/b/o_c_ref.htm accessed 21 June 2009). This definition created problems for America in the aftermath of the Katrina hurricane when many thousands of black people, displaced and abandoned outside the State of Louisiana and afraid to return, were described as refugees. However, President Bush responded by saying

'The people we're talking about are not refugees – They are Americans, and they need the help and love and compassion of our fellow citizens.' See Associated Press (7 September 2005) http://www.msnbc.msn.com/id/9232071/ (accessed 21 June 2009).

Displacement from home can take many forms: from the dramatic and media-exposed flight of residents of New Orleans in the face of Hurricane Katrina,[13] to the less publicised homelessness of Bangladeshi flooded homes, displaced persons in Palestine, Zimbabwe and Darfur, to the estimated three million silent refugees of Pakistan. Migrants forced to abandon homes for reasons of fear or survival have become a global phenomenon. At local levels, displacement of minorities, such as ethnic groups being displaced from their home,[14] women fleeing domestic violence, illegal evictions, people with disabilities being forcibly displaced to institutions and perpetual displacement through segregated housing, or indeed, lack of access to housing, all involve a denial of housing rights.

The case of *Moldovan v. Romania* in 2005, describes a violent displacement from home in Europe:

> As the fire engulfed the house, the brothers tried to flee but were caught by the mob who beat and kicked them with vineyard stakes and clubs. The two brothers died later that evening. Mircea Zoltan remained in the house, where he died in the fire. It appears that the police officers present did nothing to stop these attacks. The applicants alleged that, on the contrary, the police also called for and allowed the destruction of all Roma property in Hădăreni…[15]
>
> The applicants submitted that, in general, following the events of September 1993, they had been forced to live in hen-houses, pigsties, windowless cellars or extremely cold and deplorable conditions: 16 people in one room with no heating; seven people in one room with a mud floor; families sleeping on mud or concrete floors without adequate clothing, heat or blankets; 15 people in a summer kitchen with a concrete floor (Melenuţa, Moldova), etc. These conditions had lasted for several years and, in some cases, continue to the present day.[16]

Globalisation is also accelerating the movement of people across regions, states and continents and much of this could be described as displacement. Of course, some movements of people involve voluntary action, and are not necessarily a negative experience.[17] However, Stuart Hall views contemporary enforced migration as the

---

13 Some 200,000 people were displaced and evacuated from New Orleans to distant, unfamiliar regions without housing assistance, or the means to return to their communities or reunite with their families. See J.K. Pierre and G.S. Stephenson, 'After Katrina: A Critical Look at FEMA's Failure to provide Housing for Victims of Natural Disasters' (2008) 68 (2) *Louisiana Law Review* 443, 495.

14 See *Moldovan v. Romania* (App nos. 41138/98 and 64320/01) Judgment No. 2. 12 July 2005.

15 Ibid. para. 18.

16 Ibid. para. 69.

17 See P. Kenna, 'Globalisation and Housing Rights' (2008) 15(2) *Indiana Journal of Global Legal Studies* 397,409.

joker in the globalisation pack and describes the experience of some contemporary migrants:

> Seeking by whatever means – legal or illegal – to escape the consequences of globalization and the new world order, they move along uncharted routes, secrete themselves in the most inhospitable interstices, mortgage their worldly goods to the human traffickers, seal life-threatening contracts with gang-masters and pimps, and exploit their lateral family connections in order to subvert the physical barriers, legal constraints, and immigration regimes that metropolitan powers are vigorously putting in place. These are the overspill of the global system, the world's surplus populations, the *sans-papiers* of the modern metropolis, who slip across borders at the dead of night or stow away in the backs of lorries or under trains and silently disappear into the hidden depths of the city. This is the human face of the new globalization 'from below'. The global cities of the developed world are the sluice-gates of this new tidal movement.[18]

(4) Foreclosures

Among the most highly charged examples of displacement today are the foreclosures and repossessions from people who are unable to pay their mortgages. Since the 1990s the growth of international finance invested in housing has drawn millions of people into large-scale borrowing to access housing. Today, as economies internationally face recession and unemployment rises, many face the prospect of losing their home. Home price growth accelerated in the US in the early 2000s, prompted by low interest rates, lax underwriting standards and demand for mortgage-backed securities, which helped to flood the mortgage market with liquidity.[19] The IMF stated in 2009 that by various estimates, eight to 12 million homeowners were in negative equity, totalling about US$600 billion. As home prices continue sliding, these numbers will climb.[20] It is estimated that US home foreclosures would probably total 6.4 million by mid 2011, and inventories of foreclosed homes awaiting sale would probably have peaked in mid 2010 at about two million properties.[21]

The UN Special Rapporteur has pointed out that the biggest bubble in history, which developed from the sub-prime lending on housing, affected minorities

18 S. Hall (2006), 'Cosmopolitan Promises, Multicultural Realities', in R. Scholar (ed.), *Divided Cities, The Oxford Amnesty Lectures 2003* (Oxford University Press, Oxford 2006) 36.

19 J. Kiff and V. Klyuev, *Foreclosure Mitigation Efforts in the United States: Approaches and Challenges* (IMF Staff Position Note February 2009 – SPN/09/02) 3.

20 Ibid., 6.

21 Bloomberg News Agency http://www.bloomberg.com/apps/news?pid=20601103&sid=aHEpXU3Pg_oU.

disproportionately.[22] African Americans were five times more likely to receive a sub-prime loan than whites, even when they qualified for a loan at lower, prime rates. The proportion of sub-prime home loans by race was 52.44 per cent for African American families, 40.66 per cent for Hispanic families and 22.20 per cent for white non-Hispanic families.[23]

In the majority of cases, foreclosure has meant the loss of the unique home of a household, often resulting in homelessness or inadequate living conditions. The rise of 'tent cities' and encampments has been reported in some cases, apparently as a direct result of foreclosures.[24]

Rolnik points out that it is important to understand the impact of foreclosure – or eviction – on a household. It pushes people into more difficult situations and inadequate living conditions and impacts their ability to cope with further hardship, particularly where it results in homelessness.

It is much more difficult to maintain employment while having difficulty in accessing water and sanitation and basic services. A lot of effort is required to cope with weather changes and administrative demands, relocating belongings and maintaining an address where one can be reached. In some cases, not having a permanent address leads to exclusion from certain types of aid, or results in denial of civil and political rights, including the right to vote.

Following foreclosure, many families have no savings left, which makes them unable to afford a rental security deposit. Even if they can afford the security deposit, they are considered as less able to meet debt obligations or mortgage payment, and thus they are not eligible for a new rental contract.[25]

The UN Special Rapporteur states that the impact of eviction and homelessness on women and children can be particularly devastating, as is the reality of living in constant fear of being evicted. Homelessness has a particularly negative impact on both groups.

The discrimination faced by women can lead to a potentially higher impact on them from eviction and homelessness. The former UN Special Rapporteur

---

22 See *Report of the Special Rapporteur on Adequate Housing as a Component of the Right to an Adequate Standard of Living, and on the Right to Non-discrimination in this Context, Raquel Rolnik* (4 February 2009) UN Doc A/HRC/10/7, http://www2.ohchr.org/english/issues/housing/index.htm (accessed 21 February 2010).

23 Center for Responsible Lending, 'Updated Projections of Subprime Foreclosures in the United States and Their Impact on Home Values and Communities' CRL issue brief (Washington DC August 2008).

24 CBS News has reported tent cities in Seattle, Portland, Fresno, Columbus and Chattanooga. There were also reports of encampments in Seattle, San Diego, Columbus, Ohio and Santa Barbara and Fresno California in 2009. See http://www.msnbc.msn.com/id/26776283/ (accessed 26 June 2009).

25 See *Report of the Special Rapporteur on Adequate Housing as a Component of the Right to an Adequate Standard of Living, and on the Right to Non-discrimination in this Context, Raquel Rolnik* (4 February 2009) UN Doc A/HRC/10/7 (available at http://www2.ohchr.org/english/issues/housing/index.htm, accessed 21 February 2010) paras 67, 73.

conducted several studies on women and adequate housing and he concluded that women bear the brunt of evictions as they are forced to live in distant places and in inadequate conditions, without security of tenure, basic services, access to schools, health services and employment. When families are moved to places with no source of livelihood, men tend to migrate and leave women to fend for the family. As another result of forced evictions women are frequently left in more difficult situations than before in caring for their families.

In evictions, possessions are often destroyed, family stability jeopardised and livelihoods and schooling threatened. Affected children describe the violence, panic and confusion of the evictions and the painful experience of sleeping and managing their lives out in the open. They also face the challenge of re-establishing a stable life and dealing with frequent breakdowns in family relations as a consequence of the stress and economic challenges that are the result of homelessness.

In addition to the physical and psychological trauma of eviction and homelessness, households, especially women and children, lose the support systems they were used to and their relations with a community. The breaking of these social ties and the loss of stability lead to many other problems.[26]

(5) Displacement and Housing Rights

Housing rights address displacement and dispossession. Indeed, many cases involving displacement and dispossession have led to the development of the corpus of housing rights jurisprudence.[27] Protection from eviction legislation and consequent national court decisions constantly establish the limitations of the law in relation to the displacement of people from their home, even when confronted by the exercise of private property owners' rights.

---

26 Ibid.

27 The case of *Residents of Joe Slovo Community v.Thubelisha Homes, Minister for Housing and others*. Western Cape Constitutional Court of ZA. Case CCT 22/08 [2009] ZACC 16 amplified South African constitutional housing rights, where 20,000 residents of a large informal housing settlement were being displaced to make way for a housing development. The court held that the evicted people should be provided with temporary serviced housing and be allocated 70 per cent of the homes built on the site. In *Government of South Africa and others v. Grootboom and others*, CCT 11/00 2001 (1) SA 46 (CC), 4 October 2000, 2000 (11) BCLR 1169 (CC) the court required the public authorities to consider the needs of people being displaced from temporary accommodation on a site being redeveloped for housing. See also: *Jaftha & Another v. Van Rooyen & Another,* Constitutional Court of South Africa, 2004 Case No. CCT 74/03; *Port Elizabeth Municipality v. Various Occupiers,* 2005 (1) SA 217 (CC). Case No. CCT 53/03; *Occupiers of 51 Olivia Road, Berea Township and 197 Main Street Johannesburg v. City of Johannesburg and Others* (24/07) [2008] ZACC 1; 2008 (3) SA 208 (CC) (19 February 2008); see van der Walt in this volume.

The UN *Guiding Principles on Internal Displacement* sets out a number of rights:

> *Principle 14*
> 1. Every internally displaced person has the right to liberty of movement and freedom to choose his or her residence.
> 2. In particular, internally displaced persons have the right to move freely in and out of camps or other settlements.
>
> *Principle 18*
> 1. All internally displaced persons have the right to an adequate standard of living.
> 2. At the minimum, regardless of the circumstances, and without discrimination, competent authorities shall provide internally displaced persons with and ensure safe access to:
> (a) Essential food and potable water;
> (b) Basic shelter and housing;
> (c) Appropriate clothing; and
> (d) Essential medical services and sanitation.
> 3. Special efforts should be made to ensure the full participation of women in the planning and distribution of these basic supplies.
>
> *Principle 21*
> 1. No one shall be arbitrarily deprived of property and possessions.
> 2. The property and possessions of internally displaced persons shall in all circumstances be protected, in particular, against the following acts:
> (a) Pillage;
> (b) Direct or indiscriminate attacks or other acts of violence;
> (c) Being used to shield military operations or objectives;
> (d) Being made the object of reprisal; and
> (e) Being destroyed or appropriated as a form of collective punishment.
> 3. Property and possessions left behind by internally displaced persons should be protected against destruction and arbitrary and illegal appropriation, occupation or use.[28]

General Comment 7 on Forced Evictions of the UN Committee on Economic, Social and Cultural Rights points out that:

> The practice of forced evictions is widespread and affects persons in both developed and developing countries. Owing to the interrelationship and interdependency which exist among all human rights, forced evictions frequently

---

28 *Guiding Principles on Internal Displacement* (11 February 1998) UN Doc E/CN.4/1998/53/Add.2.

> violate other human rights. Thus, while manifestly breaching the rights enshrined in the Covenant, the practice of forced evictions may also result in violations of civil and political rights, such as the right to life, the right to security of the person, the right to non-interference with privacy, family and home and the right to the peaceful enjoyment of possessions (para. 4).[29]

However, protection from eviction is not absolute within international human rights law, which respects property rights above housing rights.[30] The UN Committee on this issue emphasised the procedural safeguards in the eviction process. International human rights law does not propose countering evictions through redistribution of property or housing rights. Indeed, many international housing rights cases now revolve around protecting property rights from appropriation by the state for a public purpose.[31]

In its 1997 General Comment the Committee explained that the procedural protections it considers should be applied in relation to forced evictions include:

> (a) an opportunity for genuine consultation with those affected; (b) adequate and reasonable notice for all affected persons prior to the scheduled date of eviction; (c) information on the proposed evictions, and, where applicable, on the alternative purpose for which the land or housing is to be used, to be made available in reasonable time to all those affected; (d) especially where groups of people are involved, government officials or their representatives to be present during an eviction; (e) all persons carrying out the eviction to be properly identified; (f) evictions not to take place in particularly bad weather or at night unless the affected persons consent otherwise; (g) provision of legal remedies;

29 See UN ECOSOC (Committee on Economic, Social and Cultural Rights), The Right to Adequate Housing (Art. 11.1): Forced Evictions: CESCR General Comment 7. (General Comments) (20/05/97) UN Doc E/C.12/1997/10 (available at http://www.unhchr.ch/tbs/doc.nsf/(Symbol)/959f71e476284596802564c3005d8d50?Opendocument).

30 See *Report of the Special Rapporteur on Adequate Housing as a Component of the Right to an Adequate Standard of Living, and on the Right to Non-discrimination in this Context, Raquel Rolnik* (4 February 2009) UN Doc A/HRC/10/7. The UN Special Rapporteur on Adequate Housing has provided detailed guidance on the implementation of international human rights obligations with reference to evictions: *Basic Principles and Guidelines on Development-Based Evictions and Displacement, Annex 1 to the Report of the Special Rapporteur on Adequate Housing as a Component of the Right to an Adequate Standard of Living*, Miloon Kothari (11 June 2007) UN Doc A/HRC/4/18, http://www2.ohchr.org/english/issues/housing/docs/guidelines_en.pdf.

31 The majority of cases relating to housing at that European Court of Human Rights involve claims for compensation arising from former redistribution policies of socialist states.

and (h) provision, where possible, of legal aid to persons who are in need of it to seek redress from the courts. (para. 15)[32]

The Council of Europe Committee on Social Rights has defined forced eviction as 'deprivation of housing which a person occupied on account of insolvency or wrongful occupation'.[33]

Legal protection for persons threatened by eviction must include, in particular, an obligation to consult the affected parties in order to find alternative solutions to eviction and the obligation to fix a reasonable notice period before eviction. The law must also prohibit evictions carried out at night or during the winter period and provide legal remedies and offer legal aid to those who are in need so they may seek redress from the courts. Procedural safeguards are important. Compensation for illegal evictions must also be provided. Even when an eviction is justified, authorities must adopt measures to re-house or financially assist the persons concerned.[34]

The concept of 'unlawful occupier' or 'wrongful occupier' implicit in this approach signifies the overriding legal priority of property ownership.

(6) Housing Rights as Promoters of Adequate Housing for All

Housing rights can act as a barrier to displacement, but can they deliver adequate safe and secure homes? It is widely accepted that housing rights are forging a new discourse and jurisprudence across the world.[35] At an international level public international human rights instruments have led to a legal discourse based on human dignity and other universal values where states mutually agree to offer certain guarantees of minimum standards, in areas of public and private life, individual

32 See UN ECOSOC (Committee on Economic, Social and Cultural Rights), The Right to Adequate Housing (Art. 11.1): Forced Evictions: CESCR General Comment 7. (General Comments) (20/05/97) UN Doc E/C.12/1997/10.

33 European Committee of Social Rights, *Conclusions 2003* (Sweden), 89 (available at http://www.coe.int/t/dghl/monitoring/socialcharter/Conclusions/State/Sweden2003_en.pdf, accessed 18 September 2010).

34 The European Committee on Social Rights has accepted that a two-months' period after formal notice has been served before the actual eviction as sufficient to protect housing rights. See European Committee on Social Rights *FEANTSA v. France*, Complaint No 39/2006, Decision on the Merits of 5 December 2007, § 88 and 89.

35 For a comprehensive collation of all these housing rights see Centre on Housing Rights and Evictions, Sources No. 4: *Legal Resources for Housing Rights*: *International and National Standards* (COHRE, Geneva 2000). See also Jeanne Woods and Hope Lewis, *Human Rights and the Global Marketplace: Economic, Social and Cultural Dimension* (Transnational, New York 2005).

freedom and socio-economic rights, such as housing.[36] For example, Article 25(1) of the Universal Declaration of Human Rights (1948) (UDHR) states that:

> Everyone has the right to a standard of living adequate for the health and well-being of himself and his family, including food, clothing, housing and medical care and necessary social services, and the right to security in the event of unemployment, sickness, disability, widowhood, old age or other lack of livelihood in circumstances beyond his control'.[37]

Housing rights within international human rights law have developed through the UN system, largely since 1945 and establishing a general hegemony of human rights principles throughout the world.[38] Donnelly points out that this moral universality of human rights must be realised through the particularities of action at national level, in order to be effective. The rights are based on the inherent dignity and possessed by every human being, and provide a moral compass for the development of law and policy across the globe. Housing rights are viewed as an integral part of economic, social and cultural rights within the UN, European, Inter-American and African human rights instruments. These include the Universal Declaration of Human Rights (1948) Article 25(1), the International Covenant on Economic, Social Cultural Rights (1966) Article 11, Convention on the Rights of the Child (1989) Articles 16.1 and 27.3, Convention on the Elimination of All Forms of Discrimination against Women (1979) Article 14.2 and the Convention on the Rights of Persons with Disabilities (2008),[39] as well as many International Labour Organisation Conventions and Recommendations. The UN Committee on Economic, Social and Cultural Rights' General Comment 4, issued in 1991,

---

36 See Matthew Craven, *The International Covenant on Economic, Social and Cultural Rights* (Clarendon Press, Oxford, 1995); Asbjørn Eide, Catarina Krause and Allan Rosas (eds), *Economic, Social and Cultural Rights: A Textbook* (2nd edn Martinus Nijhoff Publishers, Dordrecht 2001). See also the UN Millennium Goals, agreed at international level in 2001 (http://www.un.org/millenniumgoals/environ.shtml). Among the targets in Goal 7 to ensure environmental sustainability are halving the proportion of the population without sustainable access to safe drinking water and basic sanitation and, by 2015, to have achieved a significant improvement in the lives of at least 100 million slum dwellers.

37 The housing provision is elaborated in the International Covenant on Economic, Social and Cultural Rights (adopted 16 December 1966, entered into force 3 January 1976) 993 UNTS 3 (1967)(ICESCR) at Article 11, which states, 'The States Parties to the present Covenant recognize the right of everyone to an adequate standard of living for himself and his family, including adequate food, clothing and housing, and to the continuous improvement of living conditions. The States Parties will take appropriate steps to ensure the realization of this right, recognizing to this effect the essential importance of international co-operation based on free consent.'

38 See Jack Donnelly, *Affirming Universal Human Rights* (Cornell University Press, Ithaca NY,2003) 40.

39 Articles 2, 5.3., 9.1., 19, 22.1 and 28.

clarifies the international human rights obligations is relation to housing. It sets out the essential elements of housing rights as legal security of tenure, availability of services, materials and infrastructure, affordability, habitability, accessibility, suitable location and cultural adequacy.[40]

International housing instruments translate to a requirement on a state to meet a minimum core obligation in terms of the rights concerned, without discrimination – a minimum threshold approach, below which no person should have to endure. This minimum core obligation corresponds to a level of distributive justice assessing the evenness of the distribution of socially guaranteed minimal levels of certain goods and benefits among individual groups within a country.[41] In terms of housing rights, the minimum core obligations of states would involve a guarantee that everyone enjoyed a right to adequate shelter and a minimum level of housing services, without discrimination. Indeed, these principles of minimum core obligation and progressive realisation form a major contribution to housing rights discourse. While the minimum standards or core obligations approach is well developed in housing law, the concept of progressive realisation, based on increasing normative standards is interpreted within housing systems as arising from increased development, and is widely incorporated into political and consumerist norms.

In Europe, the Council of Europe has developed a range of normative housing rights standards, although not directly corresponding to the minimum core obligations and progressive realisation models of the UN.[42] The Social Charter contains important rights to social and medical assistance for those without adequate resources, establishing housing obligations in relation to physically and mentally disabled persons, migrant workers, children and young persons, and rights to social, legal and economic protection for families, those who are poor and socially excluded, homeless and those unable to afford accommodation; it includes a state obligation to provide family housing.[43] Indeed, in 2009, clarifying further the actual extent of state obligations arising from its housing rights

40 UN ECOSOC (Committee on Economic, Social and Cultural Rights), The Right to Adequate Housing (Art.11.1): Forced Evictions: CESCR General Comment 4 (General Comments) (13/12/91) UN Doc E/C.12/1771/4.

41 See Sigrun I. Skogly, 'Human Rights Reporting: The 'Nordic' Experience' (1990) 12 *HRQ* 513.

42 This is not the same organisation as the European Union. See Council of Europe, *About the Council of Europe* (http://www.coe.int/aboutCoe/default.asp, accessed 19 September 2010), giving a brief summary of the Council, its history, and its aims. The European Social Charter and Revised Charter have been adopted to some degree by all 47 members states of the Council of Europe.

43 Articles 13, 15, 16, 17, 19, 23, 30 and 31. The European Court of Human Rights of the Council of Europe develops housing rights in an indirect and oblique way through its articles on prevention of inhuman and degrading treatment, protection for home, family life and correspondence, fair procedures and non-discrimination. See *Botta v. Italy* (App no 153/1996/772/973) (1998) 26 EHRR 241; *Marzari v. Italy* (1999) 28 EHRR CD 175;

instruments, the Council of Europe Commissions for Human Rights has published *Recommendation of the Commissioner for Human Rights on the Implementation of the Right to Housing*.[44]

The European Union protects some fundamental rights which address housing and provides housing rights protection through its Charter of Fundamental Rights,[45] as well as laws prohibiting discrimination in public or private access on grounds of migrant workers status,[46] race or ethnicity[47] and gender.[48]

The Organization of American States (OAS) Charter of the Organization of American States (1948) and the American Declaration on the Rights and Duties of Man (1948) recognize housing rights.[49] The Protocol to the African Charter on Human and Peoples' Rights on the Rights of Women in Africa of the African Union reaffirms housing rights.[50]

At national level housing rights are widely enshrined in constitutions, legislation and established case law. Approximately 40 percent of the world's constitutions refer to housing or housing rights including:

Lopez-Ostra v Spain (1991) 14 EHRR 319; *Geurra v Italy* (1998) EHRR 357; *Fadeyeva v Russia* (2007) 45 EHRR 10; *Moreno-Gomez v Spain* (2005) 41 EHRR 40.

44 Strasbourg, 30 June 2009, CommDH(2009)5 https://wcd.coe.int/ViewDoc.jsp?id =1463737&Site=CommDH&BackColorInternet=FEC65B&BackColorIntranet=FEC65B &BackColorLogged=FFC679.

45 Charter of the Fundamental Rights of the European Union, art. 34(3), Dec. 18, 2000, 2000 O.J. (C364) 1. The Charter has now been incorporated into Part II of the Treaty Establishing a Constitution for Europe, Oct. 29, 2004, 2004 O.J. (C310) 41.

46 Council Regulation 1612/68, art. 9, 1968 O.J. (L257) 2 (EEC), amended by Council Regulation 2434/92 1992 O.J. (L245) 1. See Case 249/86 *Commission v. Germany* [1989] ECR 1263; Case 63/86 *Commission v. Italy* [1988] ECR 29.

47 See Council Directive 2000/43, 2000 O.J. (L180) 22. Article 13 of the Amsterdam Treaty conferred to the European Community the powers to take measures to fight discrimination on grounds of sex, race/ethnic origin, religion/belief, disability, age and sexual orientation.

48 See Council Directive 2004/113, 2004 O.J. (L373) 37, 38 (EC) (implementing the principle of equal treatment between men and women in the access to and supply of goods and services). Unfair contract terms in housing contracts are prohibited across Europe under the 1993 Directive on Unfair Terms in Consumer Contracts. See Report from the Commission on the Implementation of Council Directive 93.13.EEC of 5 April 1993 on Unfair Terms in Consumer Contracts, COM (2000) 248 final (27 April 2000).

49 Article 31; See also The Additional Protocol to the American Convention on Human Rights in the Area of Economic, Social and Cultural Rights "Protocol of San Salvador" (adopted 17 November 1988, entered into force 16 November 1999). OAS Treaty Series, No. 69 (http://www.oas.org/juridico/english/sigs/a-52.html, accessed 18 September 2010).

50 Article 16 on the Right to Adequate Housing states: 'Women shall have the right to equal access to housing and to acceptable living conditions in a healthy environment. To ensure this right, States Parties shall grant to women, whatever their marital status, access to adequate housing'.

- *Belgium (1994) Article 23(3):* Everyone has the right to enjoy a life in conformity with human dignity. Towards this end, the law, the decree or rules established under Article 134 guarantee, taking into account the corresponding obligations, economic, social and cultural rights of which they determine the conditions for their implementation. These rights include, in particular, the right to adequate housing.
- *Russian Federation (1993) Article 40(1):* Each person has the right to housing. No one may be arbitrarily deprived of housing.[51]
- *South Africa (1997) Section 26(1):* Everyone has the right to have access to adequate housing. *Section 26(2):* The state must take reasonable legislative and other measures, within its available resources, to achieve the progressive realisation of this right. *Section 26(3):* No one may be evicted from their home, or have their home demolished, without an order of court made after considering all the relevant circumstances. No legislation may permit arbitrary evictions. *Section 28(1)(c):* Every child has the right to basic nutrition, shelter, basic healthcare services and social services.[52]

Many countries have introduced legislation granting specifically enforceable housing rights. The Housing (Scotland) Act 1987 (as amended) provides a right to accommodation for homeless persons, including a right to temporary accommodation for all homeless persons, and a right to long-term accommodation for broadly defined categories, encompassing the majority of homeless applicants. By 2012, the right to long-term accommodation will be extended to all. This right is enforceable in the civil courts, and courts may order in appropriate cases that accommodation be provided to homeless persons.

In France, an enforceable right to housing has also been established through the DALO Act of 5 March 2007,[53] which provides for a two-tier remedial mechanism with regional mediation committees and the possibility to take a case before administrative courts. The use of planning law to achieve integration of social/affordable and private housing, control of land use and quality of infrastructure and amenities is now becoming widely recognised as a somewhat lateral, but practical, means of realising housing rights.[54] Courts across the world have developed housing rights in such areas as security of tenure, respect for home,

51 The Housing Code of the Russian Federation (29 December 2004, entered into force 1 March 2005) offers some of the best definitions of minimum core obligations in relation to housing with standards of not less than five square metres of living space per each person.

52 See COHRE, *Legal Resources for Housing Rights* (COHRE, Geneva 2000).

53 Droit au logement opposable (DALO) Act 2007.

54 See Juli Ponce-Sole (ed.), *Land Use Law, Housing and Social and Territorial Cohesion* (Rocky Mountain Institute, Denver 2006).

non-discrimination, decent physical standards and fair procedures in evictions.[55] A legacy of judicial activism has led to a corpus of jurisprudence in many countries which has established housing rights, even within common law principles.[56]
All of this suggests that there now exists a matrix of housing rights on implementing such across the world, drawing on a variety of precedents, legislation, constitutions, ratifications of international instruments and measures from other law applying indirectly to housing rights. The internationally accepted UN minimum core obligations and progressive realisation obligations on ratifying states, as well as the obligations to recognize, to respect, to protect and to fulfil these obligations are influencing new lawmaking. UN General Comments have clarified obligations, while many national and local laws and cases have defined standards and rights at local level. Consumer and other national private and public laws grant further housing rights in relation to housing provided by markets. Yet, without diminishing the significance of democratic participation as a means of implementing housing rights, much remains to be done in properly defining these concepts in actual contemporary housing law and policy terms.

(7) Transposing International Housing Rights

International public law instruments are voluntary agreements between states which undertake to perform certain obligations. In relation to housing rights, appropriate policies and laws must underpin the minimum core obligations, without discrimination, progressive realisation of rights and the requirement to recognise, respect, protect, promote and fulfil the required obligations.[57] This 'transmission belt' model of international human rights (see Figure 6.1), where states accept certain obligations at international level, and transpose these to national law, guaranteeing rights to individuals, faces a number of obstacles. Ideally, these rights must integrate the norms, standards and principles of

55 See D.B. Bryson, 'The Role of Courts and a Right to Housing', in R.G. Bratt, M.E. Stone and C. Hartman (eds), *A Right to Housing; Foundation for a New Social Agenda* (Temple University Press, Philadelphia 2006).

56 See for example the development of housing rights using local and state provisions and common-law principles in the US in Beth Harris, *Defending the Right to a Home* (Ashgate Publishing, Aldershot 2004). See also the historic decision in England of *R v. Sec of State ex parte Adam and Others* [2005] UKHL 66, where the highest appeal court in England had to define what level of abject destitution such homeless individuals must sink before their suffering or humiliation reaches the 'minimum level of severity' to amount to 'inhuman or degrading treatment' under Article 3 of the ECHR, prompting positive state action under the Convention.

57 UN ECOSOC (Committee on Economic, Social and Cultural Rights), The Right to Adequate Housing (Art.11.1): Forced Evictions: CESCR General Comment 4. (General Comments) (13/12/91) UN Doc. E/C.12/1771/4.

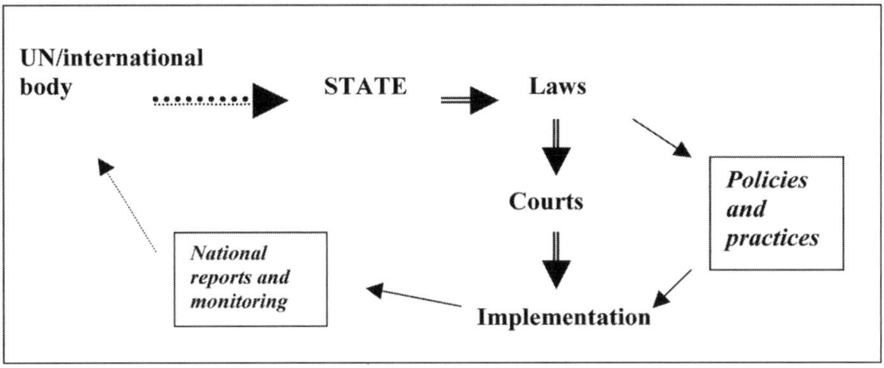

Figure 6.1 'Transmission belt' approach of public international human rights law

the international human rights system into the laws, policies, budgets and administration of the state, based on principles of equality, accountability, empowerment, participation and attention to vulnerable groups.

Effective implementation of housing rights through this 'transmission belt' approaches raises issues of dualism/monism in national legal systems, the specificity, clarity[58] and contextual definition of rights terminology,[59] as well as the relationship between human rights law and the systems it seeks to address.[60] Indeed, there is a major question as to whether such human rights can be incorporated at all into liberal economic systems.[61] At UN level there has been extensive analysis of transposing legally defined standards for housing rights on to national housing systems and standards, through indicators and benchmarks.[62] Yet,

58 Much work has been carried out on defining the specific rights contained in the Covenant especially by the UN Committee on Economic, Social and Cultural Rights in its Conclusions and Reports. See generally Office of the High Commissioner for Human Rights, Committee on Economic, Social and Cultural Rights, http://www.unhchr.ch/html/menu2/6/cescr.htm (listing examples of Committee on Economic, Social and Cultural Rights documents).

59 See Christopher McCrudden, 'Human Dignity and Judicial Interpretation of Human Rights' (2008) 19 (4) *EJIL* 655, 724. See also P. Carozza, 'Human Dignity and Judicial Interpretation of Human Rights: A Reply' (2008) 19 (5) *EJIL* 931, 944.

60 For a discussion on the role of law *vis-à-vis* other systems see Niklaus Luhmann, *Law as a Social System* (Oxford University Press, Oxford 2004); Gunther Teubner, *Autopoietic Law: A New Approach to Law and Society* (Walter de Gruyter, Berlin 1987).

61 See Paul O'Connell, 'On Reconciling Irreconcilables: Neo-liberal Globalisation and Human Rights' (2007) 3 *HRLR* 483, 509.

62 *Report of Secretary General on Indicators and Benchmarks* UN Doc. E/EN4/2000/47; UNGA, Report of the Seminar on Appropriate Indicators to Measure Achievements in the Progressive Realization of Economic, Social and Cultural Rights (Geneva, 25–29 January 1993) UN Doc. A/CONF.157/PC/7; UN Doc. E/EN4/2000/47; UN Doc. E/C.12/1994/11; UN

many UN monitoring processes can amount to little more than reports illustrating mere creative compliance by recalcitrant states.[63]

At the level of progressive realisation of rights, Robertson has pointed out that such words as 'maximum' in relation to the level of resources to be devoted to realising rights, form the sword of human rights rhetoric, while words like 'available' facilitate 'wriggle room' for the state.[64] Hunt has highlighted the variable and elusive nature of such terms as 'progressive realisation', and 'maximum of their available resources.'[65] These imply that some state obligations could vary over time: '[T]hese variable elements of States parties' obligations under ICESCR contribute to the sense of uncertainty which remain a feature of international economic, social and cultural rights.'[66] Jheelan has highlighted the imprecision and vagueness, aspirational nature and ultimately reliance on a 'reasonableness' curial test which acts a delimitation on the effectiveness of universal minimum core obligations.[67]

Other limitations on the legal liberalist 'transmission belt' approach are highlighted in legal realism, critical legal studies and feminist analyses, as well as the myopic treatment of formal over substantive equality. Indeed, legal liberal models of individually enforceable rights may act to displace, restructure or reprioritise innovative or radical programmatic approaches to state provision. Many acclaimed housing rights cases involve only the prioritisation of access to new homes, or more responsive 'decanting' procedures, ultimately leading

Doc. E/CN.4/Sub.2/1994/20; UN Doc. E/C.12/1991/SR.21; UN Doc. E/CN.4/Sub.2/1991/15; Round-Table Discussion Organized by the High Commissioner for Human Rights (Geneva, 25 March 1998); Report by Office of the High Commissioner for Human Rights (Geneva, 1998); UNCHS Official UN Guidelines for Monitoring Progress in Implementing the Habitat Agenda (http://www.unhabitat.org/, accessed 18 September 2010); Housing and Urban Indicators, Report of the Secretary-General, UN Doc. A/CONF.165/CRP; UN Millennium Development Goals Indicators (http://mdgs.un.org/unsd/mdg/Host.aspx?Content=Indicators/OfficialList.htm, accessed 18 September 2010); Methodology for Monitoring the Human Right to Adequate Housing. The Housing and Land Rights Network 'Toolkit' (http://www.hlrn.org/english/home.asp, accessed 18 September 2010).

63 See A.F. Bayefsky, *The UN Human Rights Treaty System in the 21st Century: Universality at the Crossroads* (Kluwer, The Hague 2001).

64 R. Robertson, 'Measuring State Compliance with the Obligation to Devote the Maximum Resources to Realizing Economic, Social and Cultural Rights' 16 *HRQ* 693, 714.

65 See UN Committee on Economic, Social and Cultural Rights, *State Obligations, Indicators, Benchmarks and the Right to Education* (16 July 1998) UN Doc. E/C.12/1998/11/, background paper submitted by Paul Hunt, para. 3

66 UN Committee on Economic, Social and Cultural Rights, *Report of the 19th Session. State Obligations, Indicators, Benchmarks and the Right to Education*, para. 4, UN Doc. E/C.12/1994/11; 'State Obligations, Indicators, Benchmarks and the Right to Education', background paper submitted by Paul Hunt, para. 3.

67 See N. Jheelan, 'The Enforceability of Socio-economic Rights' (2007) 2 *EHRLR* 146, 157.

to no increase in or improvement in housing. Housing rights cases, corralled within the legal liberalist discourse, often only differentiate socio-economic rights from civil and political rights, or reduce legal arguments to juxtaposing the role of politicians and courts in allocating resources in society. Indeed, the esoteric, exclusive and often intimidating language of law, combined with the costs and lack of universal access to courts, as well as the alienation of many of those in housing need from state institutions, all act to diminish the impact of enforcement of legally based housing rights. In any case, there is no effective enforcement of penalties for housing rights violations at international level, despite some very valuable principles and guidelines in this area.[68]

While the 'transmission belt' approach also proposes that rights be incorporated into policies and administration, this leaves a wide area of discretion in policy making and interpretation of obligations. Despite the development of the Human Rights Based Approach (HRBA),[69] and National Action Plans,[70] the language of human rights can easily be incorporated into public administration and management systems of consultation, participation and strategies for service delivery, often acting to buttress existing policies and processes. Effective implementation of housing rights requires a deconstruction of the elaborate context within which these rights are being advanced.[71] Implementation can involve a complex process or sub-process. Indeed, '[T]he longer the chain of causality, the more numerous the reciprocal relationships among the links and

68 See the Limburg Principles on the Implementation of the International Covenant on Economic, Social and Cultural Rights (June 1986) UN Doc E/CN.4/1987/17; Maastricht Guidelines on Violations of Economic, Social and Cultural Rights (January 1997) 20 *HRQ* 691, 705. See also Housing and Land Rights Network (Habitat International Coalition) Housing Violations database at http://www.hlrn.org/english/home.asp.

69 Five interconnected principles have been internationally recognised as forming the core of HRBA: express application of the international human rights framework; empowerment; participation; non-discrimination and prioritisation of vulnerable groups; and accountability. See J. Kirkemann Boesen and T. Martin, *Applying a Rights Based Approach: An Inspirational Guide for Civil Society* (The Danish Institute of Human Rights, Copenhagen 2007); André Frankovits, *UNESCO Strategy on Human Rights, The Human Rights Based Approach and the United Nations System* (2006) 12 (available at http://www.unssc.org/web/programmes/LS/unep-unssc-precourse-material/12_UNESCO%20HRA%20and%20Evaluation.pdf, accessed 18 September 2010).>

70 This framework developed from the Office of the High Commission for Human Rights and its promotion of national human rights plans of action. See *Handbook on National Human Rights Plans of Action* (OHCHR, Geneva 2002) Professional Training Series No. 10.

71 For a critique of rights-based approaches generally, see Duncan Kennedy, 'The Critique of Rights in Critical Legal Studies' in W. Brown and J. Hally (eds), *Left Legalism/Left Critique* (Duke University Press, Durham NC and London 2002).

the more complex implementation becomes'.[72] Comparing what is achieved and what was expected can lead to the observation of an 'implementation gap'.[73]

(8) Macro, Meso, Micro

A fundamental weakness in the implementation of housing rights instruments is the failure to appreciate that in market societies, access to basic and higher standard housing is initially more dependent on a person's labour market position than the prevalence of state obligations. There is often a tendency to equate housing rights with shelter and social housing, alongside a perception that housing rights involve creating an obligation on the state to provide a minimum level of shelter and housing for all.[74] Equally, there can be a tendency to shun the structures and dynamics of the housing systems, in favour of more complex definitions and descriptions of failures of housing rights implementation. Housing rights must be directed to the whole of housing systems, rather than merely social housing entitlements.[75] Of course, the basic right to shelter will always remain a minimum core requirement of the implementation of housing rights. But housing rights must involve more than this minimalist proposition. Effective implementation of international housing rights requires their integration into the macro, meso, micro framework of housing systems.[76] What follows is an

72 J.L. Pressman and A. Wildavsky, *Implementation* (3rd edn University of California Press, Berkeley, Los Angeles 1984) xxiv.

73 See A. Dunsire, *The Execution Process, Vol. 1: Implementation in a Bureaucracy* (Martin Robertson, Oxford 1978).

74 See Schlomo Angel, *Housing Policy Matters; A Global Analysis* (Oxford University Press, New York 2000) at 74, where he points out that 'there is little merit in a housing policy that's solely focuses on the poor, hoping against hope that "the market" will take care of the rest, without paying any attention to whether the market is functioning properly. When the market is not functioning properly, the poor are squeezed as well.'

75 There is a process referred to as 'mainstreaming' within the language of New Public Management, where new policies and perspectives, laws and obligations are integrated into policy documents and are intended to be incorporated into service delivery etc. However, here we are referring to a greater impact on states, power, large-scale institution reform, changing and inventing new social practice. See Pierre Bourdieu, *Outline of a Theory of Practice* (Cambridge University Press, Cambridge 1977). Bourdieu's 'habitus' is the ideological unconscious practice which creates a 'common-sense', world, and has the ability to create and engender practices whose limits are set by historically determined conditions of its production.

76 The analytic framework and terminology of macro, meso, micro are widely used to denote different of society or systems. See for instance K. Dopfer, J. Foster and J. Potts, 'Micro-meso-macro' (2004) 14 *Journal of Evolutionary Economics* 263, 279. This is an area where there is a dearth of research and where there is great potential for an interdisciplinary approach.

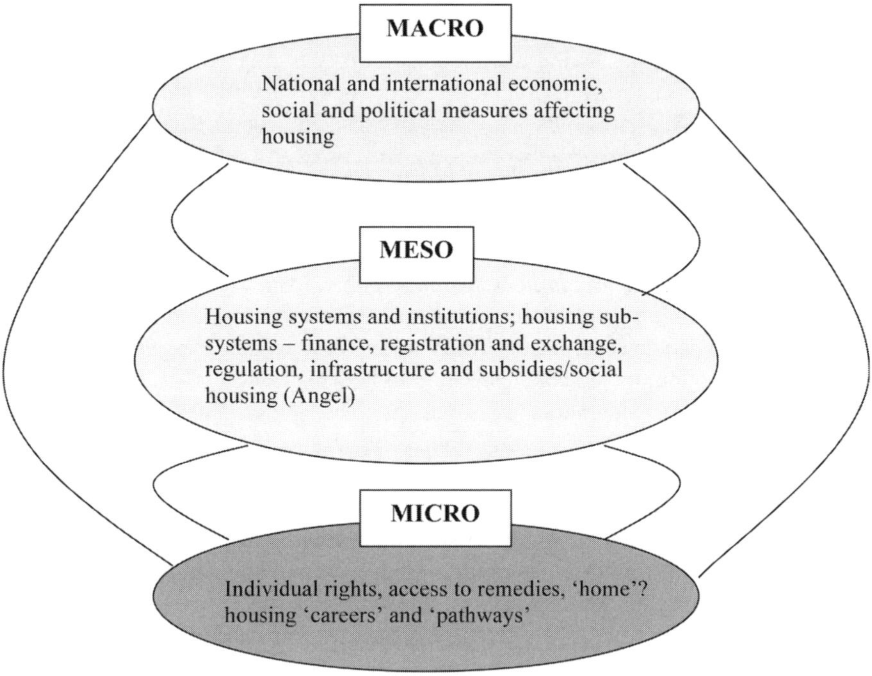

Figure 6.2 Macro meso micro perspectives on housing rights implementation

attempt to develop this implementation model, which requires an interdisciplinary but non-compromising approach to housing rights.

Housing rights must be engaged at all three levels – the *micro* (the level of individual aspirations, interactions and micro political struggles), the *meso* (including the housing systems, its sub-systems and institutional contexts) and the *macro* (broadly the national, regional and international context within which housing systems interact with other systems (see Figure 6.2).

Macro Level

Integrating housing rights at macro level of housing systems requires a focus on national and international economic, social and political measures impacting on housing systems.[77] Indeed, this also requires an understanding that states have entered an era when the processes of government have been transformed into 'governance'. Simple hierarchical concepts of command and control, involving the establishment

77 While many national macro housing system measures, such as housing rights legislation, may actually address housing rights and home, these may be coincidental or unrelated to international human rights law.

and implementation of laws and policies, have given way to the involvement of a broader range of 'actors' in the implementation process.[78] The idea of governance was described by the World Bank as the 'process by which authority is exercised in the management of a country's economic and social resources for development, and the capacity of governments to design, formulate and implement policies and discharge functions.'[79] In reality, it involves taking a perspective from outside the state, to effectively observe and evaluate progress. Governance 'describes the hybridity of legal interferences within a society'.[80] It accepts a fusion of public and private institutions, and brings an approach to public institutions primarily oriented towards efficiency and output in achieving goals. These goals, which largely relate to profit and capital enhancement, are already widely described in neo-liberal economic literature and seldom include the realisation of housing rights.

In many ways this model of supra national governance, evaluating the outcomes of institutions, laws and other measures of states in terms of results can be appropriated to the monitoring and development of housing rights. The template for this approach, being results oriented, is less concerned with actual laws and measures, but how they ensure that the objectives of housing rights are achieved. An obligation of results, rather than obligation of conduct in the implementation of housing rights is required. Of course, the UN monitoring systems, especially the UN Committee on Economic, Social and Cultural Rights, regularly examine and evaluate broader outcomes, alongside legislative

78 For an examination of the many uses of the term see M. Hill and P.L. Hupe, *Implementing Public Policy* (2nd edn Sage, London 2009) 13, 14. Some new approaches such as the Open Method of Coordination of the EU have sought to overcome this problem, where internationally accepted guidelines are consolidated into agreed national plans, in areas of employment, pensions and social inclusion. See http://ec.europa.eu/social/main.jsp?catId=753&langId=en, accessed 18 September 2010 .

79 See World Bank, *Governance: The World Bank's Experience* (Washington, World Bank 1994) XIV. The concept was first used in World Bank, *Sub-Saharan Africa: From Crisis to Sustainable Growth* (Washington, World Bank 1989). The bank's Worldwide Governance Indicators (WGI) project reports aggregate and individual governance indicators for 212 countries and territories over the period 1996–2007, for six dimensions of governance: voice and accountability, political stability and absence of violence, government effectiveness, regulatory quality, rule of law and control of corruption. Its current definition of governance is: 'Governance consists of the traditions and institutions by which authority in a country is exercised. This includes the process by which governments are selected, monitored and replaced; the capacity of the government to effectively formulate and implement sound policies; and the respect of citizens and the state for the institutions that govern economic and social interactions among them.' See http://info.worldbank.org/governance/wgi/index.asp, accessed 18 September 2010.

80 See Christopher Mollers, 'European Governance: Meaning and Value of a Concept' (2006) 43 *Common Market Law Review* 313–36 at 316.

provisions in its regular monitoring of states.[81] Indeed, the national level and future individual level monitoring systems of this UN Committee are ideally placed to address housing rights at the macro level, although resource constraints have inhibited this to date.[82] The recent approach of the European Committee of Social Rights, applying the European Social Charter, in the *FEANTSA v. France*[83] collective complaint is advancing this approach in relation to laws, policies and measures applying to all aspects of housing systems and outcomes arising from other systems.

There is a powerful interdependency between rights and regulation.[84] Regulation and governance measures and the reform of the international financial institutions offer the potential to integrate housing rights into housing systems at macro level. Surprisingly, the language of 'home' often already appears at this level within international proposals. The new international regulation and governance approaches to global finance offer an opportunity for implementing housing rights at macro level. Indeed, the UN Special Rapporteur on Adequate Housing has proposed that housing rights are integrated at the international level in the regulation of financial markets:

> The Special Rapporteur believes that the current crisis represents also an opportunity for reflection and to consider how to improve housing systems, policies and programmes so as to ensure adequate housing for all. (para. 75)
>
> States should ensure appropriate regulation of international financial activities in order to avoid future financial crises and their subsequent effect on human rights and adequate housing. (para. 89)[85]

---

81 Detailed reports on monitoring of the implementation of the ICESCR by the UN Committee on Economic, Social and Cultural Rights may be found at http://www2.ohchr.org/english/bodies/cescr/, accessed 18 September 2010.

82 See United Nations High Commissioner for Human Rights (UNHCHR) and the United Nations Committee on Economic, Social and Cultural Rights (UNCESCR), *Plan of Action to Strengthen the Implementation of the International Covenant on Economic, Social and Cultural Rights* (New York, 1997); the Optional Protocol on Economic, Social and Cultural Rights allows individual complaints of violations of such rights including housing rights (see http://www2.ohchr.org/english/issues/escr/intro.htm, accessed 18 September 2010).

83 http://www.coe.int/t/dghl/monitoring/socialcharter/Complaints/CC39Merits_en.pdf, accessed 18 September 2010.

84 See B. Morgan, *An Introduction to Law and Regulation* (Cambridge University Press, Cambridge 2006); B. Morgan (ed.), *The Intersection of Rights and Regulation: New Directions in Socio-legal Scholarship* (Ashgate, London 2007).

85 *Report of the Special Rapporteur on Adequate Housing as a Component of the Right to an Adequate Standard of Living, and on the Right to Non-discrimination in this Context, Raquel Rolnik* (4 February 2009) UN Doc A/HRC/10/7.

The Global Plan for Recovery and Reform Global Plan, which failed to mention housing, issued by the G20 leaders in April 2009, states:

> We have today also issued a Declaration, *Strengthening the Financial System.* In particular we agree:
>
> - to establish a new Financial Stability Board (FSB) with a strengthened mandate, as a successor to the Financial Stability Forum (FSF), including all G20 countries, FSF members, Spain, and the European Commission;
> - to reshape our regulatory systems so that our authorities are able to identify and take account of macro-prudential risks;
> - to extend regulation and oversight to all systemically important financial institutions, instruments and markets. This will include, for the first time, systemically important hedge funds;
> - to take action, once recovery is assured, to improve the quality, quantity, and international consistency of capital in the banking system. In future, regulation must prevent excessive leverage and require buffers of resources to be built up in good times…[86]

The G20 statement pointed out that it accepts that the current crisis has a disproportionate impact on the vulnerable in the poorest countries and recognise our collective responsibility to mitigate the social impact of the crisis to minimise long-lasting damage to global potential. To this end:

> - we reaffirm our historic commitment to meeting the Millennium Development Goals and to achieving our respective ODA pledges, including commitments on Aid for Trade, debt relief, and the Gleneagles commitments, especially to sub-Saharan Africa…
> - we call on the UN, working with other global institutions, to establish an effective mechanism to monitor the impact of the crisis on the poorest and most vulnerable.[87]

Meso Level – Housing System and Institutions

Even the most elaborate and comprehensive national housing rights legislation and policies do not always result in the anticipated level of international housing rights implementation. Many explanations have been given for this, such as the dichotomy of symbolic versus instrumental laws, bureaucratic inertia, problems of interpretation and deference to the state in the courts etc. Indeed, the weakness

86 G20. *The Global Plan for Recovery and Reform* 2 April 2009 (see http://www.g20.org/Documents/final-communique.pdf, accessed 18 September 2010).

87 Ibid. See also US measures such as Hope for Homeowners Act 2008 and Helping Families Save Their Homes Act of 2009.

of the human rights model is illustrated in its failure to recognise that access to housing and increased enjoyment of socio-economic rights is almost always directly related to income and labour market position. A fundamental structural requirement for the effective implementation of such measures is that the systems on which they rely are addressed appropriately. Thus measures which rely simply on lawmaking or policy can fail to realise the outcome intended. There is a requirement to understand the system through which housing rights will have to permeate. This requires an understanding of the meso level of the housing system, positioned between the macro level and micro level. It requires an examination of the institutional elements and behaviour of the actors within those institutions. It must also be recognised that the legal aspects of housing systems, and the protection of property rights, constitute a significant of the workload and income of lawyers worldwide, in all capitalist countries.

Housing systems around the world today are predominantly organised around the market system or enablement approach. One influential international writer identifies the components of the contemporary 'enabling policy' model of housing markets systems as encompassing five essential elements, sub-systems or regimes:

- property rights regime
- housing finance regime
- residential infrastructure regime
- regulatory regime
- housing subsidies/public housing regime.[88]

The establishment of individual and enforceable property rights in land and housing are seen as the cornerstone of this enabling housing policy regime.

> A functional and effective property rights regime must evolve a set of transparent, predictable, non-discriminatory and stable rules that preserve the rights of individuals to use, invest, maintain, rent, mortgage and sell their land

88 See S. Angel, *Housing Policy Matters; A Global Analysis* (Oxford University Press, New York 2000). International housing rights discourse has yet to engage properly with the reality of access to housing finance as a means of securing housing rights. However, this 'enabling policy' model fails to adequately consider the role of rented housing and its impact on other parts of the system, such as first-time buyers and social housing. Rent control and regulation measures have been imposed by governments of all hues since the 1800s. Kemeny argues that genuine market competition can be fostered by encouraging cost rental housing to compete directly with profit renting, thereby dampening rents, raising housing standards and increasing security of tenure. Segregating cost renting into a state-run public rental (or social housing) sector shelters private renting from competition from the costs rented or social housing sector. See J. Kemeny, *From Public Renting to the Social Market: Rental Policy Strategies in Comparative Perspective* (Routledge, London 1995).

> and housing properties without hindrance and with the full protection against arbitrary action by the authorities.[89]

Housing is by far the most widely distributed form of private wealth, and investment in housing requires law facilitating certainty, exclusivity, transferability and constitutional protection. Complex legal ownership arrangements involving family law systems, with rules on ownership and division of property on marriage, separation, divorce, death and co-habitation are required. Innovative legal mechanisms have also been developed to deal with unregistered land, transfer and conveyancing procedures, disputes and the regulation of actors involved in housing markets.

The housing finance regime requires the creation and maintenance of an effective, enforceable lending and regulatory regime for housing finance, as well as the development of housing finance institutions and sustainable mortgage markets.[90] This regime involves legal measures relating to mortgages, equity release, charges, consumer credit legislation and regulation of lenders, market liberalisation and competition. The third requirement for the enabling market approach is an effective residential infrastructure regime. This requires legislation and regulation in relation to zoning, planning, public health, control of nuisance and sanitation measures, and planning controls on urban land development and supply. Detailed legislation and case law have developed in relation to roads and walkways, water, sewage, drainage, transport, public facilities and other services, which contribute to housing quality. The fourth and most important element of this approach for industrialised countries is the regulatory regime for quality in housing systems.[91] Building control measures exercised by the state are critical elements in the development of housing markets. Indeed, these markets actually require a legal and regulatory framework that only governments can provide.[92]

Housing subsidies are a central element of housing enablement policies.[93] The presence or absence of housing subsidies (and tax incentives) cannot be understood outside the broader framework of overall fiscal policy. The largesse of the state in enhancing land values through planning and zoning decisions, and the contemporary 'capitalisation' or subsidies to banks involved in reckless mortgage

---

89 Ibid., 95.

90 Ibid., ch. 8.

91 See for example *Housing Regulation in Victoria – Building Better Outcomes* (2005) (available at http://www.vcec.vic.gov.au/CA256EAF001C7B21/WebObj/VCEChousingfinalreport/$File/VCEC%20housing%20final%20report.pdf, accessed 18 September 2010).

92 See UNECE, *Compendium of Model Provisions for Building Regulations* (UNECE, Geneva 1996) UN Doc ECE/HBP/81/Rev.1.

93 See Schlomo Angel, *Housing Policy Matters; A Global Analysis* (Oxford University Press, New York 2000) at ch. 9; R.M. Buckley and J. Kalarickal, *Thirty Tears of Shelter Lending: What Have We Learned?* (World Bank, Washington 2006).

are rarely compared with the lesser costs involved in guaranteeing minimum core obligations of housing rights. Similarly, investment of capital in housing is part of overall government investment policy (percentage of GDP). Other state legal measures include control of interest rates, curbs on public expenditure, and stimulation of demand through public spending on housing, tax reliefs, etc. These can be either supply side (subsidising producers) or demand side (supporting purchasers), such as through grants for new homes. Social housing is part of a market support system and an integral part of political largesse.

At a meso level, regulatory norms that establish minimum standards and equality of access to goods and services are widespread, although more often based on historical public health legislation than international human rights.[94] In relation to housing, there are detailed legal regulations and regulatory systems on land use, housing occupancy and maintenance, building standards, housing costs, eviction procedures, facilities and equipment, and almost all have legally enforceable sanctions for violations, and compensation for breaches. This regulation machinery seeks to protect, preserve and promote the physical and mental health and social well-being of people, control nuisances, prevent and control communicable diseases and regulate privately and publicly owned dwellings in order to maintain adequate sanitation and public health.[95] Indeed, in some circumstances, it can go so far as delimit and deny property rights, such as granting extended rights of occupancy for tenants which override the legal owners powers to sell. McCrudden has outlined the extent of measures and regulatory mechanisms across the contemporary world which act to achieve socially desirable outcomes, and in many cases override civil and property rights.[96]

The integration of international housing rights norms and jurisprudence into national housing regulatory systems represents the next step in the realisation of these rights. Thus, all draft legislation on housing systems can be housing rights proofed. House planning and building regulatory agencies, such as local authority and institutional housing finance regulators, can incorporate housing rights objectives into their regulatory systems. Equally, all development plans and zoning approvals could be required to demonstrate how they address housing rights criteria. Regulatory agencies could refer violations, as set out in the Limburg Principles and Maastricht Guidelines, to the courts to be adjudicated and appropriate sanctions enforced for violations of housing rights across all elements of housing systems.

Some legal measures can involve controls on prices or rents, deemed necessary when the market fails to meet a social norm and the state should intervene. Statutory provision of social and affordable housing, with elaborate legal precedents and

---

94 Cass Sunstein, *After the Rights Revolution: Reconceiving the Regulatory State* (Harvard University Press, Cambridge MA 1990).

95 S. Angel, *Housing Policy Matters; A Global Analysis* (Oxford University Press, New York 2000) 155, 160.

96 C. McCrudden, *Buying Social Justice: Equality, Government Procurement, and Legal Change* (Oxford University Press, Oxford 2007).

legislation on allocation, management, control, sale and inheritance, also play a significant role. However, the neo-liberalist inspired contemporary 'enabling housing subsidy regime' involves a retreat from public housing production, towards privatisation of such stock and abolition of subsidies.[97] Therein lies a major challenge to contemporary housing rights advocates, who have yet to tailor housing rights standards to the nuances and dynamics of housing market systems.

Micro Level

One of the key issues in ensuring the effective enjoyment of housing rights is justiciability. Contrary to what is sometimes suggested, neither the far-reaching nature of housing rights obligations, or their character as social or economic rights, presents a major obstacle to conferring justiciable housing rights on persons within national legal systems. Courts have regularly enforced housing rights derived from case law, legislation and constitutional provisions. Indeed, a significant overlap exists between international housing rights and rights conferred by national private and public constitutional, legislative and case law.[98] However, there are many areas where national laws do not provide the equivalent protection to that set out within international legal instruments, although there is an established international consensus on the adoption of housing rights and the internalisation of associated supranational standards into domestic law and policy.

The Council of Europe *Recommendations of the Commissioner for Human Rights on the Implementation of the Right to Housing* strongly proposes that housing rights be made individually justiciable at local level and highlights the benefits of this approach:

- specific legislation is more likely to clarify who precisely (i.e. which government agencies or private parties) is/are responsible for implementing international obligations;
- specific legislation is more likely to result in the creation of effective remedies for violations of housing rights;
- national judicial institutions are more likely to treat questions relating to housing rights as justiciable when given the task of interpreting specific legislation rather than the more broadly stated provisions of treaty obligations or constitutional guarantees;
- the process of enacting legislation focuses the attention of the political authorities on the conditions needed to ensure effective realisation of rights in practice, e.g. the resources required and allocation of responsibilities;
- the existence of specific legislation better enables states to assess the extent of

97 P. Cammack, 'Attacking the Poor' (2002) 13 *New Left Review* 125.

98 See Centre on Housing Rights and Evictions, *Sources No. 4: Legal Resources for Housing Rights: International and National Standards* (COHRE, Geneva 2000).

their compliance with international standards.[99]

Hammarberg points out that housing rights can be made justiciable in a variety of ways, but there are important issues to be considered:

> Most obviously, there is a distinction between, on the one hand, relying on administrative bodies to enforce housing rights – whether by administrative or judicial procedures or a combination of both – and on the other providing legal remedies which may be invoked by individuals or by groups/NGOs acting on their behalf. Whilst administrative enforcement may be highly effective, the provision of both administrative and individual enforcement should prove even more effective in practice. The reasons for this are:
>
> - administrative bodies may have limited resources for monitoring and detecting violations and for taking enforcement action;
> - individual and group/NGO enforcement broadens the range of those engaged in enforcement, allows people to take the initiative in protecting their own rights, and harnesses the resources of civil society;
> - the possibility of individual enforcement increases the likelihood that violations will be detected and remedies sought;
> - the greater frequency with which remedies for violation are sought will feed through into greater incentives for both public bodies and private parties to respect housing rights.[100]

To facilitate instrumental rather than formal or symbolic implementation of housing rights at national level the Human Rights Commissioner proposed a number of measures in 2009, addressing the 47 States of the Council of Europe. In implementing the right to housing member states should:

> - Enact specific legislation which clarifies how the housing rights guaranteed by international law are to be made effective in a national jurisdiction without discrimination. National laws should spell out housing rights, identify those who are responsible for their implementation at different levels, and provide for effective remedies when they are violated…
> - Include housing rights in the scope of general non-discrimination legislation both in the public and private sectors and specify that positive measures are justified in order to promote full and effective equality provided that there is an

99 Council of Europe, Commissioner for Human Rights, *Recommendation of the Commissioner for Human Rights on the Implementation of the Right to Housing*, CommDH(2009)5 (https://wcd.coe.int/ViewDoc.jsp?id=1463737&Site=CommDH&BackColorInternet=FEC65B&BackColorIntranet=FEC65B&BackColorLogged=FFC679, accessed 18 September 2010).

100 Ibid.

objective and reasonable justification for such measures. Those countries which have not yet done so should ratify Protocol No. 12 on the general prohibition of discrimination to the European Convention on Human Rights.

- Establish minimum standards in all areas of housing provision for accessibility, adequacy and affordability in accordance with the European standards developed by the European Committee of Social Rights and the European Court of Human Rights.
- Prevent and reduce homelessness through general and targeted policy measures designed to promote access to housing. Such measures include legal protection of tenants against unfair and disproportionate contractual conditions, indiscriminate termination of contracts and forced eviction, as well as the availability of a sufficient stock of rental housing and temporary shelters to provide housing for disadvantaged and vulnerable groups.
- Adopt and implement a national housing strategy which incorporates targets to be achieved for the realisation of housing rights to an extent consistent with the maximum use of available resources. A national housing strategy should also apply a gender perspective, identify disadvantaged and vulnerable groups and include positive measures for ensuring their effective enjoyment of the right to housing.
- Enable the individual enforcement of the right to housing. The individual enforcement of housing rights should be accompanied by other measures aimed at providing sufficient accommodation to meet the demand from persons classified as homeless.[101]

Other methods of making housing rights applicable at local level transcend the transmission belt approach, and rely on the HRBA, where 'rights holders' are involved in the development of policies which affect them, advanced within an international human rights framework, where they are empowered and effectively participate in the process, which is non-discriminatory, prioritises vulnerable groups and is publicly accountable.

(9) Conclusion

The concept of home and displacement from home offer powerful justifications for the strengthening of housing rights protection. In modern societies housing rights jurisprudence is growing in its content, relevance and sophistication, reflecting new principles of personal and social development, as well as the influences of public international human rights law. State action is transcending traditional civil and political rights guarantees towards giving effect to contemporary expectations,

101 Ibid.

through legal and other intervention in housing systems.[102] However, there are limitations to the international human rights approach in enforcing rights within contemporary housing systems. Housing rights now need to be integrated, not just into political policies and laws, with their traditional emphasis on social housing solutions, but into the macro, meso and micro frameworks of the housing field, involving all these elements of housing systems. This may yet provide an appropriate basis for the evolution of an effective international and national governance model for the advancement of these rights.

102 *The Vienna Declaration* (1993) states that both civil and political rights and socio-economic rights, such as housing rights are 'universal, indivisible, interdependent and interrelated'. See The Secretary-General, *Report of the Secretary General on the Vienna Declaration Programme of Action* (13 October 1993) UN Doc A/CONF 157/24 (Part I).

Chapter 7
The International Law Rights to Home and Homeland

Susan Breau[1]

(1) Introduction

The history of the twentieth century was plagued with cases of forced massive displacement of people from their homes and homeland, particularly during the Second World War. As a reaction to the mass murder of many of these displaced peoples in the Holocaust, there have been various efforts within a number of international law regimes both to prevent such events from taking place, providing for people who are forced to leave their homes, and developing rights to return. Nevertheless, the twenty-first century thus far has revealed no significant change. Massive forced displacements already evident in the twenty-first century are:

- Darfur – more than two million people homeless in the civil war in Sudan.
- Pakistan – three million people internally displaced in the North-west Frontier Province as a result of fighting with the Taliban.
- Zimbabwe – 'Operation Murambatsvina' – 'clear the filth' – hundreds of thousands evicted from their homes.
- Israel – the continuation of the settlement policy introducing Jewish people to Palestinian homelands and the construction of a wall between Israel and Palestine.

This chapter concentrates on forced displacement as a result of man-made or natural disaster and considers the following research questions:

1. Does an individual have an international law right to his or her particular residence?
2. Do groups of people have international law rights to their homeland?
3. Can these rights be enforced by the international community?
4. Is the 'Responsibility to Protect' an appropriate framework to deal with the phenomenon of forced displacement?

---

1 My sincere gratitude to University of Surrey School of Law graduate Ms Jenni Hollis for her outstanding research assistance for this chapter.

In order to begin to respond to these questions the analysis will firstly assess those doctrines developed in international human rights law that might result in a legal right to a home or homeland. This part will review what if any enforcement mechanisms exist within this framework. This part of the chapter will also focus on the European Convention of Human Rights which has within it a developed enforceable right to property, missing from the other human rights instruments. As the enforcement arm to this treaty is the European Court of Human Rights, there is limited jurisprudence in this area. This topic is canvassed in much more detail in both Antoine Buyse and Padraic Kenna's chapters in this book so that the case law here will be viewed through the lens of displacement of large groups of people. The second part of the chapter will introduce and discuss the framework of international humanitarian law which is the *lex specialis* applicable in international and non-international armed conflict. The third part of the chapter will discuss the treaty regime for refugee protection. The fourth part of the chapter will review the 'soft law' principles dealing with internal displacement and query whether these principles may have become part of customary international law. The fifth and final part of the chapter will introduce a new mechanism to prevent, react and rebuild after forced displacement, the 'Responsibility to Protect',[2] which this author will suggest is the only mechanism that could be developed for truly and finally combating this regrettable phenomenon of displacement from home and homeland.

(2) International Human Rights Law

Although there were minority rights provisions within the League of Nations system,[3] the first major post-war human rights law instrument was the Universal Declaration of Human Rights adopted by the General Assembly in 1948. This instrument confirmed the existence of individual rights and combined civil rights with economic, social and cultural rights. The general statement of economic rights was Article 25 which stated that:

> (1) Everyone has the right to a standard of living adequate for the health and well-being of himself and of his family, including food, clothing, housing and medical care and necessary social services, and the right to security in the event

---

2 For the major report on this concept see International Commission on Intervention and State Sovereignty, *The Responsibility to Protect* (International Development Research Centre, Ottawa 2001).

3 R.K.M. Smith, 'The Fate of Minorities – Sixty Years On' [2009] 1 *Web JCLI* 4–5 (http://webjcli.ncl.ac.uk/2009/issue1/smith1a.html, accessed 14 September 2009) in which she discussed the numerous peace treaties protecting minority rights and the League system of minority protection.

> of unemployment, sickness, disability, widowhood, old age or other lack of livelihood in circumstances beyond his control.[4]

Among the individual civil rights was Article 13 which stated that:

> (1) Everyone has the right to freedom of movement and residence within the borders of each state.
> (2) Everyone has the right to leave any country, including his own, and to return to his country.

This first statement of individual rights has now been argued to be part of the International Bill of Rights and part of customary international law.[5]

Two international treaties were negotiated that provided great specificity to these rights. The International Covenant on Civil and Political Rights[6] provided specific rights to family life and privacy which includes non-interference with home as part and parcel of the right.[7]

Article 17 sets out that:

> 1. No one shall be subjected to arbitrary or unlawful interference with his privacy, family, home or correspondence, nor to unlawful attacks on his honour and reputation.
> 2. Everyone has the right to the protection of the law against such interference or attacks.

The International Covenant on Economic Social and Cultural Rights,[8] Article 11, states that:

---

4 Universal Declaration of Human Rights (adopted 10 December 1948 UNGA Res 217 A(III) (UDHR).

5 Several international lawyers have argued the customary nature although unlike International Humanitarian Law there has not been a study of the customary nature of International Human Rights Law; for example see Myers McDougal, Harold Lasswell and Lung-chu Chen, *Human Rights and World Public Order* (Yale University Press, New Haven 1980) 274, 325 and 338.

6 International Covenant on Civil and Political Rights (adopted 16 December 1966), 999 *UNTS* 171.

7 UN Doc. HRI/GEN/1/Rev.6 at 142 (2003), Human Rights Committee General Comment No. 16 to the International Covenant on Civil and Political Rights, 'The Right to Respect of Privacy, Family, Home and Correspondence, and Protection of Honour and Reputation' which interprets privacy as the right to be free from interference with one's home.

8 International Covenant on Economic Social and Cultural Rights (adopted 16 December 1967) 999 *UNTS* 3.

> 1. The States Parties to the present Covenant recognize the right of everyone to an adequate standard of living for himself and his family, including adequate food, clothing and housing, and to the continuous improvement of living conditions. The States Parties will take appropriate steps to ensure the realization of this right, recognizing to this effect the essential importance of international co-operation based on free consent.

In dealing with the first and second research questions in this chapter it is evident that this right clearly does not provide for the right to one's own home or to live in one's homeland; rather that the right is directed to adequate housing, leaving open the possibility that one could lose one's own home. None of these rights contains any provision preventing the phenomenon of ethnic cleansing or massive displacement of peoples for any reason. The Genocide Convention of 1948 contains a provision prohibiting anyone from 'forcibly transferring children of the group to another group' but nothing preventing the forcible transfer of the national, ethnic, racial or religious group.[9] With the advent of ethnic cleansing in the 1990s, particularly with respect to the conflict in Yugoslavia, that omission in existing treaty law is regrettable.

The Committee on Economic, Social and Cultural Rights (CESCR) released two General Comments on the right to housing. The first was General Comment No. 4 on the right to adequate housing. The Committee in their interpretation of Article 11 of the Covenant takes a wide view of the right to housing. The General Comment states:

> In the Committee's view, the right to housing should not be interpreted in a narrow or restrictive sense which equates it with, for example, the shelter provided by merely having a roof over one's head or views shelter exclusively as a commodity. Rather it should be seen as the right to live somewhere in security, peace and dignity.[10]

Within the General Comment, the particular rights to housing are defined according to the following concepts:

1. Legal security of tenure
2. Availability of services, materials and infrastructure
3. Affordable housing; attainment of other basic needs not threatened
4. Habitable housing' physically safe and minimally comfortable
5. Accessible housing; vulnerable individuals can apply and get housing
6. Location allows access to employment and other services

---

9 Convention on the Prevention and Punishment of Genocide, 9 December 1948, 78 *UNTS* 277.

10 UN Doc. HRI/GEN/1/Rev.6 at 18 (2003) Committee on Economic, Social and Cultural Rights (CESCR), General Comment 4, Right to Adequate Housing, para. 7.

7. Culturally adequate housing.[11]

Another important component to this right is the interrelationship with other human rights. The General Comment states;

> As noted above, the right to adequate housing cannot be viewed in isolation from other human rights contained in the two International Covenants and other applicable international instruments. Reference has already been made in this regard to the concept of human dignity and the principle of non-discrimination. In addition, the full enjoyment of other rights – such as the right to freedom of expression, the right to freedom of association (such as for tenants and other community-based groups), the right to freedom of residence and the right to participate in public decision-making – is indispensable if the right to adequate housing is to be realized and maintained by all groups in society. Similarly, the right not to be subjected to arbitrary or unlawful interference with one's privacy, family, home or correspondence constitutes a very important dimension in defining the right to adequate housing.

This statement comes very close to enunciating a right to a specific home and with the interrelationship with other rights – a right to one's own homeland, rather than a right to adequate housing.

This view is further supported by General Comment No. 7 which concerns forced evictions.[12] The first statement in the comment is that forced evictions are prima facie incompatible with the requirements of the ICESCR. The General Comment defines forced evictions as the permanent or temporary removal against their will of individuals, families and/or communities from the homes and/or land which they occupy, without the provision of, and access to, appropriate forms of legal or other protection.[13] The CESCR argues that many instances of forced eviction are associated with violence, such as evictions resulting from international armed conflicts, internal strife and communal or ethnic violence.[14] The General Comment urges that the state itself must refrain from forced evictions and ensure that the law is enforced against its agents or third parties who carry out forced evictions. They argue that this obligation is reinforced by Article 17 of the International Covenant on Civil and Political Rights, the right to be protected against "arbitrary or unlawful interference" with one's home.[15] The Committee

11 C.F. Doebbler, *International Human Rights Law; Cases and Materials, Volume 1* (CD Publishing, Washington 2004) 322 and General Comment 4, ibid., para. 8.

12 UN Doc. HRI/GEN/1/Rev.6 at 45 (2003). Committee on Economic Social and Cultural Rights, General Comment 7, Forced Evictions and the Right to Adequate Housing.

13 Ibid., para. 3.

14 Ibid., para. 6.

15 Ibid., para. 8.

also relied upon the obligations enshrined in the Geneva Conventions of 1949 and Protocols of 1977 concerning prohibitions on the displacement of the civilian population and the destruction of private property as these relate to the practice of forced eviction.[16] It is evident that this General Comment is attempting to deal with the phenomenon of forced displacement for whatever reason and this comment comes close to supporting the right to home and homeland but a note of caution must be sounded as General Comments are interpretive and cannot extend so far as to change the treaty-based rights or obligations. The plain reading of both the ICCPR and ICESCR provisions do not seem to support an extension to the right of a homeland as this General Comment might imply.

The organisation responsible for developing standards with respect to housing is the UN Human Settlements Programme, UN-Habitat. The mandate for the organisation is to promote socially and environmentally sustainable towns and cities with the goal of providing adequate shelter for all.[17] They produced a Global Strategy for Shelter in 2001 and require governments to report on specific indicators every two years to the Commission on Human Settlements. They also have a specific mandate to deal with disaster management which includes natural and man-made disasters. The Committee on Economic, Social and Cultural Rights expects and reviews national reports every five years.[18] On 5 March 2009 the General Assembly adopted an Optional Protocol to the Convention on Economic, Social and Cultural Rights which would consider communications from individuals or groups of individuals claiming to be victims of violations of the Convention.[19] However, these communications would only be from those states that become party to the Optional Protocol and it does not come into effect until after the 10th instrument of ratification (which at the time of the writing of this article had not yet taken place).[20]

The Convention on the Rights of the Child (CRC) also contains a housing provision Article 27 (3):

> States Parties, in accordance with national conditions and within their means, shall take appropriate measures to assist parents and others responsible for the child to implement this right and shall in case of need provide material assistance and support programmes, particularly with regard to nutrition, clothing and housing.[21]

---

16 Ibid., para. 12.

17 http://www.unhabitat.org/categories.asp?catid=10, accessed 14 September 2009.

18 C.F. Doebbler, *International Human Rights Law; Cases and Materials, Volume 1* (CD Publishing, Washington 2004) 322.

19 UN Doc. A/Res/63/117, General Assembly Resolution 63/117, 5 March 2009.

20 Ibid., Resolution containing Optional Protocol to the International Covenant on Economic, Social and Cultural Rights, Articles 2 and 18.

21 Convention on the Rights of the Child (adopted 20 November 1989) 1577 *UNTS* 3.

The Convention on the Elimination of Racial Discrimination (CERD) also has two applicable rights, the right to housing and the right to own property alone or in association with others.[22] The ICESCR, CERD and the CRC provide for positive obligations on the state to provide such housing and the ICCPR is a negative obligation prohibiting unlawful interference in the home. These rights are premised on the right of the individual and not groups as in the post Second World War period the focus was on individual liberty. None of these provisions can even remotely be seen to deal with the issue concerning this paper except on a tangential basis to argue that everyone is entitled to adequate housing and displacement from that housing by conflict or disaster certainly deprives individuals of these rights. A further difficulty within the international system is that only the ICCPR among these instruments has a facility for individual complaints but the Human Rights Committee only issues views not a binding decision.

There is a regional instrument that provides for binding enforcement of housing rights, the European Convention on Human Rights and it includes a specific Protocol 1(1) with respect to protection of property.[23] Article 8 within the Convention itself, specifies that 'Everyone has the right to respect for his private and family life, his home and his correspondence.' Protocol 1, Article 1 states:

> Every natural or legal person is entitled to the peaceful enjoyment of his possessions. No one shall be deprived of his possessions except in the public interest and subject to the conditions provided for by law and by the general principles of international law.
>
> The preceding provisions shall not, however, in any way impair the right of a State to enforce such laws as it deems necessary to control the use of property in accordance with the general interest or to secure the payment of taxes or other contributions or penalties.[24]

These are not absolute rights as property can be confiscated for state interests on payment of compensation. However, this provision can be argued to be pertinent for those who face displacement as it is the individual possessions that are affected and an offer of adequate housing elsewhere cannot compensate the person for losing their individual home and possessions. This has been confirmed in the case law and one leading case in particular deals with an issue arising from armed conflict, the *Loizidou* case.[25] Mrs Loizidou claimed that she had been prevented

---

22 International Convention on the Elimination of All Forms of Discrimination (adopted 21 December 1965) 660 *UNTS* 195, Article 5.

23 European Convention for the Protection of Human Rights and Fundamental Freedoms (adopted 4 November 1950) 213 *UNTS* 222.

24 Protocol I (1) to the ECHR 1950 (adopted 4 November 1950) 213 *UNTS* 222.

25 *Loizidou v. Turkey* (App no 15318/89) ECHR 18 December 1996.

from enjoying her property in Kyrenia as a result of the Turkish invasion in 1974. The court supported her contention and ruled:

> as a consequence of the fact that the applicant has been refused access to the land since 1974, she has effectively lost all control over, as well as all possibilities to use and enjoy, her property. The continuous denial of access must therefore be regarded as an interference with her rights under Article 1 of Protocol No. 1 (P1-1)...It has not, however, been explained how the need to rehouse displaced Turkish Cypriot refugees in the years following the Turkish intervention in the island in 1974 could justify the complete negation of the applicant's property rights in the form of a total and continuous denial of access and a purported expropriation without compensation...In such circumstances, the Court concludes that there has been and continues to be a breach of Article 1 of Protocol No. 1 (P1-1).[26]

Although Mrs Loizidou applied individually, this decision impacted on all those who had been displaced by the Turkish invasion of Cyprus; regrettably there is no mechanism for a type of class action and each family would have to bring their own claim. Subsequently, there have been a number of cases of deprivation of property within the cases of the Kurdish conflict with the Turkish authorities in south-east Turkey. The European Court of Human Rights has found in numerous cases that security forces deliberately destroyed the homes and property of the respective applicants, depriving them of their livelihoods and forcing them to leave their villages in the state of emergency region of Turkey.[27] In one of the cases *Doğan and others v. Turkey*, 15 applications in cases of displacement from home by Kurdish people were brought together in one case. The court held unanimously that there was a violation of Article 8 and Article 1, Protocol 1.[28] The press release concerning this judgment said there were 1,500 other cases pending concerning the inability of Kurdish people to return to villages in south-east Turkey.[29] Therefore, it can be argued that within the European system there is at least some enforcement mechanism for and a remedy for displacement from one's home and homeland. A drawback is that once again the system is based on individual rights and groups that face massive displacement such as the Kurds have to bring individual complaints of deprivation of individual property rather than destruction of traditional homelands. Furthermore, the enforcement mechanism results in financial compensation rather than restitution of homes and possessions.

---

26 Ibid., paras 63 and 64.

27 See for example: *Bilgin v. Turkey* (App no 23819/94) ECHR 16 November 2000, and *Dulaş v. Turkey*, App no 25801/94) ECHR 30 January 2001 and *Doğan and others v. Turkey* (App nos 8803-8811/02, 8813/02 and 8815-8819/02) ECHR 18 November 2004.

28 *Doğan and others v. Turkey* (App nos. 8803-8811/02, 8813/02 and 8815-8819/02) ECHR 18 November 2004.

29 http://www.echr.coe.int/Eng/Press/2004/June/ChamberJudgmentDoganandothersvTurkey290604.htm, accessed 20 September 2009.

The Council of Europe's European Social Charter has a specific right, Article 31, that states 'Everyone has the right to housing'. The Charter also states:

> With a view to ensuring the effective exercise of the right to housing, the Parties undertake to take measures designed:
> 1. to promote access to housing of an adequate standard;
> 2. to prevent and reduce homelessness with a view to its gradual elimination;
> 3. to make the price of housing accessible to those without adequate resources.[30]

The Council of Europe Commissioner for Human Rights on 30 June 2009 released a recommendation on the implementation of the right to housing calling for the justiciability for such a right, but at this point that remedy is not available to victims of forced displacement.[31]

Another human right for the specific right to a homeland is within the international law of self-determination. Dussias argues that the right of self-determination includes a right to a homeland. From the perspective of indigenous rights she argues that the homelands of the indigenous peoples of the United States provide 'the necessary base for the exercise of self-government and also for the preservation of cultural integrity'.[32] Yet none of the international instruments with respect to self-determination either in the UN Charter or the international covenants have any specific reference to a homeland. Dussias' argument is certainly provocative as often groups of peoples have a great attachment to their ancestral lands; the conflict in the Middle East is emblematic of this fact.[33] However, this does not mean that there is an international law right of a homeland that is enforceable. As Haslam argues the right to a homeland is 'at most only emerging under international law' and that its precise ambit is unclear.[34] She also points out that it is uncertain whether the right to a homeland is an individual or collective right and how it would interact with other controversial areas of international law such as nationality, territory and state succession.[35]

The international human rights regime, therefore, has a lacuna with respect to rights to an individual home or homeland, save for the limited jurisprudence of the European Court of Human Rights only applicable to states in the Council

30 European Social Charter (revised) 3 May 1996, ETS 163.

31 Council of Europe Document; CommDH(2009) 5, 30 June 2009 (one of the authors in this collection, Padraic Kenna, was a consultant to this report).

32 A.M. Dussais, 'Does the Right of Self-Determination Include a Right to a Homeland?' (2004) 31 *Syracuse Journal of International Law and Commerce* 83, 84.

33 For discussion of this issue see Eyal Benvenisti and Eyal Zamir, 'Private Claims to Property Rights in the future Israeli-Palestinian Settlement' (1995) 89 *AJIL* 295.

34 Emily Haslam, 'Unlawful Population Transfer and the Limits of International Criminal Law' (2002) 61 *CLJ* 66, 74.

35 Ibid.

of Europe. In fact, the treaty regime that comes closest to providing such specific rights is the regime applicable in armed conflict, international humanitarian law.

(3) International Humanitarian Law

One of the most grievous crimes of the Second World War was the Holocaust which resulted in the murder of six million Jews. Prior to the gas chambers, Jews were forcibly removed from their homes and either murdered on the spot or placed in ghettos. Therefore, post-war humanitarian law was most concerned with the deportation of persons from their homes particularly when the territory was occupied by another foreign power. Geneva Convention IV with respect to protection of civilian persons in time of war includes Article 49 which is the most important provision with respect to protection of residence. It states:

> Individual or mass forcible transfers, as well as deportations of protected persons from occupied territory to the territory of the Occupying Power or to that of any other country, occupied or not, are prohibited, regardless of their motive. Nevertheless, the Occupying Power may undertake total or partial evacuation of a given area if the security of the population or imperative military reasons so demand. Such evacuations may not involve the displacement of protected persons outside the bounds of the occupied territory except when for material reasons it is impossible to avoid such displacement. Persons thus evacuated shall be transferred back to their homes as soon as hostilities in the area in question have ceased. ...The Occupying Power shall not deport or transfer parts of its own civilian population into the territory it occupies.[36]

The enforcement of international humanitarian law is within the realm of criminal law and individuals could be prosecuted either domestically or internationally. Parties who sign the Geneva Conventions (which now has universal ratification) agree to criminalise grave breaches of the Convention. Article 147 specifies that:

> Grave breaches to which the preceding Article relates shall be those involving any of the following acts, if committed against persons or property protected by the present Convention: wilful killing, torture or inhuman treatment, including biological experiments, wilfully causing great suffering or serious injury to body or health, unlawful deportation or transfer or unlawful confinement of a protected person, compelling a protected person to serve in the forces of a hostile Power, or wilfully depriving a protected person of the rights of fair and regular trial prescribed in the present Convention, taking of hostages and extensive

36 Geneva Convention IV Relative to the Protection of Civilian Persons in Time of War (adopted 12 August 1949) 75 *UNTS* 287.

> destruction and appropriation of property, not justified by military necessity and carried out unlawfully and wantonly.

This important provision is given greater specificity in Additional Protocol I to the Geneva Conventions of 1977.[37]

Article 85 states in paragraph 4:

> In addition to the grave breaches defined in the preceding paragraphs and in the Conventions, the following shall be regarded as grave breaches of this Protocol, when committed wilfully and in violation of the Conventions or the Protocol: (a) the transfer by the occupying Power of parts of its own civilian population into the territory it occupies, or the deportation or transfer of all or parts of the population of the occupied territory within or outside this territory, in violation of Article 49 of the Fourth Convention...

This treaty has not received universal ratification and Israel, which does transfer people into their occupied territories, has not ratified this treaty. These two Conventions are applicable in an international armed conflict but many of the conflicts that concern the international community and involve massive displacement from home and homeland are non-international armed conflicts known often as civil wars or insurgencies. In the four Geneva Conventions of 1949 there is a common Article 3 applicable to non-international armed conflict. It states:

> In the case of armed conflict not of an international character occurring in the territory of one of the High Contracting Parties, each Party to the conflict shall be bound to apply, as a minimum, the following provisions:
>
> (1) Persons taking no active part in the hostilities, including members of armed forces who have laid down their arms and those placed ' hors de combat ' by sickness, wounds, detention, or any other cause, shall in all circumstances be treated humanely, without any adverse distinction founded on race, colour, religion or faith, sex, birth or wealth, or any other similar criteria. To this end, the following acts are and shall remain prohibited at any time and in any place whatsoever with respect to the above-mentioned persons:
> (a) violence to life and person, in particular murder of all kinds, mutilation, cruel treatment and torture;
> (b) taking of hostages;
> (c) outrages upon personal dignity, in particular humiliating and degrading treatment;

37 Protocol I Additional to the Geneva Conventions of 12 August 1949, and relating to the Protection of Victims of International Armed Conflict (adopted 8 June 1977) 1125 *UNTS* 3.

(d) the passing of sentences and the carrying out of executions without previous judgment pronounced by a regularly constituted court, affording all the judicial guarantees which are recognized as indispensable by civilized peoples.
(2) The wounded and the sick shall be collected and cared for.

It is evident that this provision does not include massive deportations of peoples as was specified in Article 49 in the Fourth Convention. The reason for this is that those states' representatives viewed internal armed conflict as the sole purview of state authority and not a matter for international supervision. Notwithstanding this position by 1977 states parties were willing to negotiate a treaty to deal with humanitarian law and non-international armed conflict. This is Protocol II to the Geneva Conventions. Article 17 sets out a prohibition of forced movement of civilians, stating:

1. The displacement of the civilian population shall not be ordered for reasons related to the conflict unless the security of the civilians involved or imperative military reasons so demand. Should such displacements have to be carried out, all possible measures shall be taken in order that the civilian population may be received under satisfactory conditions of shelter, hygiene, health, safety and nutrition.
2. Civilians shall not be compelled to leave their own territory for reasons connected with the conflict.

The difficulty with this provision is that once again Protocol II is not a universally ratified treaty and for example a noted non-party is Turkey, which has continually cleared Kurdish villages during that ongoing non-international armed conflict. Israel is also not a party to this Convention.

A long-standing project initiated by the International Committee of the Red Cross is the Customary International Humanitarian Law Study,[38] released by the ICRC in 2005. The study identified 161 rules which were found to be customary. Rules 129–33 deal with displacement of peoples. These are set out here in total and the initials after the rule indicates whether it is applicable in international armed conflict (IAC) or non-international armed conflict (NIAC).

Rule 129. A. Parties to an international armed conflict may not deport or forcibly transfer the civilian population of an occupied territory, in whole or in part, unless the security of the civilians involved or imperative military reasons so demand. [IAC]
B. Parties to a non-international armed conflict may not order the displacement of the civilian population, in whole or in part, for reasons related to the conflict, unless the security of the civilians involved or imperative military reasons so demand. [NIAC]

38 Jean-Marie Henckaerts and Louise Doswald-Beck, *Customary International Humanitarian Law* (2 vols Cambridge University Press, Cambridge 2005).

> **Rule 130**. States may not deport or transfer parts of their own civilian population into a territory they occupy. [IAC]
> **Rule 131**. In case of displacement, all possible measures must be taken in order that the civilians concerned are received under satisfactory conditions of shelter, hygiene, health, safety and nutrition and that members of the same family are not separated. [IAC/NIAC]
> **Rule 132**. Displaced persons have a right to voluntary return in safety to their homes or places of habitual residence as soon as the reasons for their displacement cease to exist. [IAC/NIAC]
> **Rule 133**. The property rights of displaced persons must be respected. [IAC/NIAC]

Although Piotrowicz has some problems with the methodology used to support the customary nature of these rules, particularly the reliance on the Guiding Principles on Internal Displacement (as they may not in themselves be customary), he does support the customary status of most of these rules.[39] This is a critical argument as then the provisions against forced displacement from home and homeland bind *all states* who are involved in armed conflict, whether internal or international.

This is probably the most comprehensive regime of protection for home and homeland but the situation must be classified as an armed conflict. The difficulty is that in these situations many of the national authorities involved classify the conflict such as the Kurdish/Turkish conflict as an insurgency and argue that peoples are displaced for 'security reasons'. However, an analysis outside of the scope of this chapter can be conducted that many of the situations of non-natural disaster type of massive displacements are related to a non-international armed conflict such as the situations in Darfur and Pakistan. This legal regime seems at first glance to be just the type of treaty regime needed to deal with massive displacement of peoples in armed conflict, but as with every other international legal regime the difficulty is the enforcement. National governments are required to criminalise only those provisions they agree to and there is no obligation to criminalise these violations of customary international law, even though strictly speaking perhaps there should be. The international legal system has developed a rudimentary and consensual system of criminal justice but only for those that bear the greatest responsibility. The Darfur situation is currently under investigation by the International Criminal Court and indictments have been issued against Ahmad Muhammad Harun, former Minister of State for the Interior of the Government of Sudan and current Minister for Humanitarian Affairs of Sudan, and against

39 Ryzard Piotrowicz, 'Displacement and Displaced Persons' in Elizabeth Wilmshurst and Susan Breau (eds), *Perspectives on the ICRC Study on Customary International Humanitarian Law* (Cambridge University Press, Cambridge 2007) 337–53.

Omar Hassan Ahmad Al Bashir, President of the Republic of Sudan.[40] If these trials ever take place they would be extremely important on the issue of criminal accountability for forced displacement from home and homeland within the context of an internal armed conflict.

The specific provision in the Statute of the International Criminal Court is:

> 2. For the purpose of this Statute, 'war crimes' means:
> (a) Grave breaches of the Geneva Conventions of 12 August 1949, namely, any of the following acts against persons or property protected under the provisions of the relevant Geneva Convention:...
> (vii) Unlawful deportation or transfer or unlawful confinement...
> (e) Other serious violations of the laws and customs applicable in armed conflicts not of an international character, within the established framework of international law, namely, the following acts:...
> (viii) The transfer, directly or indirectly, by the Occupying Power of parts of its own civilian population into the territory it occupies, or the deportation or transfer of all or parts of the population of the occupied territory within or outside this territory...[41]

The *Legal Consequences of the Construction of a Wall in the Occupied Palestinian Territory* Advisory Opinion decided by the International Court of Justice in 2004[42] considers the treaty provisions discussed here in both international humanitarian law and international human rights law. The referral to the court by the General Assembly was to consider whether the construction of a wall between Israel and the Occupied Palestinian Territory was in compliance with international law. The court found on a number of reasons that the Israeli government was in breach of its international treaty and customary law obligations. With respect to displacement and housing the court found a breach of Article 49 of Geneva Convention IV as it was of the view that since 1977 Israel had conducted a policy of settlement of Israelis within the Occupied Territories that violated this provision. Furthermore, the court found that the wall would cause demographic changes within the Palestinian Occupied Territories a violation of the obligations of occupation. Furthermore, the majority of ICJ judges held that there was also a violation of international human rights law on the right to adequate housing as the Palestinians would be separated from some of their lands and residences as a result of the wall. However, as with the treaty provisions themselves there are difficulties in enforcement as this was an

---

40 http://www.icc-cpi.int/Menus/ICC/Situations+and+Cases/Situations/Situation+ICC+0205/ for details of the arrest warrants issued (accessed 20 September 2009).

41 Statute of the International Criminal Court (adopted 17 July 1998) 2187 *UNTS* 90.

42 *Legal Consequences of the Construction of a Wall in the Occupied Palestinian Territory*, Advisory Opinion of 9 July 2004 [2004] *ICJ Reports* 36.

Advisory Opinion to the General Assembly to advise the United Nations in their dealings with the Israelis and Palestinians and not an opinion binding on Israel. It would be up to the Security Council to act on this opinion but due to threatened vetoes by the United States they have not done do.

(4) 1951 Refugee Convention

The other important post-war development was the construction of a treaty concerning those persons forced to cross international frontiers to seek safety. These persons are known as refugees and in 1951 a Refugee Convention was adopted.[43] The definition of 'refugee' in Article 1 states:

> owing to well-founded fear of being persecuted for reasons of race, religion, nationality, membership of a particular social group or political opinion, is outside the country of his nationality and is unable or, owing to such fear, is unwilling to avail himself of the protection of that country; or who, not having a nationality and being outside the country of his former habitual residence as a result of such events, is unable or, owing to such fear, is unwilling to return to it.

Once a person is classified as a refugee and is granted asylum, within their new country they are also granted limited housing rights:

> *Article 13. – Movable and immovable property*
> The Contracting States shall accord to a refugee treatment as favourable as possible and, in any event, not less favourable than that accorded to aliens generally in the same circumstances, as regards the acquisition of movable and immovable property and other rights pertaining thereto, and to leases and other contracts relating to movable and immovable property.
>
> *Article 21. – Housing*
> As regards housing, the Contracting States, in so far as the matter is regulated by laws or regulations or is subject to the control of public authorities, shall accord to refugees lawfully staying in their territory treatment as favourable as possible and, in any event, not less favourable than that accorded to aliens generally in the same circumstances.

The latest figures available show that the number of refugees of concern to the UNHCR is 10.45 million refugees as at the beginning of 2009.[44] There is no specificity in the Convention about the right to return to one's home or

---

43 Convention Relating to the Status of Refugees (adopted 28 July 1951) 89 *UNTS* 150.

44 http://www.unhcr.org/pages/49c3646c1d.html (accessed 14 September 2009).

homeland although the right to voluntary return may be established in customary international law. An example is Committee on the Elimination of Racial Discrimination, in General Recommendation XXII(1996) on Article 5 of the Convention on Refugees and Displaced Persons affirmed that all 'refugees and displaced persons have the right freely to return to their homes of origin under conditions of safety'.[45] With respect to state practice, Annex 7 of the Dayton Peace Agreement for Bosnia and Herzegovina[46] states that all refugees and displaced persons have the right to 'freely to return to their homes of origin'. It also specifies that they have the right to have restored to them property of which they were deprived in the course of hostilities since 1991 and to be compensated for any property that cannot be restored to them.[47] A right to return is also set out in:

> (1) the 1994 Abkhazia Quadripartite agreement on voluntary return of refugees and displaced persons (Art. 3(a));[48]
> (2) the 1995 Basic Agreement on the Region of Eastern Slavonia, Baranja and Western Sirmium (Erdut Agreement) (para. 7);[49]
> (3) The 2006 Darfur Peace Agreement (para. 176);[50] and
> (4) The 2006 Comprehensive Peace Accord for Nepal (para. 7.3.3).[51]

There was literally no enforcement mechanism built into the Refugee Convention and so it is left to individual nations to implement their treaty obligations, but the provisions in the peace agreements cited above give some hope to the implementation of the obligation of a right to return. In fact it has been left to the soft law principles discussed below to provide specificity to a right of return and restitution.

---

45 UN Doc. HRI\GEN\1\Rev.6 at 211 (2003), Committee on the Elimination of Racial Discrimination, General Recommendation 22, Refugees and Displaced Persons (Forty-ninth Session, 1996).

46 Dayton Peace Agreement for Bosnia and Herzegovina of 14 December 1995, Annex 7, Article 1 (http://www.ohr.int/dpa/default.asp?content_id=379 accessed 20 September 2009).

47 Ibid., Annex 7, Article 1.

48 http://www.incore.ulst.ac.uk/services/cds/agreements/pdf/geo7.pdf (accessed 20 September 2009).

49 http://www.reliefweb.int/rw/rwb.nsf/db900SID/MHII-68JC6Z?OpenDocument (accessed 20 September 2009).

50 Darfur Peace Agreement 2006, http://allafrica.com/peaceafrica/resources/view/00010926.pdf (accessed 20 September 2009).

51 http://www.satp.org/satporgtp/countries/nepal/document/papers/peaceagreement.htm (accessed 20 September 2009).

(5) Guiding Principles on Internal Displacement and UN Declaration on the Rights of Indigenous Peoples

In December 2008, the Internal Displacement Monitoring Centre estimated that there were 26 million internally displaced people (hereafter IDPs) worldwide, as a result of armed conflict.[52] Sudan alone is estimated to have 4.9 million IDPs. The number of people who have been forcibly displaced from their homes is estimated at 1 per cent of the world's population.[53] While refugees are eligible to receive international protection and assistance under the 1951 Refugee Convention and the 1967 Protocol to the Convention, the international community is not under the same legal obligation to protect and assist internally displaced people. The primary responsibility for the security and well-being of all displaced peoples is left with the national governments but they are often unable or unwilling to live up to this obligation.

There had not been an agreed international law definition of internal displacement. According to Phuong the root causes of displacement varies but includes natural disasters, inter-state conflict, intra-state conflicts, human rights violations, development projects and internal strife.[54] As a response to this major lacuna in international law, the Guiding Principles on Internal Displacement[55] were developed by in 1998 by the Representative of the Secretary-General on Internally Displaced Persons, Francis Deng, and submitted to the UN Commission on Human Rights, but they were never adopted by way of treaty of UN General Assembly Declaration. These Guiding Principles compile and restate the various relevant norms of international human rights and humanitarian law and apply these to situations of internal displacement. The Guiding Principles on internally displaced persons propose a definition suitable for this chapter which is:

> internally displaced persons are persons or groups of persons who have been forced or obliged to flee or to leave their homes or places of habitual residence, in particular as a result of or in order to avoid the effects of armed conflict, situations of generalized violence, violations of human rights or natural or human-made disasters and who have not crossed an internationally recognized State border.[56]

52 http://www.fmreview.org/FMRpdfs/GP10/GP10.pdf (accessed 14 September 2009).

53 Ibid.

54 Catherine Phuong, *The International Protection of Internally Displaced Persons* (Cambridge University Press, Cambridge 2004), 26.

55 UN Doc. E/CN.4/1998/53/Add.2 Guiding Principles on Internal Displacement, 11 February 1998.

56 Ibid., para. 2.

The Guiding Principles are not a UN declaration on the rights of internally displaced peoples, nor do they constitute, as such, a binding instrument. However, it is argued that they reflect and are consistent with international human rights law and international humanitarian law and to a large extent thus codify and make explicit guarantees protecting internally displaced persons that are inherent in these bodies of law.[57] The relevant principles with respect to home and homeland are as follows:

> **Principle 14**
> 1. Every internally displaced person has the right to liberty of movement and freedom to choose his or her residence.
> **Principle 15**
> Internally displaced persons have the right to
> (b) leave their country
> (d) be protected against forced return to or resettlement in any place where their life, safety, liberty and/or health would be at risk.
> **Principle 18**
> 1. All internally displaced persons have the right to an adequate standard of living.
> 2. At the minimum, regardless of the circumstances, and without discrimination, competent authorities shall provide internally displaced persons with and ensure safe access to:
> (b) Basic shelter and housing...

Kalin has provided an influential commentary to these guidelines, seeking to argue their customary status.[58] His commentary to Principle 18 states:

> The right to shelter and housing is explicitly guaranteed by Article 25(1) UDHR, Article 11(1) CESCR, Article 27(3) CRC, Article 38 ArCHR and Article 31 ESC as an aspect of the right to an adequate standard of living. General Comment 7 (1997) of the Committee on Economic, Social and Cultural Rights sets out the protection provided by this guarantee against forced evictions. Such protection also applies to internally displaced persons who had access to housing during their displacement but are at risk of losing it as a consequence of being evicted.

Kalin also applies international humanitarian law to the principle stating:

> Even though humanitarian law does not contain any explicit provision protecting civilian housing and shelter, Article 54(2) Protocol I protects objects that are indispensable for survival. The ICRC Commentary points out that 'it cannot be

57 Walter Kalin, 'Legal Annotations on the Guiding Principles' 2008 (http://www.asil.org/pdfs/stlp.pdf, accessed 14 September 2009).

58 Ibid., 46.

excluded that as a result of climate or other circumstances, objects such as shelter or clothing must be considered as indispensable to survival' and are, therefore, protected against attack, removal or destruction. This issue is also covered, at least implicitly, by the prohibition against destruction of property belonging to private persons as embodied in Article 53 Geneva Convention IV.[59]

Principle 21
1. No one shall be arbitrarily deprived of property and possessions.
2. The property and possessions of internally displaced persons shall in all circumstances be protected, in particular, against the following acts:
(a) Pillage;
(b) Direct or indiscriminate attacks or other acts of violence;
(c) Being used to shield military operations or objectives;
(d) Being made the object of reprisal; and
(e) Being destroyed or appropriated as a form of collective punishment.
3. Property and possessions left behind by internally displaced persons should be protected against destruction and arbitrary and illegal appropriation, occupation or use.

The Commentary to this provision is also illuminating particularly with respect to the third paragraph. Kalin has to concede that the principle of protection against destruction or appropriation 'is not based on explicit language in present human rights or humanitarian law', but that it 'reflects a strong trend in present international law towards deducing from human rights guarantees the duty of authorities not only to refrain from violations but to provide protection against violations by others.'[60] However, his only support for this trend is the UN Secretary General's 2007 report on the protection of civilians in armed conflict, which recommended to the Security Council the following measures:

(a) Preventive and deterrent actions, such as the strategic deployment of peacekeeping troops to prevent evictions and the illegal appropriation of land and property, and the identification and prosecution by national courts or the International Criminal Court of those criminally responsible for the illegal appropriation or destruction of land and property; (b) Preparatory actions, such as the early identification and registration of land and property abandoned by internally displaced persons and refugees to facilitate restitution or, where necessary, compensation, and the issuance of ownership documentation where this has been lost or destroyed.[61]

---

59 Ibid.
60 Ibid., 54.
61 UN Document, S/2007/643, Secretary-General's Annual Report 2007, para. 59.

Regrettably, none of this can be said to be evidence of an emergence of a customary norm prohibiting confiscation of property as a Secretary-General's report cannot be argued to be state practice or *opinio juris*.[62] Only the European Convention on Human Rights has a specific guarantee on the right to property as seen above.

> **Principle 28**
> 1. Competent authorities have the primary duty and responsibility to establish conditions, as well as provide the means, which allow internally displaced persons to return voluntarily, in safety and with dignity, to their homes or places of habitual residence, or to resettle voluntarily in another part of the country. Such authorities shall endeavour to facilitate the reintegration of returned or resettled internally displaced persons.
> 2. Special efforts should be made to ensure the full participation of internally displaced persons in the planning and management of their return or resettlement and reintegration.

The commentary to this rule acknowledges that 'there is no general rule in present human right law that explicitly affirms the right of internally displaced persons to return to their original place of residence or to move to another safe place of their choice within their own country.'[63] Kalin argues that this right can be deduced from the right to the liberty of movement and the right to choose one's residence as embodied in Article 12 ICCPR, which, however, can be limited under certain conditions. Support for this provision can also be found in international humanitarian law as discussed above, particularly Article 49, paragraph 2 Geneva Convention IV. But once again Kalin acknowledges that the provision is applicable only during interstate armed conflicts. He also admits that in situations of internal armed conflict neither common Article 3 nor Protocol II contains rules governing the right of the internally displaced to return to their residences, and relies on Rule 132 in the ICRC customary international humanitarian law study to argue that internally '[d]isplaced persons have a right to voluntary return in safety to their homes or places of habitual residence as soon as the reasons for their displacement

---

62 Statute of the International Court of Justice (adopted 26 June 1945) *TS* 993. Article 38 of the Statute states:

1. The Court, whose function is to decide in accordance with international law such disputes as are submitted to it, shall apply:

a. international conventions, whether general or particular, establishing rules expressly recognized by the contesting states;

b. international custom, as evidence of a general practice accepted as law;

c. the general principles of law recognized by civilized nations;

d. subject to the provisions of Article 59, judicial decisions and the teachings of the most highly qualified publicists of the various nations, as subsidiary means for the determination of rules of law.

63 Walter Kalin, 'Legal Annotations on the Guiding Principles' 2008 (http://www.asil.org/pdfs/stlp.pdf, accessed 14 September 2009).69.

cease to exist' arguably has become part of customary international humanitarian law applicable in both international and non-international armed conflict.[64]

In support of this principle, the practice of the UN Security Council is extensive as it has not only called on governments and the international community to facilitate the return of internally displaced persons but on several occasions explicitly recognised and affirmed the right of persons to return to their former homes. See for example resolutions with regard to: Bosnia-Herzegovina (S/RES/820 (1993), para. 7); Croatia (S/RES/1009 (1995), para. 2); Georgia (S/RES/876 (1993) and S/RES/1781 (2007), para. 15); Kosovo (S/RES/1244(1999), preambular para. 7). The Security Council has also mandated peacekeeping operations under Chapter VII of the UN Charter to work towards facilitating the voluntary return of internally displaced persons to their former homes (e.g., E/RES/ S/RES/1778 (2007) para. 1 (Chad) and S/RES/1756 (2007), para 3(b)(Democratic Republic of Congo)). Similarly, the General Assembly has reaffirmed the right of all displaced persons to return to their homes or former places of residence in the territories occupied by Israel since 1967 (A/RES/51/126).[65]

At the regional level, the European Court on Human Rights explicitly refers to Principles 18 and 28 and stresses that:

> the authorities have the primary duty and responsibility to establish conditions, as well as provide the means, which allow the applicants to return voluntarily, in safety and with dignity, to their homes or places of habitual residence, or to resettle voluntarily in another part of the country.[66]

Although it may well be that the practice of the UN Security Council may not in itself result in customary international law, the practice of the states whose membership rotates through the Security Council in agreeing to these resolutions may be reflecting a customary norm of a right to restitution and return to one's own home and homeland.

> **Principle 29.2**
> Competent authorities have the duty and responsibility to assist returned and/or resettled internally displaced persons to recover, to the extent possible, their property and possessions which they left behind or were dispossessed of upon their displacement. When recovery of such property and possessions is not possible, competent authorities shall provide or assist these persons in obtaining appropriate compensation or another form of just reparation.

---

64 Ibid., 69–71.

65 As cited in the Kalin commentary, ibid.

66 *Doğan and others v. Turkey* (App nos. 8803-8811/02, 8813/02 and 8815-8819/02) ECHR 29 June 2004, para. 154.

The issue of recovery of property and/or compensation is a fundamental part of a right to home and homeland. People who return to their former homes often find their property destroyed, confiscated, expropriated or occupied by other people.[67] The legal issue is whether the former owner has a right of restitution of the property or to financial compensation. This issue was addressed in the Advisory Opinion on the *Legal Consequences of the Construction of a Wall in the Occupied Palestinian Territory*. The International Court of Justice quoting the Chrorzow Factory case referred to the fundamental customary principle that breaches of international law entail a duty to provide reparation that:

> must, as far as possible, wipe out all the consequences of the illegal act and re-establish the situation which would, in all probability, have existed if that act had not been committed. Restitution in kind, or, if this is not possible, payment of a sum corresponding to the value which a restitution in kind would bear; the award, if need be, of damages for loss sustained which would not be covered by restitution in kind or payment in place of it – such are the principles which should serve to determine the amount of compensation due for an act contrary to international law...[68]

The court importantly held that these principles apply to reparation in the form of restitution of or compensation for the requisition and destruction of homes, businesses and agricultural holdings owned by natural or legal persons that was a consequence of the construction, in violation of international human rights and humanitarian law, of the wall in the Occupied Palestinian Territory.[69]

Regional human rights tribunals have ordered compensation for victims of displacement from home and homeland in the European and Inter-American systems. As discussed above the case of *Doğan v. Turkey* awarded compensation for human rights abuses involving denial of access to property and possessions, including unregistered land to which the applicants were attributed rights in accordance with local custom.[70] The Inter-American Commission on Human Rights has recommended payment of just compensation to returning internally

67 Walter Kalin, 'Legal Annotations on the Guiding Principles' 2008 (http://www.asil.org/pdfs/stlp.pdf, accessed 14 September 2009).72.

68 *Legal Consequences of the Construction of a Wall in the Occupied Palestinian Territory*, Advisory Opinion of 9 July 2004 [2004] *ICJ Reports* 36, para. 152; and *Case Concerning the Factory at Chorzów* (*Germany v Poland*) (Merits) PCIJ Rep Series A No 17, p. 47.

69 *Legal Consequences of the Construction of a Wall in the Occupied Palestinian Territory*, Advisory Opinion of 9 July 2004 [2004] *ICJ Reports* 36 para. 152.

70 *Doğan and others v. Turkey* (App nos. 8803-8811/02, 8813/02 and 8815-8819/02) ECHR 29 June 2004, para. 154.

displaced persons for the loss of their property, including homes, crops, livestock and other belongings, in the *Miskito* case.[71]

Finally, there is an important treaty on restitution and compensation for displacement. The Rome Statute of the International Criminal Court provides that the court 'shall establish principles relating to reparations to, or in respect of, victims, including restitution, compensation and rehabilitation'.[72] This is an essential provision to deal with the situation of displacement in the context of an international crimes such as grave breaches of international humanitarian law. The Statute of the War Crimes Tribunal for the former Yugoslavia (ICTY) allows the Tribunal to order the return of any property and proceeds acquired by criminal conduct, including by means of duress, to their rightful owners.[73]

These principles embody what might be needed in terms of rights to home and homeland both before and after displacement. However, these provisions should be incorporated into an international instrument with an enforcement mechanism which will deal with serious violations of these rights as in their current form the principles remain soft law and are not binding.[74] The principles could be seen as rights and these could be developed into an instrument. However, once again, as these situations are often the result of internal conflict, there is reluctance on the part of sovereign states to agree to such an instrument.[75] The argument that the principles are evolving into customary law is very important as that might allow concerned parties to argue that a nation that does preserve and protect a displaced person's home and not facilitate a return to a specific residence is in violation of its obligations under international law.

Principles on Housing and Property Restitution for Refugees and Displaced Persons

Another important development that further refines the right of return and restitution is the Pinherio Principles on Housing and Property Restitution for Refugees and Displaced Persons.[76] The development of these principles began in 1997 when the Committee on the Elimination of Racial Discrimination (CERD) proposed to the Sub-Commission on the Promotion and Protection of Human Rights to study the

71 Report on the situation of human rights of a segment of the Nicaraguan population of Miskito origin, OEA/Ser.L/V/II.62, doc. 10, rev. 3, 29 November 1983.

72 Statute of the International Criminal Court (adopted 17 July 1998) 2187 *UNTS* 90, Article 75 (1).

73 UN Doc. S/75704, 25 May 1993, Statute of the International Criminal Tribunal for the former Yugoslavia, Article 24 (plunder of property and displacement are crimes under the statute).

74 Susan Carr, 'From Theory to Practice: National and Regional Application of the Guiding Principles' (2009) 21 *International Journal of Refugee Law* 34, 35.

75 Ibid., 34.

76 http://www.unhcr.org.ua/img/uploads/docs/PinheiroPrinciples.pdf (accessed 19 September 2009).

return of refugee or displaced persons' property. In 1998, the Sub-Commission adopted a resolution on Housing and Property Restitution in the Context of the Return of Rights for Refugees and Internally Displaced Persons, which affirmed the Sub-Commission's serious attention to restitution of lost property as a fundamental human rights concern.[77] In 2002, the Sub-Commission appointed Paulo Sérgio Pinheiro, of Brazil, as Special Rapporteur on Housing and Property Restitution for Refugees and Internally Displaced Persons. After considering his preliminary study in 2003, the Sub-Commission asked the Special Rapporteur to prepare draft principles or guidelines on housing and property restitution based on the initial conclusions of the preliminary study. In 2004, Pinheiro presented a preliminary set of principles to the Sub-Commission for consideration and review. After detailed responses to the principles, the final text was presented to the Sub-Commission on the Promotion and Protection of Human Rights and they were formally endorsed on 11 August 2005.[78]

These principles are not treaty provisions and are again soft law principles but as with the Guiding Principles on Internal Displacement they do have the potential at some point to become customary international law. Principle 2.1 provides that refugees and IDPs 'have the right to have restored to them any housing, land and/or property of which they were arbitrarily or unlawfully deprived, or to be compensated for any housing, land and/or property that is factually impossible to restore as determined by an independent, impartial tribunal'. These rights are extended to 'tenants, social occupancy rights holders and other legitimate occupants or users of housing, land and property' and that such claimants should (as set out in Principle 16.1), 'to the maximum extent possible', be 'able to return to and re-possess and use their housing, land and property in a similar manner to those possessing formal ownership rights'. In terms of the relationship between restitution of property and compensation, the Restitution Principles give clear priority to restitution (as set out in Principle 21.1) 'that the remedy of compensation is only used when the remedy of restitution is not factually possible or when the injured party knowingly and voluntarily accepts compensation in lieu of restitution, or when the terms of a negotiated peace settlement provide for a combination of restitution and compensation'.[79]

77 Sub-Commission on the Promotion and Protection of Human Rights, formerly Sub-Commission on the Prevention of Discrimination and Protection of Minorities, Resolution 1998/26 Housing and Property Restitution in the Context of the Return of Refugees and Internally Displaced Persons, adopted 26 August 1998; see also Resolution 2002/7 Housing and Property Restitution in the Context of Refugees and Other Displaced Persons, adopted 14 August 2002. Both are found at: http://www.unhabitat.org/list.asp?typeid=23&catid=463&start=11&page=2&ContentByTheme=277 (accessed 20 September 2009).

78 http://www.ohchr.org/Documents/Publications/pinheiro_principles.pdf (accessed 20 September 2009).

79 Ibid.

Another pertinent declaration which is also not a treaty but was adopted by General Assembly resolution deals with a particular group often subject to displacement, indigenous peoples.

UN Declaration on the Rights of Indigenous Peoples 2007[80]

> *Article 8*
> 1. Indigenous peoples and individuals have the right not to be subjected to forced assimilation or destruction of their culture.
> 2. States shall provide effective mechanisms for prevention of, and redress for:
> (*a*) Any action which has the aim or effect of depriving them of their integrity as distinct peoples, or of their cultural values or ethnic identities;
> (*b*) Any action which has the aim or effect of dispossessing them of their lands, territories or resources;
> (*c*) Any form of forced population transfer which has the aim or effect of violating or undermining any of their rights;
> (*d*) Any form of forced assimilation or integration;
> (*e*) Any form of propaganda designed to promote or incite racial or ethnic discrimination directed against them.
>
> *Article 10*
> Indigenous peoples shall not be forcibly removed from their lands or territories. No relocation shall take place without the free, prior and informed consent of the indigenous peoples concerned and after agreement on just and fair compensation and, where possible, with the option of return.

This is a statement on a right to a homeland but there is no agreed definition of indigenous peoples in this declaration. The United Nations Economic and Social Council established the UN Permanent Forum on Indigenous Peoples (UNPFII) with its first meeting in May 2002. There is no enforcement mechanism for the declaration and it remains to be seen if it becomes part of customary international law.

A final soft-law instrument is The Millennium Declaration by the General Assembly in 2000 which confirmed collective responsibility for all peoples by stating:

> We recognise that, in addition to our separate responsibilities to our individual societies, we have a collective responsibility to uphold the principles of human dignity, equality and equity at the global level. As leaders, we have a

80 UN Doc. A/Res/ 61/295, General Assembly Resolution, UN Declaration on the Rights of Indigenous Peoples (adopted 13 September 2007).

> duty therefore to all the world's people, especially the most vulnerable and, in particular the children of the world, to whom the future belongs.[81]

In the Millennium Development goals under 'Protecting Our Common Environment' is a statement resolving 'to adopt in all our environmental action a new ethic of conservation and stewardship and, as first steps, resolves...to intensify cooperation to reduce the number and effects of natural and man-made disasters'.[82] This declaration points to the only mechanism to truly deal with displacement is international responsibility to prevent and respond to man-made and natural disasters.

(6) The Responsibility to Protect in International Law

An important development that has emerged in this new century is the notion of international responsibility as set out above. It has been further refined in the doctrine of the 'Responsibility to Protect' (R2P) which has been endorsed by the international community as a responsibility on all nations to protect populations of every state from genocide, crimes against humanity, ethnic cleansing and war crimes. This endorsement was a key positive outcome of the United Nations 60th Anniversary Summit. The General Assembly resolution incorporating the summit outcomes states:

> The international community, through the United Nations, also has the responsibility to use appropriate diplomatic, humanitarian and other peaceful means, in accordance with Chapter VI and VIII of the Charter, to help protect populations from genocide, war crimes, ethnic cleansing and crimes against humanity. In this context, we are prepared to take collective action, in a timely and decisive manner, through the Security Council, in accordance with the UN Charter, including Chapter VII, on a case by case basis and in cooperation with relevant regional organizations as appropriate, should peaceful means be inadequate and national authorities manifestly failing to protect their populations from genocide, war crimes, ethnic cleansing and crimes against humanity…[83]

This declaration was the end result of a series of reports on the disputed right of humanitarian intervention, including the High Level Panel on Threats, Challenges and Change, *A More Secure World* and the Secretary-General's report for the

81 UN Doc. A/Res/55/2, General Assembly Resolution, United Nations Millennium Declaration (adopted 18 September 2001).

82 Ibid.

83 UN Doc. A/Res./60, *UN Summit Outcome Document*, 24 October 2005, para. 139.

60th anniversary Summit, *In Larger Freedom*.[84] Earlier, an influential report, *The Responsibility to Protect*, prepared by the International Commission on Intervention and State Sovereignty, proposed three separate stages of intervention for human protection purposes: the responsibility to prevent, the responsibility to react and the responsibility to rebuild.[85] This report also proposed criteria for intervention, if necessary by force, by the international community. These criteria are:

> **(1) The Just Cause Threshold**
> Military intervention for human protection purposes is an exceptional and extraordinary measure. To be warranted, there must be serious and irreparable harm occurring to human beings, or imminently likely to occur, of the following kind:
> A. **large scale loss of life**, actual or apprehended, with genocidal intent or not, which is the product either of deliberate state action, or state neglect or inability to act, or a failed state situation; or
> B. **large scale 'ethnic cleansing'**, actual or apprehended, whether carried out by killing, forced expulsion, acts of terror or rape.[86]

It should be noted that none of the reports cited above supports a state acting on its own to intervene in another sovereign state and that the 'right authority' means that there is no better or more appropriate body than the United Nations Security Council to authorise military intervention for human protection purposes.[87]

However, on the face of it, this new doctrine does not include a specific international obligation to prevent internal displacement or to protect persons who have been displaced. Yet this is precisely how the doctrine is being interpreted in academic literature. Barbour and Gorlick argue that R2P should be interpreted as a positive obligation on states to take steps to prevent victimisation, reduce statelessness and redress the dire circumstances for those who have no human rights protection or national rights.[88] This certainly could be extended to victims of disasters when their home nations are unwilling or unable to address the displacement issues. Wong argues that the doctrine should authorise the international community to react when a government demonstrates a 'criminal

---

84 Secretary-General's High-Level Panel on Threats, Challenges and Change, *A More Secure World* (United Nations, New York 2004); UN Doc. A/59/2005, *In Larger Freedom*, 21 March 2005.

85 International Commission on Intervention and State Sovereignty, *The Responsibility to Protect* (Ottawa, 2001).

86 Ibid., see synopsis pp.XI-XIII.

87 Ibid.

88 Brian Barbour and Brian Gorlick, 'Embracing the "Responsibility to Protect": A Repertoire of Measures Including Asylum for Potential Victims' (2008) 20 *International Journal of Refugee Law* 533.

failure' to protect its people from natural or man-disasters based on omissions that are arguably crimes against humanity.[89]

Barber discusses an excellent case study to support R2P in disaster and displacement: the situation in Myanmar in 2008.[90] This controversy erupted in May 2008 as a result of the Cyclone Nargis when the Myanmar regime refused to allow delivery of aid. French Foreign Minister Kouchner called on the Security Council to impose, by force if necessary, the international delivery of aid on the Myanmar government.[91] It was noted by Wong that the threshold for this international responsibility was not the disaster itself but the state's failure to protect its citizens in the aftermath of the disaster.[92] The inaction would have to be deliberate to amount to a crime against humanity under international law. This interpretation met with favour by the Co-Chair of the International Commission on Intervention and State Sovereignty, Gareth Evans, who argued that if the generals of Myanmar were 'in effect denying relief to hundreds of thousands of people at real and immediate risk of death' this could be 'characterised as a crime against humanity, then the responsibility to protect principle does indeed cut in'.[93] These arguments could be called a 'constructive interpretation' of R2P grounded in international criminal jurisprudence that an omission may be the basis of a finding of a crime against humanity.

Furthermore, Barber argues that the Security Council is competent to declare a humanitarian crisis to be a threat to international peace and security, and thus exercise its Chapter VII powers to authorise the use of force. She argues that this competence has been so widely accepted that it may reasonably be said to have found a place within customary international law.[94] The practice of the United Nations confirms her view when one examines the situations in Somalia and Yugoslavia, but she may be taking the argument further than the current practice because as of yet the United Nations has not declared massive displacement in the context of natural disaster as a threat to international peace and security. She is correct that displacement of peoples in the context of armed conflict as seen by the Security Council resolutions discussed earlier are threats to international peace and security.

Nevertheless, R2P in itself is a very new concept only emerging in 2000 (in a Dutch report entitled *Humanitarian Intervention*) and it may not yet be a doctrine

---

89 Jarrod Wong, 'Reconstructing the Responsibility to Protect in the Wake of Cyclones and Separatism' (2009) *Tulane Law Review* 84 (available at SSRN: http://ssrn.com/abstract=1446364, accessed 18 September 2010).

90 Rebecca Barber, 'The Responsibility to Protect the Survivors of Natural Disaster: Cyclone Nargis. A Case Study' 14 *Journal of Conflict and Security Law* 3.

91 Ibid.

92 Jarrod Wong, 'Reconstructing the Responsibility to Protect in the Wake of Cyclones and Separatism' (2009) *Tulane Law Review* 84 (available at SSRN: http://ssrn.com/abstract=1446364).

93 Rebecca Barber, The Responsibility to Protect the Survivors of Natural Disaster: Cyclone Nargis. A Case Study' 14 *Journal of Conflict and Security Law* 3, 4.

94 Ibid.

of international law.[95] To call on international responsibility at this juncture may only be a political tool rather than a legal obligation. In any event as a result of intensive diplomatic efforts, perhaps with the threat of international intervention, the regime in Myanmar allowed limited relief efforts. Action in a situation such as Myanmar would have confirmed the extension of the doctrine of collective security which cannot be said to have happened as a result of the peaceful resolution to the humanitarian disaster.

The most regrettable part of the practice of the Security Council is the delay in authorising a robust response to disaster. The general practice is to wait until a society disintegrates before there is any type of intervention. Prevention is a rarely utilised part of the toolkit of peace and security. As we have seen from the human rights and humanitarian law discussion, it is difficult to facilitate a right to return to home and homeland after displacement. Unless there is an acceptance that the 'Responsibility to Protect' includes the 'Responsibility to Prevent' the right to home and homeland will not be a realisable and enforceable right.

The other characteristic that is lacking is the sense of legal obligation necessary to truly implement the responsibility to protect. Darfur is the key example of where the international community is failing in its responsibility as millions of displaced persons are still in very insecure camps and there are not enough troops on the ground to truly protect people. Returning to home and homeland is not possible in that situation. However, there are other missions such as the Democratic Republic of Congo and Burundi where robust mandates are given to troops to use force to protect peoples and have allowed internally displaced people to return home. Another excellent example of R2P in action is the Great Lakes Peace Process which includes arrangements for return of property to IDPs and refugees.[96]

The fact that the three responsibilities of preventing, reaction and rebuilding might be legal obligations may well be some time in the future. It will involve a fundamental shift in understanding as to when a 'threat to the peace' might actually emerge, as the fact is that Chapter VII mandates are needed at a much earlier stage in the process. This will be seen by many countries as an attack on the notion of state sovereignty and without the adoption of the specific criteria for the use of force as set out in the original report these states may well have a point. The notion of a legal obligation of a responsibility to protect may be some time off but there is clear movement in that direction in the practice of the United Nations in peace enforcement.[97]

---

95 Advisory Council on International Affairs and Advisory Committee on Issues of Public International Law, *Humanitarian Intervention* (The Hague 2000).

96 For a text of the peace pacts see https://www.lse.ac.uk/collections/law/projects/greatlakes/ihl-greatlakes-summary.htm (accessed 22 September 2009).

97 Susan Breau, 'The Impact of the Responsibility to Protect on Peacekeeping' (2006) 11 *Journal of Conflict and Security Law* 429.

(7) Conclusion

It seems from this analysis that taking all the instruments in total there can be an argument of an international law right to a home and homeland. The rights derived from both human rights law and humanitarian law includes: (1) protection from arbitrary displacement in the first instance; (2) protection and assistance after displacement has taken place; and (3) assistance with safe and voluntary return or resettlement and rehabilitation. It cannot be unequivocally argued that the second and third part of these rights are established within customary law but the large volume of state and international practice certainly seems to point in that direction and it seems likely that the Guiding Principles on Displacement will be part of that legal regime.

However, most critical in the protection of the right to home and homeland is the obligation on the international community to ensure that these massive displacements of persons do not occur in the first place and the only possible mechanism to do that is the 'Responsibility to Protect'. This places the responsibility firmly in the hands of the international community as represented by the United Nations. It is critical that early warning mechanisms be developed so that the 'Responsibility to Prevent' can be realised.

Chapter 8
Loss of the Home during Armed Conflict: ECHR Case Law on Destruction, Eviction and Denial of Access

Antoine Buyse[1]

(1) Introduction

In his *Tristia* the Roman poet Ovid, banished to the shores of the Black Sea, laments his fate and longs to go back to his home in his beloved Rome. Far from being solely a source of inspiration for classical poetry, today the loss of one's home still has far-reaching consequences for private life and security of families and individuals. In times of peace a new home may be difficult enough to find, but in situations of conflict this can be impossible altogether. In the latter case the loss of home causes long-term uprooting of people and large-scale movements of displaced people. In the light of these grave consequences it is important to see what obligations rest upon states to protect persons against such occurrences.

This contribution will focus on what arguably is the strongest system of international human rights protection: the European Convention on Human Rights (ECHR). Article 8 ECHR protects *inter alia* the right to respect for the home. The European Court of Human Rights, the supervisory body of the ECHR, has developed the notion of respect of the home along two strands of case law: a qualified prohibition of interference by the state and positive obligations. In this article I will review the Court's case law on the loss of the home under Article 8 and delve into the question of what factors are taken into account in such an assessment.

Before undertaking this analysis, it is important to emphasize that the notion of the home in the case law of the European Court has developed beyond its original context of privacy and even beyond the mere notion of shelter, although both still play a significant role. The continuing links, and thus the social, physical and emotional attachment of a person to his or her home, seem to be the defining

---

1 Antoine Buyse is a researcher and associate professor at the Netherlands Institute of Human Rights (SIM) at Utrecht University, the Netherlands. This contribution is based on parts of his PhD research on housing restitution after conflict from the perspective of the European Convention of Human Rights. The author thanks Laura Henderson for her editorial assistance. The author can be contacted at: A.C.Buyse@uu.nl.

underlying principle in the Court's assessment when deciding whether a particular place of dwelling can be considered as someone's home.[2] Obviously, this is of major importance for displaced people seeking to regain their house, instead of being forced to resettle elsewhere.

(2) Duties of Non-interference

Respect for the home entails first of all a protection against arbitrary interference.[3] Interference with this right is only allowed under the conditions enumerated in paragraph 2 of Article 8: the interference should have a legal basis and a legitimate aim and must be necessary in a democratic society.[4] Limiting the right in another way than the method of paragraph 2 is not allowed. There is no room for so-called implied limitations not mentioned in the Article itself.[5] In addition, Article 8 ECHR provides that the limitations permitted under the Convention 'shall not be applied for any purpose other than those for which they have been prescribed'. Finally, since an interference constitutes an exception to a right, the Court has adopted a narrow interpretation of paragraph 2 of Article 8.[6] National authorities thus have to follow a specified legal track when interfering with the right to respect for the home.

A legal basis for the interference means that the interference should be carried out in accordance with the law. There must therefore be a basis for the interference in domestic law as a safeguard against arbitrariness. This domestic law should, according to the criteria developed by the Court, be accessible and foreseeable. Accessibility means that an individual should be able to know what the applicable rules are. Laws in any form should not be secret but public. Secondly, foreseeability entails that the individual should be able to regulate his conduct to keep it within the confines of the law. The consequences of his actions should be reasonably foreseeable, if needed with 'appropriate advice'. In order for him to do so, the law should be sufficiently precise. Such precision should not amount to complete rigidity. Otherwise it would be impossible for states to make laws. The court has therefore consistently held that 'many laws are inevitably couched in terms which, to a greater or lesser extent, are vague and whose interpretation and application

2 See for a much more elaborate discussion of this issue my 'Strings Attached: The Concept of "Home" in the Case Law of the European Court of Human Rights' (2006) *European Human Rights Law Review* 294–307.

3 See as one of the earliest among many references: *Gillow v the United Kingdom* (App no 9063/80) (1986) Series A no 109 [51].

4 These requirements are common to Articles 8–11 of the ECHR. Interpretations developed under one of these articles can thus be applied to all of them by the Court. See e.g. *Silver a.o. v The United Kingdom* (Appl no 5947/72) (1983) Series A no 61 [85].

5 *Golder v The United Kingdom* (App no 4451/70) (1975) Series A no 018 [44].

6 *Klass v Germany* (App no 5029/71) (1978) Series A no 28 [42].

are questions of practice.'[7] It is thus up to the state to find the right equilibrium between precision and broad applicability.

The second condition to be fulfilled is the existence of a legitimate aim. Article 8 contains an exhaustive list of the permitted aims: national security, public safety, the economic well-being of the country, the prevention of disorder or crime, the protection of health or morals and the protection of the rights and freedoms of others. The state concerned has to argue convincingly that it interfered with the right to respect for the home in the interest of one of these aims. This condition is usually not a stumbling block: most of the time, the Court accepts the legitimate aim the state invokes.

For loss of housing four of the stated aims could possibly be relevant. Rather arguably, national security and public safety could be at stake when the home concerned belongs to a person who by affiliation, conviction or ethnicity is, according to the state, likely to cause problems or tensions. In conflict situations where groups find themselves opposing each other, this is easily conceivable. The same may apply in post-conflict situations of return: the state may continue to block returns, and thus interfere with an individual's rights, with the same justification. The economic well-being of the country may also be invoked, especially since post-conflict states are often in shortage of funds and housing in general may be in short supply. Finally, the protection of the rights and freedoms of others may play a role. In post-conflict situations of housing restitution, for instance, eviction of illegal occupants will often be necessary. The return of the home to one person or family then entails the loss of housing to another. To protect these others, the state may choose to interfere with the right to respect of the home of the occupant of the house. Whichever course of action – or inaction – the state chooses it will always touch the right of respect for the home of one of the parties.

The third and final test is that of necessity: is the interference 'necessary in a democratic society'? In the leading *Handyside* case the Court developed an interpretation of this test that still stands today.[8] First of all the respondent state must show that the interference corresponds to a pressing social need. Secondly, the interference must be 'proportionate to the legitimate aim pursued'. Effectively, this means that the general interest should be balanced against the interests of the individual whose rights are interfered with. Thirdly, the reasons adduced by the state to justify the interference should be 'relevant and sufficient'. This latter condition entails that the Court should not only ascertain that a state 'exercised its discretion reasonably, carefully and in good faith' nor that it should just look at the national decisions at stake in isolation, but also that it 'must look at them

7 *The Sunday Times v The United Kingdom* (App no 6538/74) (1979) Series A no 30 [49].

8 *Handyside v The United Kingdom* (App no 5493/72) (1976) Series A no 024 [48–50]. See, for a later summary of the necessity test also: *Silver a.o. v The United Kingdom* (Appl no 5947/72) (1983) Series A no 61 [97].

in the light of the case as a whole'.[9] The third condition is in fact a substantive appraisal of what the Court would only assess *in abstracto* under the second test: the legitimate aim. The second block may not lead to stumbling, but the third one is often a difficult hurdle for the state to take. When the aim and its relevancy are not contested at all, the Court does not need to apply the third condition of the necessity test. This explains why it does not figure in every judgment.

The court looks at the facts of a case from a distance and after the event. It is not in the same position as a national authority. It has thus chosen to leave to each state a certain margin of appreciation, a freedom within the bounds allowed by paragraph 2 of Article 8 to make and implement law and policy. The margin leaves room for cultural and other differences between the parties to the ECHR. Additionally it supports the rule that the primary responsibility for securing the rights of the Convention falls upon the national authorities.[10] The margin does not always emerge in the Court's case law: certain rights are so absolute that no margin is left (prohibition of torture). Other rights, including Article 8, are more vaguely formulated and leave more room for national implementation choices.[11] Moreover, sometimes it is so clear that there has been a disproportionate interference or no interference at all that the margin of appreciation is irrelevant.

In those cases in which the margin does play a role, it may vary in scope depending on the situation. Four different factors can help and determine it: (1) the nature of the legitimate aim, (2) the nature of the individual's interest, (3) the nature of the right at stake and finally (4) the divergence in Europe on the issue involved.[12] Certain legitimate aims, such as natural security, are deemed of such importance that their invocation by the state may broaden the scope of the margin of appreciation.[13] The same goes for planning policies,[14] which are of particular importance to housing issues. On the other hand when a high interest for the individual is at stake, such as one that touches the most intimate aspects

9 *Olsson v Sweden (No. 1)* (App no 10465/83) (1988) Series A no 130 [68].

10 See Article 1 ECHR and also: Paul Mahoney, 'Marvellous Richness of Diversity or Invidious Cultural Relativism?' (1998) 19 *Human Rights Law Journal* 1, 2.

11 R.A. Lawson and H.G. Schermers, *Leading Cases of the European Court of Human Rights* (2nd edn Ars Aequi Libri, Nijmegen 1999) 39.

12 Mahoney distinguishes even more than these four – among them the difference between times of peace or war. In the latter situation the state could apparently be given a larger margin. This would of course be highly relevant in case of forced evictions and housing restitution. Issues of conflict, however, seem to surface in more situations than the Article 15 ECHR emergency situations to which Mahoney appears to refer. Nevertheless, I have not been able to find case law to substantiate his claim. See Paul Mahoney, 'Marvellous Richness of Diversity or Invidious Cultural Relativism?' (1998) 19 *Human Rights Law Journal* 1, 5. As to the divergence within Europe, the Court has held that a state cannot rely on the margin in that context by mere unquestioning and passive adherence to a historic tradition: *Hirst v The United Kingdom* (App no 74025/01) ECHR 30 March 2004 [41].

13 See e.g. *Leander v Sweden* (App no 9248/81) (1987) Series A no 116 [59].

14 *Buckley v The United Kingdom* (App no 20348/92) ECHR 1996-IV 16 [75].

of his private life, then the margin narrows down again. The nature of the right I have already mentioned above: some rights are formulated such as to inherently require a balancing by national authorities whereas others are of an absolute nature. Finally, a large divergence of views between the parties to the Convention on an issue may serve to stretch the scope.[15] A high level of consensus may decrease it.

The margin of appreciation gives leeway to the states, but not infinitely. It is elastic, but may snap when a state goes too far. The court may then find a violation of a Convention right. The margin thus goes 'hand in hand with a European supervision'.[16] The path that the state follows towards safeguarding human rights may vary from country to country but is guarded from above and marked by three flags: legal basis, legitimate aim and necessity.

Let us now turn from the path to the actual footsteps. In the context of the right to respect to the home a range of interferences can be imagined: destruction, eviction, searches and nuisance from noise[17], fumes or smells.[18] I will focus on the three interferences that result in loss of the home: destruction, eviction and denial of access.

Destruction may very well be considered as the worst and most far-reaching interference with the right to respect for the home. It turns housing restitution into an empty shell. It also is the most extreme, irreversible form of eviction. The court has dealt with destruction in a series of applications against Turkey. These applications originated in the armed conflict between the Turkish security forces and the Kurdish Workers' Party (PKK) which started in the 1980s and lasted until a ceasefire in 1999.[19] During this conflict a large number of villages were attacked and houses were burnt down, both by the PKK and by government forces. The applications in Strasbourg concerned, among others, allegations of Turkish involvement in the destruction of houses.

In the very first case on the issue,[20] *Akdivar and others*,[21] the Commission went on a fact-finding mission to Turkey, since the facts of the case were heavily disputed. Turkey denied allegations of involvement of its security forces in the destruction of houses in the village of Kelekçi in the south-eastern part of the country. But

15 See e.g. *Stjerna v Finland* (App no 18131/91) (1994) Series A no 299 [39].

16 *Handyside v The United Kingdom* (App no 5493/72) (1976) Series A no 024 [49].

17 See e.g. *Hatton a.o. v The United Kingdom* (App no 36022/97) ECHR 2 October 2001; *Hatton a.o. v The United Kingdom* (Grand Chamber) ECHR 8 July 2003; *Moreno Gómez v Spain* (App no 4143/02) ECHR 16 November 2004.

18 Eg *López Ostra v Spain* (App no 16798/90) (1994) Series A no 303.

19 Jonathan Sugden, 'Housing and Property Restitution in Turkey', in Scott Leckie (ed.), *Returning Home: Housing and Property Restitution Rights of Refugees and Displaced Persons* (Transnational Publishers, Ardsley 2003) 335–6.

20 The cases on destruction dealt with here are the leading ones from the total number of cases. They were found by using the HUDOC search engine in looking for destruction cases under Article 8. 'Leading' in this respect means those cases in which the Court used principles or formulated *dicta* on destruction for the first time.

21 *Akdivar a.o. v Turkey* (App no 21893/93) ECHR 1996-IV 1211.

the Court concurred with the Commission's view that the security forces were responsible. It held that the deliberate destruction of the houses by burning them was a serious interference with the right to respect for the home. Since Turkey had only denied and not offered subsidiary justification for the alleged actions, the Court did not even use the paragraph 2 test but simply concluded that Article 8 had been violated. Nevertheless, it did not establish the existence of an administrative practice of wanton destruction.[22]

The *Akdivar* judgment left one question unanswered: is destruction an interference that is so grave in general that it can never be justified under the second paragraph of Article 8? Or could the Court's reasoning be explained by the particular fact that Turkey denied the allegation altogether? The *Selçuk & Asker* case offered a similar set of facts, with security forces destroying the houses of the applicants on purpose. Again the government denied any involvement whatsoever, but this time the Court did not even explicitly weigh this denial in its establishment of a violation of Article 8. It dubbed the interference 'particularly grave and unjustified'.[23] Can it indeed be induced from this that deliberate destruction can never be justified? It seems to be the case if we follow the pithy statement of the Court. One may of course easily imagine many cases in which buildings are destroyed, for example in the context of urban regeneration. This in itself could be justified. The difference with these cases would be that the buildings to be destroyed are no longer people's homes: they have been expropriated or offered alternative accommodation. By contrast, in the Turkish cases the destroyed houses were still inhabited and used as homes.

An even more conclusive court statement followed in the *Menteş and others* case. The burning of houses by security forces was 'a measure devoid of justification'.[24] Based on these and a range of later cases in which the Court expressed itself in similar ways, it would seem possible to conclude that the deliberate destruction of the home is an act that does not lend itself for justification under paragraph 2 of Article 8.[25] The fact that a conflict is raging in a certain area does not alter that conclusion. On the other hand, it would be more theoretically sound to view things slightly differently. Article 8 provides for justifications to restrict the right to respect for the home. In the cases of destruction dealt with here the state concerned often did not even bother to try and justify its actions. This kind of interference so clearly would not pass one or more of the tests of paragraph 2, even *prima facie*,

22 Ibid. [88].

23 *Selçuk & Asker v Turkey* (App nos 23184/94 and 23185/94) (1998) ECHR 1998-II 891 [86].

24 *Menteş a.o. v Turkey* (App no 23186/94) ECHR 1998-IV 80 [73]. The seriousness of destruction for the applicants and its grave consequences are also recognised by the Court sometimes in finding a violation of Article 3. E.g. *Selçuk & Asker v Turkey* (App nos 23184/94 and 23185/94) (1998) ECHR 1998-II 891 [72–80].

25 See e.g. *Dulas v Turkey* (App no 25801/94) ECHR 30 January 2001 [60]; *Bilgin v Turkey* (App no 23819/94) ECHR 16 November 2000 [108].

that the Court would not even deem it necessary to apply them. Apparently then, destruction of the home in such a case could never be proportionate or would not serve any legitimate aim.[26]

A less far-reaching interference, but one having the same effect of not being able to enjoy one's house, is eviction. Evictions play a role in several contexts: housing and planning issues and conflict situations, or combinations of these. The context involved influences the assessment of the European Court. Before delving deeper into these contexts, I would emphasise that even where eviction proceedings have started, but the eviction itself has not been carried out, a violation of Article 8 may be established. The existence of a real threat is sufficient.[27]

Housing and tenancy issues are a context in which evictions often occur. In this context evictions are allowed, as long as they fulfil the criteria of paragraph 2 of Article 8. When for example a tenant is evicted for refusal of paying rent, this may be justified. The court has accepted that the legitimate aim in such a case is the protection of the rights of others.[28] In a series of judgments on the situation of Gypsies in the United Kingdom planning issues formed the core of the matter. The authorities tried to prevent urban sprawl of large cities into the surrounding countryside by adhering to a so-called Green Belt policy. Under this policy the residential use of land in these Green Belts was severely restricted. Several Gypsy families who established their caravan homes on plots of land they owned were thus obliged to move. These orders to move can be considered as evictions, although in these situations the home moves together with the inhabitants. In this series of cases the legal basis and the legitimate aim – the rights of others to protection of the environment – were not disputed. The considerations of the Court thus centred on the necessity test. The illegality of the settlement weighed against the applicants, whereas a legal establishment would have worked in their favour.[29] This is thus one of the relevant elements in assessing whether a fair balance has been struck.

A second element, and a highly relevant one to the general topic of housing restitution, is the Court's considerations on alternative accommodation in these British cases. The existence of alternatives makes the interference less serious,

---

26 Matters may be different when a house is at risk of collapsing and it is preventively destroyed to safeguard the lives of both its inhabitants and the neighbours. If the inhabitants are unwilling to leave their home in such a case, a state would have to carry out an eviction that does comply with Article 8.

27 *Larkos v Cyprus* (App no 29515/95) ECHR 18 February 1999 [28]. See also the partly dissenting opinion of Judge Repik in *Buckley v The United Kingdom* (App no 20348/92) ECHR 1996-IV 16 [75].

28 *Natale Marzari v Italy* (admissibility) (App no 36448/97) ECHR 4 May 1999.

29 *Chapman v The United Kingdom* (Appl.no. 27238/95) ECHR 18 January 2001 [102]. Similar judgments issued on the same day: *Beard* (App no 24882/94) ECHR; *Coster* (App no 24876/94) ECHR; *Lee* (App no 25289/94) ECHR; *Jane Smith* (App no 25154/94) ECHR. No violation of Article 8 was found in these cases.

according to the Court.[30] So does the suitability of the alternative to the particular needs of the evicted individual, including their family situation and financial resources:

> The more suitable the alternative accommodation is, the less serious is the interference constituted by moving the applicant from his or her existing accommodation.[31]

On the other end of the suitability scale are the rights of the local inhabitants to protection of their immediate environment. A large margin of appreciation in planning matters is left to the authorities.[32]

A third element of importance for the fair balance appeared in the Italian case of *Marzari*. The applicant was a disabled man who refused to pay rent and was therefore evicted. He did not accept the alternative accommodation offered by the authorities. Marzari was never cooperative, whereas the authorities did their utmost to provide him with suitable accommodation. The court concluded that in this case a fair balance existed and found no violation of Article 8.[33] Thus both the conduct of the state (due diligence) and of the applicant (cooperation or obstruction) were of importance.

Generally, the practical legal and administrative framework of evictions should contain sufficient safeguards to protect the interests of the individual. A situation in which local authorities are not even required to justify an eviction based on the particular facts of the case can thus lead to a violation of Article 8.[34] *A fortiori* every eviction should be carried out in accordance with the existing legal framework. An eviction carried out illegally is a violation in itself.[35]

In the context of conflict matters may be different. Rarely if ever will the state be able – or even try to – to show that a fair balance between the interests of the individual and those of society as a whole has been struck. Consequently, justification of an interference is nearly impossible. Eviction may be an automatic consequence of housing destruction. The latter may be done with the purpose of causing the former. The combination as such of destruction and consequent eviction can be a violation of Article 8,[36] as can be the combination of eviction and

30 One may caution here that this moving around of people may in general be differently viewed in the case of a nomadic lifestyle where home and inhabitants move together than in case of someone living in a 'fixed' home.

31 *Chapman v The United Kingdom* (Appl.no. 27238/95) ECHR 18 January 2001 [103].

32 Ibid. [103–104].

33 *Natale Marzari v Italy* (admissibility) (App no 36448/97) ECHR 4 May 1999.

34 *Connors v The United Kingdom* (App no 66746/01) ECHR 27 May 2004 [92–5].

35 *Prokopovich v Russia* (App no 58255/00) ECHR 18 November 2004 [44–5].

36 *Yöyler v Turkey* (App no 26973/95) ECHR 24 July 2003 [79–80].

subsequent denial of access.[37] An eviction in such a context thus is often a serious and unjustified interference.

Finally, turning to the last of the three relevant interferences, denial of access is the barring of return to one's home that has been left either forcibly through eviction or under the pressure of circumstances. The largest-scale situation of this kind that has come under the consideration of the European Court is the conflict on Cyprus. In 1974 Turkish armed forces conducted military operations in Northern Cyprus which led to a division of the island and the displacement of many people on both sides. Hundreds of thousands of displaced Greek-Cypriots have been denied access to their homes in the north. Visits were not allowed, let alone re-occupation of the homes at stake. In 1994 the government of Cyprus lodged a state complaint against Turkey with the Strasbourg institutions, among others about this denial of access.[38] In 2001 the Court issued a judgment in this case. Turkey was of the opinion that the possible return of the displaced was something to be decided on in the context of the negotiations on an overall settlement. According to the Turkish government returns would enhance the risks of conflict by intermingling the Greek- and Turkish-Cypriot communities. The court held that denial of access amounted to 'complete denial of the right of displaced persons to their homes'.[39] It had no basis in domestic law within the meaning of paragraph 2 of Article 8. In the Court's view political negotiations on a future settlement could not be invoked to justify violations of the ECHR. Thus the denial of access constituted a violation of Article 8. Since this violation had endured as a matter of policy since 1974, the Court considered it to be a continuing violation.

The court's judgment in the *Cyprus v. Turkey* case seems to leave some leeway for the state: if one of the reasons leading to the finding of a violation was no basis in domestic law existed, then maybe the existence of such a law may justify similar interferences (outside the Cypriot context). Is this a convincing inference? The only later case where a violation on this point was found was the earlier mentioned case of *Demades*. In that case the Court simply reiterated its findings in the *Cyprus v. Turkey* judgment. Thus it provides no further clarity. The earlier report of the European Commission of Human Rights in the case does shed some light. The Commission held that complete denial of access was unjustified. Even if it accepted that the aim of public safety invoked by Turkey could justify a restriction on the right to respect for the home, it still was not necessary in a democratic society. A general exclusion of access could not in any way be seen as proportionate.[40] I tend to concur with the Commission's views on this point: a general policy to downgrade the respect for the home to near non-existence cannot be considered proportionate. Although the Commission's findings cannot

---

37 *Doğan and others v Turkey* (App no 8803/02 a.o.) ECHR 29 June 2004 [157–60].

38 *Cyprus v Turkey* (App no 25781/94) ECHR 10 May 2001.

39 For this and the following considerations of the Court: ibid. [174–5]. See also: *Slivenko v Latvia* (App no 48321/99) ECHR 9 October 2003 [95].

40 EComHR, *Cyprus v Turkey* (Report) (App no 25781/94) 4 June 1999 [261–71].

be automatically equalled to those of the Court, it seems hard to conceive how the complete denial of access would pass the necessity test, even if there *had* been a law in Northern Cyprus justifying the policy.

A case from a rather different context – the conflict between the Turkish armed forces and the PKK in eastern Turkey – sustains this reasoning. In *Doğan and others* a number of villagers were expelled from their village for security reasons. For almost 10 years they were not allowed to return to their homes. Taking this long span of time into account, the Court considered this to be 'a serious and unjustified interference' with Article 8.[41] The phrasing almost mirrored the 'destruction' cases mentioned above.

As we have seen thus far all three interference resulting in the loss of the home are difficult to justify. In principle the triple test of Article 8, paragraph 2 can always be applied. In times of peace, looking for example at evictions, this is what the Court does. In doing so it is quite strict. In the context of conflict the test is rarely applied at all. Presumably because the interference involved would so clearly fail on one of more counts of the test. Even though such interference is not automatically unjustifiable, it will often be unjustified.

(3) Positive Obligations

The second strand of case law along which the Court has developed the notion of respect is that of positive obligations.[42] They are called thus to distinguish them from the negative obligation not to interfere. Positive obligations require states to take action to secure human rights. The court first elaborated the concept of positive obligations in cases in which it obliged states to grant individuals certain rights, privileges or legal status.[43] Later it extended the scope of positive obligations to a state duty to protect individuals against other individuals.[44] It should be noted that the extent of a positive obligation varies according to the right involved. Positive obligations are thus seldom absolute; the Court in general considers whether the state concerned has taken reasonable and appropriate measures.[45]

---

41 *Doğan and others v Turkey* (App no 8803/02 a.o.) ECHR 29 June 2004 [159].

42 For a very elaborate overview of this doctrine, see Cordula Dröge, *Positive Verpflichtungen der Staaten in der Europäischen Mensenrechtskonvention* (Springer, Heidelberg 2003).

43 *Marckx v Belgium* (App no 6833/74) (1979) Series A no 031; *Airey v Ireland* (App no 6289/73) (1979) Series A no 39.

44 *X & Y v The Netherlands* (App no 8978/80) (1985) Series A no 091.

45 See eg *Powell & Rayner v The United Kingdom* (App no 9310/81) (1990) Series A no 172 [41]. And Harris and others, *Harris, O'Boyle & Warbrick: Law of the European Convention on Human Rights* (Oxford University Press, Oxford 1995) 284–5.

Although the qualified prohibition of interference is explicit in the wording of Article 8, the positive obligations are not. Nevertheless the Court has applied more or less the same principles to test both:

> In both contexts regard must be had to the fair balance that has to be struck between the competing interests of the individual and of the community as a whole; and in both contexts the State enjoys a certain margin of appreciation in determining the steps to be taken to ensure compliance with the Convention.[46]

In addition, when the Court assesses whether this balance has been struck under a positive obligation, it takes the legitimate aims of paragraph 2 – normally used to justify an interference – into consideration.[47] Finally, the Court has held that it is not its role to 'dictate precise measures which should be adopted by the States in order to comply with their positive duties under Article 8.'[48]

Let us now step down from the higher steps of principle to the lower ones of application: what positive obligations, if any, has the Court formulated in respect of the home? The court has held that positive obligations are applicable to the right to respect for the home,[49] but the case law on this point appears piecemeal and rather scarce. In one case of interference with the home by private individuals with help of the police, the applicant complained that the authorities had failed to protect the home. Although the case provided the opportunity for the Court to elaborate on the existence and extent of such an obligation, it did not find it necessary to do so since it had already concluded that the police interference with the home was unjustified.[50] In the earlier mentioned 'Gypsy'[51] cases the Court held that there was a positive obligation for states to facilitate the way of life of this group, but not to guarantee a sufficient amount of camping sites for them.[52] This connects to the fact that Article 8 does not guarantee the right to a home.[53] Concerning noise disturbance, the Court found a violation of a positive obligation in a Spanish case. The applicant was suffering from extreme disturbance caused by discotheques near her home. The court found that the authorities had not lived up to the positive obligation of enforcing their own local rules on this point. Thus they failed to protect the right to respect for the home of the applicant.[54]

46 Ibid.

47 See e.g. *Rees v The United Kingdom* (App no 9532/81) (1986) Series A no 106 [37]; *Novoseletskiy v Ukraine* (App no 47148/99) ECHR 22 February 2005 [69].

48 *Fadeyeva v Russia* (App no 55723/00) ECHR 9 June 2005 [133].

49 *Botta v Italy* (App no 21439/93) (1998) 26 EHRR 241 [33].

50 *McLeod v The United Kingdom* (App no 247455/94) (1998) 27 EHRR 493 [59–61].

51 Wording used by the Court itself.

52 *Chapman v The United Kingdom* (Appl.no. 27238/95) ECHR 18 January 2001 [96–8].

53 E.g. *Fadeyeva v Russia* (App no 55723/00) ECHR 9 June 2005 [133].

54 *Moreno Gómez v Spain* (App no 4143/02) ECHR 16 November 2004.

More specifically on the topic at hand, positive obligations on the actual loss of the home have been addressed in very few judgments. Concerning destruction and the negative consequences arising from it the earlier mentioned case of *Moldovan a.o. v. Romania* is thus far the only one. Although the actual destruction took place some months before the entry into force of the ECHR for Romania and the Court could thus not assess the destruction itself, it did look at the later consequences of it which in themselves were in violation of the Convention. These included attempts by the police to cover up the incident. The applicants, chased from their village, found no other place to live than in very overcrowded cellars, stables and even hen-houses. The involvement of the police gave rise to state responsibility in this case. No criminal proceedings were instituted against them. Only partial and very belated compensation was offered. Some houses were rebuilt by the authorities but were unfit for habitation. Due to all of this most of the victims were unable to return. On top of that national court judgments contained discriminatory remarks on Roma. The court held that these elements included both hindrance and failure to act by the authorities. Both interferences and positive obligations were dealt with together in the assessment of compliance with Article 8. Since the human rights violations in this case were so grave, the Court did not even apply a fair balance test,[55] but concluded that the situation amounted to a serious continuing violation of the ECHR, not just of Article 8 but also of Article 3.[56]

On evictions the applications against Croatia are most illuminating. In the case of *Cvijetić* the applicant was chased from her house by other individuals during the civil war in the former Yugoslavia.[57] She started judicial proceedings to be recognised as the lawful inhabitant of the house and in the end obtained an eviction order. The enforcement of the domestic court order, however, led to a host of Kafkaesque situations. At the first eviction attempt another family than the original illegal occupants suddenly inhabited the premises. The second time a group of war veterans prevented the eviction, the police standing by idly. And the third time a doctor who was assumed to help the illegal but disabled occupants did not show up. Eventually, after more than eight years the case was settled without help of the state: the occupants agreed with the applicant to vacate her house.

The applicant complained before the European Court of Human Rights about the fact that the proceedings exceeded the reasonable time requirement protected in Article 6 ECHR and also about the failure of the authorities to protect her right to respect for the home under Article 8. The court held a violation of Article 6: the execution of a judgment (in this case the eviction) is part of the period to be taken

55 The same approach as in the Turkish destruction cases mentioned in section 2. It is interesting to note that the Court also stated that the general attitude of the authorities perpetuated the feelings of insecurity of the victims (para. 108), thus emphasising this underlying concept of the home.

56 *Moldovan a.o. (No.2, merits)* (App nos 41138/98 and 64320/01) ECHR 12 July 2005 [102–14].

57 *Cvijetić v Croatia* (App no 71549/01) ECHR 26 February 2004.

into account and this period lasted far too long, the length being attributable to the state. As to Article 8, the Court held that Croatia had not complied with its positive obligation. The elements taken into account were: the apartment in question was the applicant's home, the occupants lived in it without any legal ground and the applicant could only repossess her apartment through judicial proceedings. Since the latter took so long to execute, as found already under Article 6, the Court also found a breach under Article 8. The *Cvijetić* judgment was the first case in which the Court found that a state has the positive obligation to assist an individual to recover his or her home if there is a domestic court order requiring so. Earlier it had held that such a positive obligation to evict existed in relation to the right to property under Article 1 of Protocol 1.[58] It now extended this principle to the right to respect for the home.

In the second judgment on eviction issues, *Pibernik v. Croatia*, the factual background was almost the same. The court thus easily came to the same conclusion as in *Cvijetić*: the state had not complied with its positive obligations under Article 8, since it 'created or at least enabled a situation where the applicant was prevented from enjoying her home for a very long time'.[59]

A few points are relevant about these cases in the context of the present inquiry. Firstly, the applicants in both cases were recognised by the state as the legal inhabitants of their apartment, whereas the occupants held no legal title to them whatsoever. This considerably strengthened the applicants' claims and was relevant in the Court's assessment of the facts. Secondly, the fact that the situations at stake took place during and shortly after the war in Croatia did not alter Croatia's obligations. The court made no reference to this context whatsoever when holding, in both cases, that a state should organise its legal system in such a way as to prevent obstruction of the execution of domestic court judgments. The fact that these very institutions may be weakened by recent conflict is apparently immaterial. Thirdly, the Court's judgments in these cases cannot be interpreted as an unqualified positive obligation to provide for housing restitution. It is not clear how the case would have been assessed, had the domestic courts not recognised that the apartments were the legal homes of the applicants. But even then, I would submit, the Court could have ruled in favour of the applicants. Depending of course on the convincingness of the domestic courts' reasoning, the claim of a formerly legal inhabitant vis-à-vis someone who broke into a house and chased him or her would still be strong. It would be difficult for a state to hold that in such a scenario a fair balance had been struck.

Apart from evictions like the ones described above, the Court has also issued a judgment in a case which holds the middle ground between grave disturbance and denial of access. In the Romanian case of *Surugiu* different national authorities issued contradictory titles of ownership.[60] The applicant claimed ownership of his

58 *Immobiliare Saffi v Italy* (App no 22774/93) ECHR 28 July 1999.

59 *Pibernik v Croatia* (App no 75139/01) ECHR 4 March 2004 [70].

60 *Surugiu v Romania* (App no 48995/99) ECHR 20 April 2004.

home and the adjoining land, whereas another family claimed ownership of that land too. During the different national procedures on this conflict, tensions rose to such heights that the other family started to use the land, beat on the applicant's house with sticks when the latter was away at a hospital and dropped manure in front of the house. Witnesses heard by the police declared that the family had threatened to beat the applicant up if he returned to his home. The applicant did not dare to return. Only once in the course of the more than five years that the conflict lasted was the interfering family fined for a breach of the peace, and then they only had to pay a very low amount.

Whereas the authorities claimed not to bear any responsibility since this concerned a conflict between private parties, the Court reiterated the existence of positive obligations to secure the respect for the home. Importantly, the Court held that the property dispute did not exonerate the state from all its responsibility for the interferences by private parties with the applicant's right to respect for the home. The court also held that an applicant can legitimately expect that once his title of ownership has been established, the authorities implement such recognition by concrete action against repeatedly interfering third parties. In this case nothing of that kind had been done. The authorities 'n'ont pas déployé les efforts auxquels on pouvait normalement s'attendre'.[61] Thus the Court found a violation of Article 8.

The two Croatian cases and the Romanian case of *Surugiu* show that once title of ownership or even mere recognition of legal tenancy have been officially established, a positive duty is incumbent upon the state. This consists of taking reasonable measures and thus showing due diligence to enforce such a recognition vis-à-vis third parties. Put differently, the *effective* respect for the home must be secured. All these cases, just as the Spanish noise disturbance case[62], centre on a state's failure to enforce its own rules, laws and decisions.[63] The positive obligations involved here entail that states organise their judicial and enforcement systems to render them effective.[64] An individual thus can expect from the state a reasonable amount of protection for his home against interferences by third parties.

---

61 Ibid. [68].

62 *Moldovan a.o. (No. 2, merits)* (App nos 41138/98 and 64320/01) ECHR 12 July 2005 being the odd one out, reflecting an even worse situation.

63 It may of course equally happen that there is something wrong with the decision or law itself. It may be discriminatory or offer insufficient safeguards against abuse. In such case, the situation would be analysed through the looking glass of an interference instead of a positive obligation.

64 Interestingly, and as far as I am aware, the Court has never considered the fact that a state has recently experienced conflict and may thus be institutionally weak as a mitigating factor. In the case Slovenia used the argument that it was experiencing radical legal and economic changes to defend the length of its domestic proceedings. The court held that it had 'no information which would indicate that the difficulties encountered during the relevant period were such as to deprive the applicant of his entitlement to a judicial determination within a "reasonable time"' (*Majarič v Slovenia* (App no 28400/95) ECHR 8 February 2000 [39]). In my view this indicates two things. Firstly – but this is a

(4) Conclusion

Respect for the home is in itself a vague notion. In the above we have seen that the text of Article 8 ECHR, but especially the judgments and decisions of the Strasbourg Court have explained and refined the meaning of the notion along two paths. Firstly, in the context of non-interference, we have seen that interferences leading to the loss of one's home (destruction, eviction and denial of access) always can be – and theoretically should be – tested on the basis of the second paragraph of Article 8. In the context of conflict, the severity of these interferences and the often existing lack of legal safeguards render them almost impossible to justify. Frequently the case is so clear that the Court does not even apply a proportionality or necessity test. Secondly, regarding positive obligations, the case law reveals that the state has the duty to protect through reasonable measures an individual's home against interferences by third parties. And in case of loss of a home, of which state authorities have recognised that an applicant is its legal inhabitant, it has the positive duty to help and return him to that home, if need be by evicting illegal occupants. This does not amount to a general right to housing restitution, let alone to a general right to housing under the Convention.

In assessing, along any of the two paths, whether a fair balance was struck by the national authorities several factors are taken into account: the legality or illegality of occupation of both the former and current inhabitant or occupant, the existence of alternatives for the applicant[65] and the conduct of both the applicant and the state (both concerning due diligence and in applying the rule of law with normal procedural guarantees protected by the Convention). It will be difficult for a state to prove that a fair balance exists under Article 8, if the alleged action or omission is in breach of other Convention articles.[66] With the help of these factors national authorities should weigh the interests involved in case of conflict between former and new inhabitants of a dwelling.

The European Court has thus been developing a framework which may serve as a guiding tool for state conduct. However, by its very nature, the Court's case law offers only a haphazard framework. Its content is to a large extent connected to the cases which reach the Court through the system of individual application. In principle the Court's dicta thus only relate to the particular facts of a given

---

general line in the Court's case law – the context of the matter plays a role in the assessment of 'reasonable time'. Secondly, this socio-economic and legal context apparently does not easily serve as an excuse, not even when it concerns the transition from communism to liberal democracy and market economy. How the Court would deal with countries facing much graver and painful transitions, such as Bosnia and Herzegovina, is thus not really clear.

65 And one would assume for the occupant, but the Court has not clarified that yet in this context.

66 E.g. Article 6 in *Cvijetić v Croatia* (App no 71549/01) ECHR 26 February 2004 or Article 14 ECHR (a discriminatory law).

case. Nevertheless, the Court does at times give broader and more principled assessments. One may add, in the Court's own words, that:

> bearing in mind that the Court provides final authoritative interpretation of the rights and freedoms defined in Section I of the Convention, the Court will consider whether the national authorities have sufficiently taken into account the principles flowing from its judgments on similar issues, even when they concern other States.[67]

This combination of an *erga omnes* effect of its judgments in practice, combined with the growing range of its case law on the loss of housing, leads to an increasingly fine-tuned net of legal obligations and considerations. Not only does this guide states directly. It also offers a very important tool for the empowerment of the dispossessed. For all those displaced persons in the Caucasus or the Balkans, the Court's judgments provide clarity where domestic law does not and justice where national authorities fail to do so. Strasbourg judgments in single cases may thereby serve as fissures in an otherwise solid wall of state unwillingness or discrimination against particular social, religious or ethnic groups. While a judgment from the European Court may be one of the final steps on the long road which an individual applicant has to take, it is often one of the first steps on the way to broader reforms to benefit larger groups of refugees and other displaced persons. The implementation of the Court's guidance needs to take place, after all, in the domestic arena.

---

67 *Opuz v Turkey* (App no 33401/02) ECHR 9 June 2009 [163].

Chapter 9
Re-thinking Responses to Displacement and Dispossession

Lorna Fox O'Mahony and James A. Sweeney[1]

The essays collected in this book address a diverse range of legal problems, from dispossession by eviction for non-payment of rent or mortgage repayments, to allow economic development, or to forced displacement in times of armed conflict. The laws and policies under scrutiny range from various countries' domestic laws to the European Convention on Human Rights, from the law of the European Union to international law, and span what Kenna describes as: 'the *micro* (the level of individual aspirations, interactions and micro political struggles), the *meso* (including the housing systems, its subsystems and institutional contexts) and the *macro* (broadly the national, regional and international context within which housing systems interact with other systems).'[2] While the terrain covered is undoubtedly wide, the essays highlight several important and common issues which characterise the human costs of displacement and dispossession; the ways in which the idea of home is present or absent in legal responses to displacement and dispossession; the apparent limitations of legal structures which this exposes; and the opportunities that a 'home' perspective presents for re-analysing problems involving displacement and dispossession. In this chapter we explore some of the synergies which emerged through our workshop and subsequent work editing the volume, and set out potential avenues for further research.

A common feature of the essays was our deliberate attempt to try to create room in our analyses for the social agent – the displaced or dispossessed individual – rather than being restricted by the dominant structure of existing law, which often excludes the experiences of these individuals. As such, our starting point broadly adopted the epistemological traditions of social constructionism,[3] in as much as the chapters have deliberately placed the lived experiences of the displaced or dispossessed people at the centre of the discussion, and in doing so, have sought to resist the discursive boundaries of current laws and policies in favour of an

---

1 lorna.fox@durham.ac.uk/j.a.sweeney@durham.ac.uk.

2 See P. Kenna in this volume.

3 See P.L. Berger and T. Luckmann, *The Social Construction of Reality: A Treatise in the Sociology of Knowledge* (Anchor Books, New York 1967); for discussion of the use of social constructionism in housing research, see K. Jacobs, J. Kemeny and T. Manzi (eds), *Social Constructionism in Housing Research* (Ashgate, Aldershot 2004).

exploratory approach. In much the same way as constructionism has sought to examine research questions independent of the demands of policy makers,[4] our goal has been to attempt to develop a research agenda that is independent from the restrictions implied by law and legal method. This approach has steered us towards examining questions which are not always deemed 'relevant' to legal proceedings, for example, Bright's focus on the personal stories of tenants and mortgagees in arrears. Thus, in a context which tends to be preoccupied by financial considerations, Bright's home perspective highlights the importance of identity – both the identity of the occupier (as borrower/private sector tenant/local authority tenant) and the identity of the person or agency seeking to dispossess – to the question of whether the occupier's personal story can find a legal voice. Similarly, Kenna highlights the need to move beyond the traditional reach of international human rights law approaches to housing policy and legal regulation, into an approach that fully comprehends the multiple levels of complexity inherent in housing systems (the macro, meso and micro), while Sweeney and Fox O'Mahony's analysis of housing and home for asylum seekers – an area which straddles immigration law and social welfare – highlights the dominance of the idea of control which has come to characterise immigration policy in the UK, to the exclusion of the human experiences of 'doubly displaced' asylum seekers.

Our approach also echoes constructionism in our attempts to 'question the status of given assumptions and interrogate the process of "claims-making"';[5] in law as it responds to and implements policy. Rather than applying positivist analyses to current law, the authors 'focus on broader social processes and…the importance of social, political and economic context';[6] to highlight issues which legal processes do not traditionally bring to the fore. For example, van der Walt's study of the eviction of residential occupiers by the state for the purposes of economic development notes that in 'ordinary' cases of eviction (where the state might be seen as performing a more 'neutral' adjudicating role), the nature of different types of claims to land and 'the hierarchical domination of ownership' means that:

> [e]ven when contextual factors enter the equation, courts' professional tendency to enforce the law of eviction 'normally', 'neutrally' or 'objectively' will more often than not still privilege the protection of stronger rights and result in more or less mechanical eviction of unlawful or weak occupiers who are unable to prove legal occupation rights that are strong enough to trump the owner's right.[7]

4 K. Jacobs, J. Kemeny and T. Manzi, 'Introduction' in K. Jacobs, J. Kemeny and T. Manzi (eds), *Social Constructionism in Housing Research* (Ashgate, Aldershot 2004) 2.

5 K. Jacobs, J. Kemeny and T. Manzi (eds), *Social Constructionism in Housing Research* (Ashgate, Aldershot 2004) 3.

6 Ibid.

7 Van der Walt, in this volume, 62.

Van der Walt goes on to add, however, that when the party seeking an eviction is the state, the contextual issues are liable to be completely lost in the debate about the legitimacy of the state's action, so that the:

> ensuing debate is mostly on the legitimacy or justifiability of the compulsory acquisition and not on the eviction or the effect it has on the former residents. The context and the personal circumstances of the individuals and groups affected often do not even feature in the discussion.[8]

On a similar note, Sweeney and Fox O'Mahony show that in the case law concerning state responsibility for asylum seekers in the UK, the debate has been derailed into the question of who is less responsible between central and local government, with the impact on the doubly displaced asylum seeker excluded from the discussion. Breau's approach to the international law rights to housing and home offers the possibility to move beyond the 'minimal' question of legitimacy when considering the conduct of the state towards vulnerable people to focus on the obligations of the international community, via the 'Responsibility to Protect'.

While the issues considered in the collection are wide-ranging, another important common feature is the vulnerability of the people who are at risk of displacement and dispossession. This vulnerability is manifest at several levels: the people most at risk of displacement and dispossession are likely to be poor and marginalised in the first place; and their vulnerability is only exacerbated by the realisation of the threat of displacement and/or dispossession, and further by the exclusion of their voices from legal processes. From the indigenous people displaced in armed conflicts, to asylum seekers, to the occupier of a South African township, occupiers who are seeking to defend their homes in these cases are too easily constructed as a class of people who are 'them' not 'us'. In his seminal analysis of the (self-imposed) limits of legal method, Thomas Ross[9] illustrated how the rhetoric of poverty – separating the poor as 'other' – is combined with the premise that we are helpless to change the 'harsh realities' of society, to place the 'problem' of poverty beyond judicial power or jurisdiction.[10] Similarly, in all of the cases considered in this collection the occupier is either vulnerable because they have no property, or because they are not in a position to defend their claim to property.

With low income obviously linked to arrears, in a benign economic climate at least, in cases of repossession (see Bright, Dyal-Chand) the vulnerability of dispossessed occupiers is likely to stem from poverty, although as Dyal-Chand reminds us, this cannot be disaggregated from other vulnerabilities, such as those resulting from racially motivated behaviour on the part of lenders. Dyal-Chand

8 Van der Walt, in this volume, 62.

9 T. Ross, 'The Rhetoric of Poverty: Their Immorality, Our Helplessness' (1991) 79 *Georgetown Law Journal* 1499.

10 Ibid., 1502, 1509.

and Bright highlight the importance of identity in legal responses to dispossession in two different jurisdictions. Bright's essay demonstrates the contrast between possession proceedings against local authority tenants, where the personal home story can be heard, and cases involving private landlords where:

> If there is a personal home story to be heard, it probably will not be. And if a buy-to-let tenant is a good tenant but it is the landlord who is in default, there is nothing to be done. The occupier has no voice, and will be lucky to receive much notice of having to move.[11]

Not only is the personal story of the occupier not likely to influence the outcome of the case, there is likely to be no opportunity for the court to hear about the likely impact of the dispossession on the occupier. So far as mortgage borrowers are concerned, much depends on the forbearance of the individual lender, with recent initiatives focusing on the development of good practice amongst lenders,[12] rather than focusing (directly at least) on the consequences of losing their home for dispossessed borrowers. Indeed, the lack of empathy on the part of the government for the human experience of repossession – and the adverse consequences that follow loss of home in these circumstances – was highlighted in the comments of then UK housing minister John Healy when he claimed that: 'For some people it can be the only, and it can in fact be the best, option for them to allow their home to be repossessed. Sometimes it is impossible for people to maintain the mortgage commitments they've got. It may be the best thing in those circumstances.'[13]

Both Dyal-Chand and Bright challenge us to think about how the legal process might take greater account of the human impacts of dispossession, and take the first steps in mapping who is privileged under the prevailing system, and who is excluded. Bright reminds us that – with UK responses to the credit crunch largely taking the form of optional 'good practice' protocols:

> The more vulnerable borrowers – those with poor credit histories, illnesses and unreliable income levels – are much more likely to fall into arrears and to have borrowed from the sub-prime lenders who, as we have seen, pursue more aggressive arrears and repossession policies and are not participants in several of these more progressive government initiatives.[14]

---

11 Bright, in this volume, 36.

12 See for example, L. Whitehouse, 'The Mortgage Arrears Pre-Action Protocol: An Opportunity Lost?' (2009) 72 *Mod. L. Rev*. 793.

13 Comments were made on a BBC Radio Five Live interview, and reported in the *Daily Express* newspaper, 15 February 2010; http://www.express.co.uk/posts/view/157650/Housing-minister-It-s-ok-to-lose-your-home (accessed 20 September 2010).

14 Bright, in this volume, 28.

Dyal-Chand, on the other hand, explains the US response to the recent housing market crisis as revealing – in a departure from its traditional focus on owners – a new focus on renters, which recognises the adverse impact of foreclosure on tenants, and which begins to allow scope for the idea of home as shelter to emergence onto the agenda alongside the dominant image of home (ownership) as an activity characterised by risk taking and individual opportunity.

If the (effectively) automatic prioritisation of the claims of creditors over the interests of occupiers in mortgage possession actions reflects the way in which the 'needs of property owners, self-interested and rational individuals in the market place, override the needs of those who are different: weaker or poorer, or in a different way defined as Other';[15] there is also evidence to suggest that it is those who are most vulnerable who are most likely to suffer adverse effects from dispossession: when a person's economic and social resources are limited, home and the neighbourhood environment play a critical role in that person's life chances and identity.[16] Ironically, those who have the most to lose – who are most vulnerable to the impacts of dispossession – are the most at risk of being dispossessed. As van der Walt observes: 'the destruction [of home] always targets those who are too weak or marginal to avoid it or to defend themselves and their interests.'[17]

A similar picture emerges in relation to displacement: Kenna describes displaced persons as migrants who are 'forced to abandon homes for reasons of fear or survival', including:

> minorities, such as ethnic groups being displaced from their home, women fleeing domestic violence, illegal evictions, people with disabilities being forcibly displaced to institutions, and perpetual displacement through segregated housing, or indeed, lack of access to housing...[18]

Richer, more educated or particularly skilled people *may* be able to avoid forced migration and flee before being expelled – although one might argue that this is akin to 'coerced' migration rather than truly voluntary or economic migration.[19] Likewise recent efforts to render processes for claiming asylum more strict have

15 K. Green, 'Being Here – What a Woman Can Say About Land Law', in A. Bottomley (ed.), *Feminist Perspectives on the Foundational Subjects of Law* (Cavendish, London 1996) 93–4.

16 S. Saegert, 'The Role of Housing in the Experience of Dwelling' in I. Altman and C.M. Werner (eds), *Home Environments* (Plenum Press, New York 1985) 289–90; see also A. Schorr, *Slums and Social Insecurity* (US Government Printing Office, Washington DC 1964).

17 Van der Walt, in this volume, 85.

18 Kenna, in this volume, 137.

19 Cf. the discussion of 'voluntary', 'coerced' and 'forced' returns of failed asylum seekers in Fox O'Mahony and Sweeney, in this volume.

the effect of favouring applicants with greater cultural capital over those who are more vulnerable. Viewed this way, stricter policies do not reduce the number of applications for asylum, but alter the qualities of the successful applicant.[20] This is potentially rather subversive since it would seem to shift the focus of the process away from the needs of the applicant on to the needs of the receiving state, for people who will be less reliant on the welfare state, or for certain categories of worker, for example, that are far more suitable for consideration under mechanisms for economic migration.

Forced migration – in circumstances which often involve violence and trauma – has major impacts on home and identity, with displacement and dispossession having 'profound and long-term implications'[21] on those who are separated from their homes and homelands, and this can only be exacerbated where the displaced people are already vulnerable. Buyse provides valuable examples of cases where displacement resulted from the deliberate and violent destruction of homes (houses burnt down by security forces) or where displaced people were denied access to their homes because they were located in a region of conflict, while Breau argues for a duty to protect based on collective responsibility for all peoples 'especially the most vulnerable'.[22]

The vulnerability of the dispossessed claimant is only heightened when the party on the other side of the dispute is relatively strong or aggressive. In the case of repossessions, this can be the 'strong' property claim of ownership,[23] which easily trumps the relatively weaker claim to use as a home as a result of the 'hierarchical domination of ownership',[24] particularly when it is advanced by creditors – in light of the tendency of the court to prioritise the needs of creditors above other considerations.[25] In the case of expropriation for economic development (van der Walt), the opposing party is the state itself, and this is also the case in relation to the exclusion of asylum seekers from housing and welfare benefits (Sweeney

20 See N. El-Enany, 'Who is the New European Refugee' (2008) 33(3) *European Law Review* 313, arguing at 335 that restrictive EU policies have filtered out: 'certain refugees from the category of the European refugee. Not only must a European refugee fulfil the requirements set out in the [EU] Qualifications Directive, but she must also possess certain other, implicit characteristics: financial resources, economic mobility, an element of power and a willingness to take risks. Though a number of the persecuted possess these traits, the most vulnerable do not.'

21 A. Blunt and R. Dowling, *Home* (Routledge, London 2006), quoting C.J. Wickham, *Constructing Heimat in Post-War Germany: Longing and Belonging* (The Edwin Mellen Press, Lewiston NY 1999) 196.

22 Breau, in this volume, pp. 190, *et seq*.

23 For an extensive analysis of the contest between 'strong' property rights and the protection of marginalised and weak land users see A.J. van der Walt, *Property in the Margins* (Hart Publishing, Oxford 2009).

24 See van der Walt, in this volume, p. 56.

25 See L. Fox, *Conceptualising Home: Theories, Laws and Policies* (Hart Publishing, Oxford 2006), ch. 2.

and Fox O'Mahony). While these cases demonstrate the relative strength of the dispossessors' legal rights, in the displacement cases discussed in Kenna, Buyse and Breau the 'displacer' may also (or instead) show strength through aggression, for example, in Buyse's discussion of security forces burning homes to the ground, or in other cases of displacement resulting from armed conflict.

Furthermore, in each case, the displaced or dispossessed person's vulnerability is compounded when they lose their home. The 'homeless' person faces both the practical dilemmas of losing their shelter and the psychological impact of losing their home, which has been shown to trigger extreme responses, including alienation and grief amongst the dispossessed occupiers.[26] Brown and Perkins' study of reactions to displacement found that 'the loss of normal attachments creates a stressful period of disruption followed by a post-disruption phase of coping with lost attachments and creating new ones.'[27] Fried[28] and Porteous[29] have both examined the impact of displacement on occupiers, in both cases where several homes in a neighbourhood had been destroyed for urban planning or development reasons (termed 'domicide'). Fried described displacement from home as 'a crisis with potential danger to mental health'[30] and as triggering:

> feelings of painful loss, the continued longing, the general depressive tone, frequent symptoms of psychological or social or somatic distress, the active work required in adapting to the altered situation, the sense of helplessness, the occasional expressions of both direct and displaced anger, and tendencies to idealise the lost place.[31]

Although the ways in which the loss of home is experienced in any given case will vary, the generally negative effects of displacement have been described as 'a widespread and serious social phenomenon'.[32] Although the most extreme reactions occur in only a minority of cases, '[f]or the greatest number, dislocation…does lead to intense personal suffering despite moderately successful adaptation to the total

---

26 See R.J. Lawrence, 'Deciphering Home: An Integrative Historical Perspective' in D. Benjamin (ed.), *The Home: Words, Interpretations, Meanings and Environments* (Ashgate, Aldershot 1995) 61–2; M. Fried, 'Grieving for a Lost Home' in J. Duhl (ed.), *The Urban Condition – People and Policy in the Metropolis* (Basic Books, New York 1963).

27 B.B. Brown and D.D. Perkins, 'Disruptions in Place Attachment' in I. Altman and S.M. Low, *Place Attachment* (Plenum Press, New York 1992) 279.

28 M. Fried, 'Grieving for a Lost Home' in J. Duhl (ed.), *The Urban Condition – People and Policy in the Metropolis* (Basic Books, New York 1963).

29 J.D. Porteous, 'Domicide: The Destruction of Home' in D. Benjamin (ed.), *The Home: Words, Interpretations, Meanings and Environments* (Ashgate, Aldershot 1995).

30 M. Fried, 'Grieving for a Lost Home' in J. Duhl (ed.), *The Urban Condition – People and Policy in the Metropolis* (Basic Books, New York 1963) 152.

31 Ibid.

32 Ibid., 167.

situation of relocation.'[33] Similarly, Porteous claimed that 'domicide has negative social and psychological effects on its human victims';[34] with the significant factor for the occupiers being the *forced* relocation from their homes. This study indicated that '[c]hange almost invariably involves loss, and bereavement-like symptoms of grief are common among those uprooted and relocated.'[35]

In addition, exiles who lose both home and homeland, particularly in violent circumstances such as armed conflict, are likely to experience what we have termed 'double displacement': dispossessed from their homes and displaced from their homeland. The state of exile has been described as:

> a painful or punitive banishment from one's homeland. Though it can be voluntary or involuntary, internal or external, exile generally implies a fact of trauma, an imminent danger, usually political, that makes the home no longer safely habitable.[36]

The impact of double displacement is captured in the following description of Croation refugees:

> It is not only their concepts of homeland that have been transformed, but also their homes in the most basic, physical sense. From sites of personal control, they were transformed into sites of danger and destruction...People were forced to leave their homes in response to threat, fears, military orders and violent attacks. Many homes literally ceased to exist.[37]

Kinnvall has described forced migrants as experiencing 'a sense of powerlessness and dependence...frequently mixed with an acute anxiety about their new circumstances and strong feelings of homelessness.'[38]

The importance of home for ontological security only exacerbates the existential anxiety experienced by dispossessed people. This in turn is heightened as the status of being without a home – with all the adverse impacts this has on

---

33 Ibid.

34 J.D. Porteous, 'Domicide: The Destruction of Home' in D. Benjamin (ed.), *The Home: Words, Interpretations, Meanings and Environments* (Ashgate, Aldershot 1995) 153.

35 Ibid., 159.

36 J.D. Peters, 'Exile, Nomadism, and Diaspora: the Stakes of Mobility in the Western Canon' in H. Naficy (ed.) *Home, Exile, Homeland: Film, Media, and the Politics of Place* (Routledge, New York 1999) 19.

37 M. Povrzanovic Frykman, 'Homeland Lost and Gained: Croatian Diaspora and Refugees in Sweden' in N. Al-Ali and K. Koser (eds), *New Approaches to Migration? Transnational Communities and the Transformation of Home* (Routledge, London 2002) 118; also S. Carter, 'The Geopolitics of Diaspora' (2005) 37 *Area* 54–63.

38 C. Kinnvall, 'Globalisation and Religious Nationalism: Self, Identity, and the Search for Ontological Security' (2004) 25 *Political Psychology* 741, 747.

well-being – significantly undermines the ability of displaced and dispossessed people to defend their claims. If we accept that home and housing are 'gateway rights' (Sweeney and Fox O'Mahony) which provide the base for civil and political participation, then we must also ask how those who are excluded from housing and home are able to argue their case: how are the voices, experiences and understandings of displaced and dispossessed people heard within the legal system, in light of their marginalised position. At the same time, we are acutely aware of the limitations of legal method in framing the types of interests we are seeking to advance. As the discussion above illustrates, it is not difficult to discover why the 'home' interests of vulnerable displaced and dispossessed people are not strongly asserted, particularly when they come up against powerful interests – for example, what are seen as the legitimate claims of creditors or landlords (Bright) or the legitimate exercise of state power (van der Walt, Sweeney and Fox O'Mahony). The 'normal' property framework of rights and entitlements does not protect the weak home interests of those in the margins. In some cases, this has led to 'law' being side-stepped by individual judges, creating a disjuncture between law in theory and law in practice. For example, Bright described how 'a judge who is uncomfortable with evicting a family may try very hard to find some way of avoiding this outcome, perhaps by a scrupulous scrutiny of the paperwork.'[39]

Another obstacle in applying legalistic approaches to the idea of home in displacement and dispossession cases is the problem of minimal compliance. Kenna and Breau both demonstrate the 'soft' nature of international law concerning the right to housing and to the protection of displaced people, while Sweeney and Fox O'Mahony discuss the difficulties of minimal compliance in domestic applications of human rights laws which set minimum standards. The problem, we argue, is that the idea of home in law is not conceptually suited to the absolute standards required of legal frameworks of rights and entitlements. One of the major obstacles to the idea of home in law is the subjective nature of home attachments, which are not subject to legal 'proof'. While the authenticity of home attachments has been well established,[40] home scholarship has recognised that the occupier's interest in property *as a home* is:

> a relative concept, not an absolute one that can be defined in a dictionary or by a linguist. Given that it transcends quantitative, measureable dimensions and includes qualitative subjective ones, it is a complex, ambiguous concept that generates confusion.[41]

39 Bright, in this volume, p. 15.

40 See for example discussion in L. Fox, *Conceptualising Home: Theories, Laws and Policies* (Hart Publishing, Oxford 2006) especially ch. 4.

41 R.J. Lawrence, 'Deciphering Home: An Integrative Historical Perspective' in D. Benjamin (ed.), *The Home: Words, Interpretations, Meanings and Environments* (Ashgate, Aldershot 1995) 58.

Similarly, Dovey has described the difficulties associated with the concept of home, since:

> *home* is not an empirical variable whose meaning we might define in advance of careful measurement and explanation. As a consequence, understanding in this area is plagued by a lack of verifiability that many will find frustrating.[42]

This challenge is compounded by the fact that the legal tools that might be identified as most relevant to the project of developing the idea of home for displaced and dispossessed people also set in place relative rather than absolute standards. Kenna explains in his essay that the right to housing in international law necessarily – as a social and economic right – sets a relative standard which, while ensuring minimum core obligations are set, pitches those obligations at the lowest common denominator. While states which are signatories to the International Covenant on Economic, Social and Cultural Rights, for example, have committed to the principle of progressive realisation of the right to housing set out in that document, it is not possible to legislate for progressive realisation, which depends on the willingness of states to engage with good practice.

Thus, Kenna argues for the need for a 'whole system' approach, which transposes international housing rights into meaningful legal and non-legal standards. We would argue that legal scholarship must play an important role in this process. For one thing, the absence of home arguments in many of the legal contexts examined in the collection demonstrates a need to begin by articulating the home claim more coherently. In order for a 'problem' to be identified as requiring policy attention – to be accepted and acted upon within the policy realm – a number of factors need to be in place. Firstly, the problem must be defined, as 'the policy approach is a problem-focused inquiry'[43] in which social problems are 'formed and framed'. Atkinson has argued that:

> the particular aspects of reality which come to be defined as a 'problem' are rarely self-evidently problems as such. For an aspect of the real to be defined as a 'problem' it needs first of all to be constructed and articulated as an object amenable to diagnosis and treatment in and through a narrative discourse which carries with it an 'authority', or in Bourdieu's terms is enunciated by an individual or organization possessing the relevant symbolic capital to make performative utterances, i.e. to develop a narrative which will be 'listened to' and heeded.[44]

42 K. Dovey, 'Home and Homelessness', in I. Altman and C.M. Werner (eds), *Home Environments* (Plenum Press, New York 1985) 34.

43 W. Parsons, *Public Policy: An Introduction to the Theory and Practice of Policy Analysis* (Edward Elgar, Cheltenham 1995) 85.

44 R. Atkinson, 'Narratives of Policy: the Construction of Urban Problems and Urban Policy in the Official Discourse of British Government 1968–1998' (2000) 20 *Crit. Soc. Policy* 211, 214.

In exploring the issues of displacement and dispossession as they are represented (or not) in legal contexts, the essays in this collection try to draw together a narrative concerning the idea of (loss of) home in law which reveals some of the problems with addressing these interests in legal frameworks. The second step in this process is to influence the policy agenda to recognise a problem as such, so that, in turn, a coalition of support can be formed to ensure that institutional measures are implemented to 'solve' the problem.[45] Jacobs et al. have also emphasised:

> the role of power in bringing housing problems into prominence, the lobbying exercised to first establish housing problems on political agendas, and then influence the policy-making process and finally the decisions to devise specific policies, including justifying the allocation of resources to legitimise interventions.[46]

We argue that legal scholarship plays an important role in defining the problem of displacement and dispossession, by scrutinising the law to reveal the presence or absence of home values in legislative policies and judicial decisions, by identifying potential avenues by which the claim to home can be articulated within and without legal frameworks, and by lobbying for greater attention to be paid to the human interests of displaced and dispossessed people. There is, of course, a strong normative dimension to what we propose. As Breau's essay indicates, whether or not the human consequences of displacement and dispossession are even discussed within the legal arena may depend on what the state thinks it is responsible for. So, while the state (including the state as manifest through the institution of law) may consider itself responsible for matters such as state security (Breau), immigration (Sweeney and Fox O'Mahony), economic development (van der Walt) and even support for the (owner-occupied) housing market (Dyal-Chand) or the property rights of creditors and landlords (Bright), it is much more difficult to 'fix' the state with responsibility for the dignity and worth of the (often marginalised) displaced or dispossessed person.

Having recognised the limitations of employing a rights and entitlements model in this context, we argue that a valuable route forward – which resonates with the theme of progressive realisation – is through seeking to develop good practice, for example, in the extent to which states engage with 'soft law' standards, and to influence policy. A clearer articulation of the problem is crucial in either case. Policy analysts recognise that 'facts are things that never speak for themselves, they require an interpreter'.[47] The power of law in influencing and supporting this

45 See K. Jacobs, J. Kemeny and T. Manzi, 'Power, Discursive Space and Institutional Practices in the Construction of Housing Problems' (2003) 18 *Housing Stud.* 429.

46 Ibid., 430.

47 W. Parsons, *Public Policy: An Introduction to the Theory and Practice of Policy Analysis* (Edward Elgar, Cheltenham 1995) 87.

process was demonstrated in Ross's seminal study of the rhetoric of poverty,[48] in which he highlighted the role of legal methodology and – significantly – the self-imposed limits on our expectations of what law can achieve, in defining the problem of poverty and law's (lack of) responsibility, through the premise that we are helpless to change the 'harsh realities' of society, thus placing the 'problem' of poverty beyond judicial power or jurisdiction.[49]

Yet, this also reveals the important and potentially powerful role of legal scholarship in articulating the problems of displacement and dispossession from home, and in indicating how they might be resolved by law. Blumer argued that 'Social problems lie in and are produced by a process of collective definition';[50] while Jones has added that 'whosoever initially identifies a social problem shapes the initial terms in which it will be debated'.[51] More recently, Atkinson has added that:

> the definition and construction of a 'problem' contains within it the 'solution' to that problem. Moreover, the construction of a 'problem' (and its 'immanent solution') involves the development of a particular discursive narrative (a 'story') depicting/portraying the evolution and causes of the problem.[52]

In 'official' policy making, the dominant discourse determines which stories are told, contains the immanent solutions to the problems which are identified, and:

> By presenting a 'problem' in this manner, a narrative attempts to foreclose debate and prevent a 'problem' from being thought of in ways that are not congruent with the dominant discourse from which the narrative is derived.[53]

We have argued elsewhere[54] for the need for legal scholarship to counter the official discourse which excludes consideration of the experiences of displaced and dispossessed people from law and policy through the development of an

48 T. Ross, 'The Rhetoric of Poverty: Their Immorality, Our Helplessness' (1991) 79 *Georgetown Law Journal* 1499.

49 Ibid., 1502, 1509.

50 H. Blumer, 'Social Problems as Collective Behaviour' (1971) 18 *Social Problems* 298, 301.

51 J.A. Jones, 'Federal Efforts to Solve Contemporary Social Problems' in E.O. Smigel (ed.), *Handbook on the Study of Social Problems* (Rand-McNally, Chicago 1971), 561.

52 R. Atkinson, 'Narratives of Policy: the Construction of Urban Problems and Urban Policy in the Official Discourse of British Government 1968–1998' (2000) 20 *Crit. Soc. Policy* 211.

53 Ibid., 215.

54 L. Fox O'Mahony and J.A. Sweeney, 'The Exclusion of (Failed) Asylum Seekers from Housing and Home: Towards an Oppositional Discourse' (2010) 37 *Journal of Law and Society* 285–314.

'oppositional discourse' shaped through the lens of human experiences. For one thing, as Smith has argued, when proposing greater reference to human (ethical and social) considerations in a similar context: 'while a certain inertia on these points might be expected among politicians and policy-makers, it is increasingly hard to justify in the research community.'[55] In addition, Ross's study of the rhetoric of poverty demonstrates the importance of the way that we (as scholars) talk about issues to the development (or not) of legal strategies to address them.

In their examinations of the various contexts in which displacement and dispossession takes place, and by framing their analyses through a focus on the human experiences of losing home, the contributors to this collection make a valuable contribution to the exposition of the issue, and provide a fresh perspective from which to seek solutions to these problems. In doing so, and in addition to the proposals set out in the individual essays, the suggestions that emerge might usefully inform further research and could form the basis for lobbying for the development of good practice in the ways that lawyers think and talk about displacement and dispossession.

Firstly, we recognise the difficulties with applying a strict legalistic approach (rights and entitlements) in relation to a very 'human' and personal problem (see Bright's discussion of how and why the 'personal home stories' of occupiers in arrears sometimes 'leak' into the decisions of individual judges; also Sweeney and Fox O'Mahony on the ways in which, left to the political will, housing and home for asylum seekers are excluded from 'official' policy but can be re-introduced by individual judges). One of the difficulties, it might be argued, in bringing the human dimensions of home considerations to bear in contests involving dispossession or displacement is the risk that attachments to home might be perceived as 'mere emotion', and so fail to carry weight within the legal arena. The key to addressing this, we argue, is to focus on the *impact* of losing home for the displaced or dispossessed occupier. As one home theorist has suggested in another context: 'the problem lies with the fact that we are dealing with environmental intangibles – attachment, grief, loss – which are immeasurable, difficult to articulate, and thus easy to ignore by the cost-benefit brigade.'[56] By focusing on the damage or detriment to the occupier, on what is lost, it is – theoretically at least – more likely to be possible to capture the harm which will be occasioned to any occupier in any given case. In one sense, the impact of losing one's home can only ever be quantified after the event, since '[b]eing intangible, qualities of home are often

55 S. Smith, 'Banking on Housing: Speculating on the Role and Relevance of Housing Wealth in Britain' (paper prepared for the Joseph Rowntree Foundation Inquiry into Home Ownership 2010 and Beyond, 2005). Smith's comments were made in support of re-evaluating the credit market for home ownership from an ethical and social, rather than merely financial, perspective.

56 J.D. Porteous, 'Domicide: The Destruction of Home' in D. Benjamin (ed.), *The Home: Words, Interpretations, Meanings and Environments* (Ashgate, Aldershot 1995) 153.

only identified when they are lost.'[57] Yet, while empirical studies are certainly capable of capturing the qualitative losses of displacement and dispossession, there are a number of practical obstacles to measuring such losses for the purposes of legal contests, including the resource implications of measuring losses on a case-by-case basis and the prospect that such measurements would effectively become a 'post-mortem' account after the adverse consequences had taken place. Once a person is displaced it becomes very difficult to 'do' anything about it: for this, and other reasons discussed below, we argue that the objective of any protection must be preventative of home loss, with a focus on particularly vulnerable groups.

One approach, which we suggest may be worth pursuing in this context, would be to focus on particular groups of individuals to reflect the idea that different individuals might attribute different types or degrees of value to their homes; or be particularly adversely affected by loss of those homes. So, the idea of home in law might focus on evidence of particular vulnerability which might indicate that the group are at a heightened risk of suffering adverse effects from displacement or dispossession. The group-based approach also resonates with the process of defining social problems for policy making discussed above, with the development of a convincing narrative as the starting point for recognising a housing problem. Atkinson has observed that 'individual narratives do not exist in isolation, but reflect (and simultaneously conceal) a deeper more pervasive narrative linked to particular social (class or group) interests.'[58] One such group interest might be the welfare of children;[59] another could be based on structural factors, for example low income;[60] or a critical gendered perspective which recognises structural inequality and the unequal distribution of responsibilities;[61] or, where people have experienced trauma and violence, for example in armed conflict, it might be appropriate to argue that, as a group, their need for protection against (further) displacement is greater as a result of the vulnerabilities caused by these experiences.[62]

At the same time, we also need to be sensitive to the risk that certain groups of occupiers who are in fact vulnerable can be portrayed as 'villains' due to their 'otherness', and that such regressive arguments can potentially subvert claims that their needs should be recognised as a priority. Ross gives the example of the rhetorical separation of 'the poor' as different, deviant, morally weak, achieved, in

57 K. Dovey, 'Home and Homelessness', in I. Altman and C.M. Werner (eds), *Home Environments* (Plenum Press, New York 1985) 56.

58 R. Atkinson, 'Narratives of Policy: the Construction of Urban Problems and Urban Policy in the Official Discourse of British Government 1968–1998' (2000) 20 *Crit. Soc. Policy* 211, 213.

59 This proposition is advanced in Fox, *Conceptualising Home: Theories, Laws and Policies* (Hart Publishing, Oxford 2006) ch. 9.

60 See above, text to n. 13.

61 See for example, L. Fox, 'Re-possessing "Home": A Re-analysis of Gender, Home Ownership and Debtor Default for Feminist Legal Theory' (2008) *Wm. and Mary J. Women and L.* 423–94.

62 See generally, Breau, in this volume.

part, through the separation and stigmatisation of people in poverty using themes of difference and deviance which enable us to distinguish groups of people as 'them' and 'us', and 'to make *their* suffering intellectually coherent'.[63] The two main categories of occupiers running throughout the papers in this collection might be described as 'the poor', on the one hand (Bright, Dyal-Chand, van der Walt) and 'exiles' – refugees, asylum seekers, internally displaced persons – (Sweeney and Fox O'Mahony, Buyse, Kenna, Breau) on the other. In both cases, there is a risk of 'demonisation'[64] which must be met head on in any attempts to establish a convincing new narrative which focuses on the human needs of displaced and dispossessed people, rather than constructing their very existence as a (social) problem. In doing so, it is also worth remembering that everyone has to 'be' somewhere: we all have to live somewhere, physically, materially and socially; and that displacement and dispossession merely move 'the problem'/the people around.

Another outcome of our symposium was that the idea of home in law, particularly in relation to displacement and dispossession, is complex and often difficult, both in respect of the range of 'legal' and 'extra-legal' strategies that might be adopted to enable home claims to be more coherently represented in the legal arena, and in relation to the interactions between these strategies and the social policy context. We have noted above that in many senses the strict legal concepts of rights and entitlements are not likely to prove fruitful, but suggest that a more valuable strategy is to adopt a 'whole system' approach, taking account of the matrix of housing rights which are recognised and acknowledged in relation to housing and home, from human rights laws at the 'hard' enforceable end of the spectrum to soft law approaches which build norms through the articulation of responsibilities towards people who live at the margins, and through these norms to influence policies. Kenna captures this process when he describes the idea of human rights functioning as a 'moral compass' for the development of law and policy around the globe. An example of this process in practice can be seen in the Participation in the Practice of Rights project in Northern Ireland and the work of the Community Action Network with the Rialto Rights in Action group in Dublin, which demonstrate how the moral norms articulated by rights-bearers can be utilised to put pressure on duty-bearers to deliver, and so to give content to the right to housing and other rights.[65] Similarly, Breau illustrates the role of norms in the emergence of customary principles, which in turn can be influential in the policy-making process.[66]

---

63 T. Ross, 'The Rhetoric of Poverty: Their Immorality, Our Helplessness' (1991) 79 *Georgetown Law Journal* 1499, 1508, emphasis added.

64 In the case of 'the poor', see ibid; in the case of 'exiles', see L. Fox O'Mahony and J.A. Sweeney, 'The Exclusion of (Failed) Asylum Seekers from Housing and Home: Towards an Oppositional Discourse' (2010) 37 *Journal of Law and Society* 285–314.

65 See http://www.pprproject.org/; www.canaction.ie/

66 See generally, Breau, in this volume.

In practice, the problems associated with displacement and dispossession raise difficult questions, which are hard to answer in a context of limited resources, and sometimes against a backdrop of media and public opinion – even political comment – which appears to demonstrate little sympathy for the displaced or dispossessed occupier – whether through framing asylum seekers as 'cheats', 'illegals', 'spongers' and 'social parasites' on the welfare state, or by casting people who cannot pay their rent or mortgage as 'failures' in the individualised, market-dominated ownership society described by Dyal-Chand. We do not suggest that eradicating displacement and dispossession, whether at a local, national or global level, is simply a matter of lawyers and policy makers choosing to make it so. Yet, on the other hand, the impact of the global recession in bringing home to all of us our vulnerability to dispossession might potentially be viewed as a 'tipping point'[67] for understanding and responding to the human consequences of losing home. In considering the role of the academic in responding to these problems, our modest aim in this collection is to demonstrate, when there are difficult choices to be made, the key importance of articulating the 'home' considerations on the side of the occupier, as well as recognising the competing interest of the 'strong' claimant on the other side. We argue that a clearer and more coherent understanding of the consequences of losing home is needed, and that, rather than allowing dominant to automatically trump less robust claims, particularly when this may lead to the loss of home by vulnerable, voiceless or marginalised people, it should be framed by focusing on how displacement and dispossession impacts on the people who are affected, adopting a 'whole system' approach, with particular attention to the role of human rights norms in transmitting the values of housing and home into the legal domain.

67 See M. Gladwell, *The Tipping Point: How Little Things Can Make a Big Difference* (Little Brown, 2002).

Index

Figures are indicated by **bold** page numbers, tables by *italic* numbers.